Human Dignity

Connecting three generations of critical theorists, this edited collection focuses on the mutual complementarity between the concept of "human dignity" and the theory and practice of human rights.

Human dignity has recently emerged as a controversial theme in the philosophy of human rights and has become the subject of a growing debate involving theological, political, juridical, moral, and biomedical perspectives. Previously, interpretations of this concept took for granted specific definitions of this term without accounting for the perspective offered by a "Critical Theory of Human Rights." This interdisciplinary perspective relies on a tradition that goes from Immanuel Kant to Jürgen Habermas, influences new generations, and sheds more light on how human dignity is used (and abused) in contemporary discourses. Based on this tradition, the contributors sustain an engaged discussion of the topic and address issues such as domination, colonialism, multiculturalism, globalization, and cosmopolitanism. Informed by different contexts, each author offers a unique contribution to distinctive aspects of the necessary internal correlation between human dignity and human rights.

This book will be of interest to students and researchers in human rights in Europe, North America, and Latin America and readers in the areas of political science, philosophy, sociology, law, and international relations.

Amos Nascimento is Professor of Philosophy at the University of Washington, Tacoma and Seattle, affiliated with Interdisciplinary Arts and Sciences, International Studies, and Germanics programs, and Principal Investigator of the Interdisciplinary Research Cluster on "Human Interactions and Normative Innovation."

Matthias Lutz-Bachmann is Professor of Philosophy, Principal Investigator of the Cluster of Excellence on "The Formation of Normative Orders," and Director of the Research Center for Humanities at the Goethe University in Frankfurt.

Rethinking Political and International Theory

Series Editors: Keith Breen, Dan Bulley, Susan McManus

Committed to show you in what ways traditional approaches in political and international theory may be applied to 21st century politics, this series will present inventive and pioneering theoretical work designed to build a common framework for the latest scholarly research on political theory and international relations. Intended to be international and interdisciplinary in scope, the series will contain works which advance our understanding of the relevance of seminal thinkers to our current socio-political context(s) as well as problematize and offer new insights into key political concepts and phenomena within the arena of politics and international relations.

For more information about this series, please visit: https://www.routledge.com/Rethinking-Political-and-International-Theory/book-series/ASHSER1348

The Concert of Civilizations
The Common Roots of Western and Islamic Constitutionalism
Jeremy Kleidosty

Virtue and Economy
Essays on Morality and Markets
Andrius Bielskis and Kelvin Knight

Revolutionary Subjectivity in Post-Marxist Thought
Laclau, Negri, Badiou
Oliver Harrison

Human Rights, Human Dignity, and Cosmopolitan Ideals
Essays on Critical Theory and Human Rights
Edited by Matthias Lutz-Bachmann and Amos Nascimento

Creativity and Limitation in Political Communities
Spinoza, Schmitt and Ordering
Ignas Kalpokas

Human Dignity
Perspectives from a Critical Theory of Human Rights
Edited by Amos Nascimento and Matthias Lutz-Bachmann

Human Dignity

Perspectives from a Critical Theory of Human Rights

Edited by
Amos Nascimento and Matthias Lutz-Bachmann

Routledge
Taylor & Francis Group

LONDON AND NEW YORK

First published 2018
by Routledge
2 Park Square, Milton Park, Abingdon, Oxon OX14 4RN

and by Routledge
605 Third Avenue, New York, NY 10017

First issued in paperback 2021

Routledge is an imprint of the Taylor & Francis Group, an informa business

Publisher's Note
The publisher has gone to great lengths to ensure the quality of this
reprint but points out that some imperfections in the original copies
may be apparent.

British Library Cataloguing-in-Publication Data
A catalogue record for this book is available from the British Library

Library of Congress Cataloging-in-Publication Data
Names: Nascimento, Amos, editor. | Lutz-Bachmann, Matthias, editor.
Title: Human dignity : perspectives from a critical theory of human rights /
edited by Amos Nascimento and Matthias Lutz-Bachmann.
Description: Abingdon, Oxon ; New York, NY : Routledge, 2018. |
Series: Rethinking political and international theory | Includes
bibliographical references and index.
Identifiers: LCCN 2018005979| ISBN 9781138204447 (hbk) |
ISBN 9781315468297 (ebk)
Subjects: LCSH: Human rights. | Dignity.
Classification: LCC JC571 .H6264 2018 | DDC 323.01--dc23
LC record available at https://lccn.loc.gov/2018005979

ISBN 13: 978-1-03-209532-5 (pbk)
ISBN 13: 978-1-138-20444-7 (hbk)

Typeset in Times New Roman
by Taylor & Francis Books

To JIM BOHMAN

friend, fellow, and distinguished colleague
Department of Philosophy
Saint Louis University
St. Louis, MO USA

Contents

Contributors

Rainer Forst is Professor of Philosophy and Political Theory at the Goethe University in Frankfurt, Director of the Research Center on "The Formation of Normative Orders" in Frankfurt, and leader of various research projects on issues related to transnational justice, human rights, and non-domination. His research focuses on theories of justice and democratic theory. He is the author of *Contexts of Justice* (2002), *Toleration in Conflict* (2012), *The Right to Justification* (2007), *Justification and Critique* (2013), *The Power of Tolerance* (2014, with Wendy Brown), and *Normativity and Power* (2017).

Jürgen Habermas is Professor of Philosophy *emeritus* at the Goethe University in Frankfurt, the leading contemporary critical theorist, with a long list of publications spanning from *Structural Transformation of the Public Sphere* (1962) and *Knowledge and Interests* (1967) through *Theory of Communicate Action* (1981) and *Between Facts and Norms* (1992), to *Postmetaphysical Thinking I* (1988), *Postnational Constellation* (1998), and *The Inclusion of the Other* (1996). His more recent publications include *Religion and Naturalism* (2005), *The Crisis of the European Union* (2011), and *Postmetaphysical Thinking II* (2012), among many others. Habermas has renewed Critical Theory with his publications and worked in areas such as philosophy of science, discourse ethics, political theory, and law. His recent interests focus on global constitutionalism, the European Union, human rights, and religion.

Cristina Lafont is Professor of Philosophy at Northwestern University. She is the author of *The Linguistic Turn in Hermeneutic Philosophy* (1999), *Heidegger, Language, and World-Disclosure* (2000), *Global Governance and Human Rights* (2012), and editor of the *Habermas Handbuch* (with Hauke Brunkhorst and Regina Kreide, 2010) and *The Future of Critical Theory: Transforming the Global Political and Economic Order* (2017). She has published numerous articles in contemporary moral and political philosophy. One of her current research projects focuses on the defense of an ideal of deliberative democracy that could be implemented beyond national borders, with an emphasis on the practice of human rights.

Matthias Lutz-Bachmann is Professor of Philosophy, Principal Investigator of the Cluster of Excellence on "The Formation of Normative Orders," and Director of the Research Center for Humanities at the Goethe University in Frankfurt. His research focuses on early modernity, Kantian practical philosophy and cosmopolitanism, philosophy of religion, and the intersection between discourse ethics and the philosophy of international relations. He is the author, editor, and co-editor of many books on these subjects, including *Geschichte und Subjekt* (1988), *Toward Perpetual Peace* (1997), *Grundkurs Philosophie: Ethik* (2013), and *Transnationale Verantwortung: Überlegungen zu einem Prinzip der Anwendung normativer Ethik* (forthcoming). Recently, he has edited *Kosmopolitanismus. Zur Geschichte und Zukunft eines umstrittenen Ideals* (with Andreas Niederberger and Philipp Schink, 2010), *Human Rights, Human Dignity, and Cosmopolitan Ideals* (with Amos Nascimento, 2014), and *Postsäkularismus. Zur Diskussion eines umstrittenen Begriffs* (2015), among other books. He is the general editor of the series "Medieval and Early Modern Legal and Political Theory," "Religion in Modernity," and "Kosmopolis."

Eduardo Mendieta is Professor of Philosophy and Associate Director of the Rock Ethics Institute at Pennsylvania State University. His books include *The Adventures of Transcendental Philosophy* (2003), *Global Fragments: Latinoamericanism, Globalizations, and Critical Theory* (2007), and *Three Pragmatist Lectures* (2008) as well as many edited books on Critical Theory, Latin America, and contemporary global and cosmopolitan issues. Among his latest projects, he edited *Reading Kant's Geography* (with Stuart Elden, 2011), *The Power of Religion in the Public Sphere: Butler, Habermas, Taylor and West in Dialogue* (with Jonathan VanAntwerpen, 2011), *Habermas and Religion* (with Craig Calhoun and Jonathan VanAntwerpen, 2013), *Maps for a Fiesta: A Latina/o Perspective on Knowledge and the Global Crisis* (2015), and *The Cambridge Habermas Lexicon* (with Amy Allen, forthcoming). His research focuses on Critical Theory and he has edited and translated works by Jürgen Habermas, Karl-Otto Apel, and Enrique Dussel into English.

Amos Nascimento is Professor of Philosophy at the University of Washington, Tacoma and Seattle, affiliated with Interdisciplinary Arts and Sciences, International Studies, and Germanics programs. He authored *Im Zwielicht der Aufklärung* (2009) and *Building Cosmopolitan Communities* (2013). He is the editor of *A Matter of Discourse: Community and Communication in Contemporary Philosophies* (1998), *Brasil: Perspectivas Internacionais* (2001), and co-editor of *Grenzen der Moderne* (with Kirsten Witte, 1997) and *Human Rights, Human Dignity, and Cosmopolitan Ideals* (with Matthias Lutz-Bachmann, 2014). He has published many articles on Critical Theory and human rights in Europe and Latin America.

Andreas Niederberger is Professor of Philosophy at the University of Duisburg-Essen, where he teaches practical philosophy and political theory. His publications include *Kontingenz und Vernunft. Grundlagen einer Theorie kommunikativen Handelns im Anschluss an Habermas und Merleau-Ponty* (2007) and *Demokratie unter Bedingungen der Weltgesellschaft? Normative Grundlagen legitimer Herrschaft in einer globalen politischen Ordnung* (2009). He is the editor of *Kosmopolitanismus. Zur Geschichte und Zukunft eines umstrittenen Ideals* (with Matthias Lutz-Bachmann and Philipp Schink, 2010), *Globalisierung: Ein interdisziplinäres Handbuch* (with Philipp Schink, 2011), and *Republican Democracy: Liberty, Law, and Politics* (with Philipp Schink, 2013), among others. He also published many articles on theories of democracy, cosmopolitanism, human rights, and environmental justice.

Preface

The first article of the *Universal Declaration of Human Rights* states that "All human beings are born free and equal in dignity and rights" and many other international documents and national constitutions reaffirm the centrality of this assertion. However, contemporary debates on this subject show a growing number of voices asking whether there is a plausible justification for such strong affirmation of *human dignity* and its intrinsic relation to *human rights*. The lack of a strong consensual justification leaves both concepts open to all kinds of appropriation, a problem that is even more prevalent in relation to the idea of human dignity. As a concept, human dignity has a long history going back to religious traditions and ancient philosophy, but it has been reinterpreted in many ways at various times. It is often assumed to be the premise upon which a full repertoire of human rights is supposed to rest. It also has been viewed as an empty concept whose ambiguity allows it to serve as a placeholder for *a posteriori* elaboration. Its openness may yield a plethora of positive reflections about the important role of this concept in promoting and protecting human rights, but there is also a risk that this vagueness is an invitation to particularistic appropriations and manipulations. Human dignity has gained the status of a legal principle functioning as the basis for the establishment of a complex structure and corresponding hierarchy of needs, interests, norms, institutions, government initiatives, and international policies on human rights, but because this legal basis does not appear to have a firm foundation, the contemporary human rights regime can be criticized for lacking stronger validation. Consequently, recent debates have begun to raise questions whether the supposedly foundational role of human dignity to human rights is sufficiently justified in philosophical terms.

Philosophers representing different theoretical traditions have contributed to an increasing literature on this topic, thus helping to establish the "philosophy of human rights" as an important new field that considers human dignity as a central concept, fosters interdisciplinary *modi* of reflection, and motivates dynamic practices worldwide. As the question concerning the definition, justification, application, and impact of human dignity in relation to human rights emerges as a core issue, these philosophers have tried to address and analyze these various themes with the help of many available theoretical tools. Amidst the variety of contributions to a philosophy of human rights there are several critical perspectives, but we need to consider the specific influence springing from the tradition of Critical Theory – conventionally spelled out in capital letters to refer to the Frankfurt School – and the emerging field of a "Critical Theory of Human Rights." This contribution is seldom mentioned more explicitly in recent overviews of international discussions on human dignity, although publications on this subject invariably mention Immanuel Kant, constantly allude to historical events in the German context as key to the renaissance in the interest on human dignity, and regularly refer – even if only *en passant* – to a few critical theorists working on these themes.

Kant is rightly acknowledged as one of the first to provide a modern and secular definition of human dignity, but we need to recognize the historical antecedents to the Kantian views on human rights and human dignity as well as the rise of Critical Theory as one of the systematic consequences of the philosophical analyses inspired on the tradition inaugurated by him. Historically, the origins of a Critical Theory of Human Rights can be traced back to the eighteenth century and to his philosophy of "Criticism," in which he proposes a new paradigm for morality, politics, and law, beyond the Westphalian model of territorial sovereignty. Based on the idea of humanity [*Menschheit*] Kant introduced an ideal of world citizenship in relation to human rights [*Menschenrechte*] and to a corresponding moral principle of human dignity [*Menschenwürde*]. Relying on and reacting to his philosophy, a new current of critical thinking developed during the nineteenth century, as thinkers such as Georg Wilhelm Friedrich Hegel and Karl Marx explicitly used "critique" as their methodology for the discussion of humanity and rights.

The importance of Germany to contemporary discussions on human rights and human dignity is difficult to deny. Many interpreters see a direct connection between the recent German past and the important role given to the concept of human dignity today. Legal debates on the contemporary meaning of terms such as crimes against humanity, humanitarian intervention, human rights, and human dignity go back to the context of World War I and the Russian Revolution. These terms were then reaffirmed in reaction to the rise of National Socialism, the impact of World War II, the systematic genocide of Jews in Europe, and the trials of those responsible for unimaginable atrocities. These proposals were also related to analyses of German constitutionalism and legal categories connected to the advent of the Weimar Republic in 1919 and the new Basic Law [*Grundgesetz*] of the German Federal Republic in 1949 – whose first and most fundamental constitutional article states that "human dignity is inviolable." To be sure, the idea of human dignity now has a foundational status beyond this particular case, as seen in new conceptions of human rights enshrined in recent constitutions in countries such as Ireland, South Africa, Switzerland, Brazil, New Zealand, and – literally – hundreds of other nations. Nevertheless, many questions concerning the justification for the inclusion of these constitutional clauses or the appeal to human dignity in judicial processes remain unanswered and motivate a critical review of these historical sources.

Critical Theory has evolved alongside these processes. At each historical juncture, a generation emerges with a group of people born around the same time, studying with the same professors, experiencing similar historical events, and facing common conceptual challenges. There are no exact years defining a cohort, the geographic boundaries are fluid, and overlapping factors are present, so we apply the term "generation" in a loose heuristic way. The so-called Frankfurt School and its proposal for a Critical Theory of Society was initially proposed in the 1920s, reflecting the culture of the Weimar Republic and involving authors such as Max Horkheimer, Herbert Marcuse, Erich Fromm, and Theodor Adorno – among many others. Together with some of their contemporaries such as Ernst Bloch and Hannah Arendt, these authors witnessed many of the key historical events related to the advancement of a new human rights regime in the twentieth century and expressed a direct concern with human oppression and the ideologies that justified domination. They reacted to challenging times and offered reflections on the meaning of human rights and human dignity. Therefore, a Critical Theory of Human Rights is deeply connected to the German context in various ways: there is a proximity of critical theorists to historical events; they were related to discussions on the meaning of human dignity; and they contributed to a program whose contours are now being defined more clearly.

Critical Theory developed further with a second generation of philosophers who were influenced by the "re-education" of German society and the linguistic turn in twentieth-century German philosophy, including Karl-Otto Apel, Jürgen Habermas, Albrecht Wellmer as well as Alfred Schmidt, Hermann Schweppenhäuser and many others who played an important role as editors of the earlier writings of Max Horkheimer, Theodor W. Adorno, Walter Benjamin, and Herbert Marcuse and other members of the first generation of Critical Theory. The second generation helped to transform the critical tradition by emphasizing the importance of discourses, their normativity, and their practical application in ethics, politics, and law. This updating of Critical Theory into Discourse Theory and Discourse Ethics also implied a dialogue with other philosophical currents in Anglo America – especially through the work of Thomas McCarthy and his mediating role in United States – and Latin America – mainly through a dialogue with Enrique Dussel. This widening of the spectrum enabled the inclusion of new voices and new themes that came to enrich this tradition even more, expanding earlier philosophical tools with new concerns.

Thus, a third generation of critical theorists emerged with Axel Honneth, Hauke Brunkhorst, Ingeborg Maus, Gunzelin Schmid Noerr, Matthias Lutz-Bachmann, Klaus Günther, Christoph Menke and many others who expanded the repertoire of topics to be analyzed from a critical perspective and promoted a more intensive dialogue with critical theorists in the United States such as Seyla Benhabib, James Bohman, Iris Young, Stephen Bonner, Lucius

Outlaw, and Nancy Fraser, among many others. This intercultural exchange promoted a richer dialogue with newer schools and philosophies, leading to a more explicit inclusion of topics such as gender relations, social justice, coloniality, multiculturalism, racism, and globalization.

It is only more recently – and in tandem with new developments related to recent debates around the global role of the United Nations and the world-wide recognition of the *Universal Declaration of Human Rights* and its nor-mativity – that a more globally oriented Critical Theory of Human Rights has emerged beyond Europe, North America, and South America, albeit in dialogue with new issues closely related to the German context. This collec-tion of essays includes a fourth generation – represented here by Cristina Lafont, Rainer Forst, Eduardo Mendieta, Amos Nascimento, and Andreas Niederberger – which is engaged in the process of making sense of these times of transition.

The main purpose of this publication is to show the connection among authors who inherit the critical tradition and expand it in a programmatic discussion of human rights and human dignity. Jürgen Habermas has been very active reflecting on human right issues for decades, proposing new con-cepts, intervening in public debates, and influencing social and political actions. Other authors such as Matthias Lutz-Bachmann and Rainer Forst have addressed questions concerning human dignity in its normativity. Cris-tina Lafont and Andreas Niederberger question some of the consequences of opening or expanding human dignity without a critical consideration of its premises. Eduardo Mendieta and Amos Nascimento connect this discussion to human rights issues in the Latin American context and other global issues. These contributions are not isolated but form part of a wider movement interested in a better understanding of the relationship between human rights and human dignity in a critical perspective. Therefore, it is important to map the formation of new generations of students and practitioners of human rights and link their research and publications which reflect on the meaning of human dignity. Because there may appear to be a lack of unity among these several initiatives, it is useful to see their institutional connections and developments, which have yielded new academic programs, spawned inter-disciplinary research projects, and led to the articulation of international net-works. All this reveals that a Critical Theory of Human Rights is a programmatic movement with long roots and wide-ranging branches that can yield plural perspectives on questions related to human dignity.

The different generations of critical theorists gathered in this collection offer readers an opportunity to engage with the plural ways of addressing questions concerning the philosophical justification of human rights in rela-tion to human dignity. Previously, interpretations of human dignity took for granted specific definitions of this term within fields such as theology, law, political science, or the biomedical sciences. Now, however, an inter-disciplinary approach is necessary to shed more light on the multiple ways in which human dignity is understood. Bringing these authors together helps us identify a plurality of perspectives based on a common background and highlight a common purpose, which is to consider what it means to be recognized as a human being, with dignity, needs, interests, rights, and duties. A Critical Theory of Human Rights is this necessary approach. It has deep historical antecedents in Germany, important contemporary representatives internationally, and future possibilities for broader considerations worldwide, which will certainly expand the scope of current debates. This approach offers many advantages in dealing with the issues mentioned thus far, especially because recent reflections by critical theorists reveal that the discussion has not remained stationed in frozen historical moments, but has evolved to include new contemporary developments. The claim for dignity has been iterated and reiterated by different social actors at different moments and in various locations. The philosophical considerations by multiple generations of critical theorists follow a corresponding plurality of challenges and concerns.

The chapters in this book also summarize a theoretical and practical concern spanning many decades of experiences and reflections. The various authors combine historical analysis and contemporary developments in the understanding of human dignity and its centrality in the justification of human rights. They highlight that human dignity and human rights need to be addressed more critically. They contribute to a contemporary Critical Theory of Human Rights that is able to discuss more clearly how issues of colonialism, capitalism, democratic participation, identity politics, gender relations, multiculturalism, racism, religious tolerance, terrorism, biomedical developments, and globalization processes as well as economic exploitation and corporate demands or interests are directly related to questions about human dignity.

This publication offers an interesting and important complement to a previous collection we published in this series: *Human Rights, Human Dignity, and Cosmopolitan Ideals*. The authors in this volume have participated in a series of events organized at the University of Washington in Seattle and Tacoma, United States, and at the Goethe University in Frankfurt, Germany. Many of the papers have been prepared for these events, others were discussed at different moments and published elsewhere, but this volume is the only publication that brings all these contributions of Critical Theory together, allowing readers to compare their differences, observe cross-references, and discover common trends.

Amos Nascimento, University of Washington, Tacoma
Matthias Lutz-Bachmann, Goethe University, Frankfurt
Summer of 2017

Acknowledgments

This is the second collection of essays we publish in the series "Rethinking Political and International Theory," sharing some of the work we have been developing at seminars and colloquia organized with the joint support of the Interdisciplinary Research Cluster on "Human Interactions and Normative Innovation" at the University of Washington in Seattle, United States, and the Cluster of Excellence "Die Herausbildung normativer Ordnungen" at the Goethe University in Frankfurt, Germany. We thank Keith Breen, Dan Bulley, and Susan McManus for accepting to include this publication in the series.

The title of our previous collection in this series, *Human Rights, Human Dignity, and Cosmopolitan Ideals*, indicated how a Critical Theory of Human Rights implies the reconsideration of the Enlightenment project as well as a reflection on morality, politics, and law through the lens of Kantian cosmopolitanism. In the present volume, *Human Dignity: Perspectives from a Critical Theory of Human Rights*, we expand on that prior initiative and focus more systematically on the concept of human dignity, its historical roots, philosophical underpinnings, and controversial implications. Both volumes complement each other and contribute to a common endeavor. The occasion for a more programmatic discussion of human dignity was offered by an event organized in the summer of 2015 by Matthias Lutz-Bachmann and Amos Nascimento and hosted by the Forschungskolleg Humanwissenschaften at Bad Homburg, a research center of Goethe University. The participants in the seminar as well as other authors involved in other activities related to our project on Critical Theory and Human Rights are also contributing to this volume. By bringing these authors together, we not only show how different generations of critical theorists maintain an ongoing dialogue, but we also demarcate more clearly the expansion and impact of an emerging field defined as Critical Theory of Human Rights.

Most of the chapters brought together in this publication have been published elsewhere since we first discussed them. However, these publications remain scattered in different venues, locations, and languages. By reprinting them in slightly updated versions, this book provides a sense of unity and visibility, helping to convey the message that a Critical Theory of Human Rights offers a robust interdisciplinary and intergenerational framework to address key questions in ethics, politics, law, international relations, and other areas. Moreover, this collection documents the engagement, cooperation, and dialogue among colleagues who inherit a critical tradition with clear roots in the German context and in the philosophy of Immanuel Kant. The authors not only receive but also transform and advance this tradition by relating it to other philosophical currents, contexts, and global issues.

As mentioned, the chapters collected in this publication had previous iterations, were published in academic journals, and are adapted with minor revisions for this volume. In what follows, we would like to register our acknowledgments to various publishers for granting us permission to reprint copyrighted materials:

Andreas Niederberger's chapter was originally published as "*Esse servitutis omnis impatientem*/Man is impatient of all servitude: Human Dignity as a Path to Modernity in Ficino and Pico della Mirandola?" in *The European Legacy: Towards New Paradigms* 20, no. 5 (2015): 513–526 and is reprinted here with slight changes. A previous version of Matthias Lutz-Bachmann's chapter was published in German as "Das Verhältnis von Ethik und Recht: Der Rekurs auf die Menschenwürde" in G. Frank, A. Hallacker, and S. Lalla (eds.), *Erzählende Vernunft* (Berlin, 2006, 367–374) and reprinted as "Menschenrechte und Menschenwürde" in J. König and S. Seichter (eds.) *Menschenrechte. Demokratie. Geschichte. Transdisziplinäre Herausforderungen an die Pädagogik, Festschrift für Micha Brumlik* (Weinheim, 2014). We publish an expanded and updated version in English, translated by Amos Nascimento and reviewed by the author. Jürgen Habermas's chapter was originally published in *Metaphilosophy* 41, no. 1 (July 2010): 464–80 and then included as a chapter of his book, *The Crisis of the European Union* (Cambridge: Polity, 2012). An earlier version of Rainer Forst's chapter was published as a Working Paper of the Excellence Cluster on "The Formation of Normative Orders" in 2011 and later included as a chapter of his book, *Justification and Critique* (Cambridge: Polity, 2013). The chapter by Cristina Lafont appeared in *Ethics and International Affairs* 30, no. 2 (2016): 233–252 and was updated for this publication. A slightly different version of Eduardo Mendieta's chapter appeared as "The Legal Orthopedia of Human Dignity: Thinking with Axel Honneth" in *Philosophy and Social Criticism* 40, no. 8 (2014): 799–815, and has been adapted for this publication. Parts of Amos Nascimento's chapter rely on his "From Plural Worldviews to Global Human Rights Discourses: On Multiculturalism, Interculturalism, and the Possibility of an Overlapping Consensus" in *Revista de Direito* [Journal of Law, Federal University of Mato Grosso do Sul], Vol. 1/2 (Jul-December 2015): 7–26.

We also acknowledge the support of our respective institutions – the University of Washington and Goethe University. We have had the opportunity to use state-of-the-art facilities and count on the support of dedicated staff. Funding for the work involved in this overarching project has been granted by the Simpson Center for the Humanities in Seattle, the Interdisciplinary Arts and Sciences program in Tacoma, and the Cluster of Excellence on

"The Formation of Normative Orders" in Frankfurt. At these institutions, many people were directly or indirectly involved in processes related to the preparation of this book and we would like to express our appreciation to Ursula Krüger and Lucas Waggoner for their support.

In the process of going from the proposal for a publication through the organization of the events where these chapters were presented to the preparation of the manuscript, we also counted on the support of our colleagues who participated in the dialogue at large and presented papers related to other subjects not included in this book. This community includes Bill Talbott, Michael Forman, Regina Kreide, Michael Rosenthal, Jamie Mayerfeld, Roseli Fischmann, Jonathan Warren, Margaret Griesse, Michael Blake, Amy Reed-Sandoval, Elizabeth Bruch, Andreas Wagner, Philipp Schink, Anselm Spindler, Turkuler Isikisel, Darrel Moellendorf, Thomas M. Schmidt, Stefan Schweighöfer, Uchenna Okeja, and Jane Compson. We thank them all for their support and cooperation.

Finally, we acknowledge the patience, support, and guidance provided by Rob Sorsby at Routledge during a time of many transitions for all of us. Anonymous peer-reviewers as well as the editorial staff, especially Claire Maloney, contributed immensely in guaranteeing the quality of the materials and the preparation of this manuscript. Translations from German texts were provided by Ciaran Cronin and Amos Nascimento, and are published here with the publishers' permission.

The editors of this volume, Amos Nascimento and Matthias Lutz-Bachmann, have collaborated systematically for over two decades. This publication is another step in an ongoing dialogue and partnership to promote a Critical Theory of Human Rights.

1 Human dignity in the perspective of a Critical Theory of Human Rights

Amos Nascimento and Matthias Lutz-Bachmann

In this introduction, we would like to define a "Critical Theory of Human Rights," provide some background to illustrate its development, explore its relation to the concept of human dignity, and introduce the authors in this volume who are contributing to the task of considering the role of human dignity in the justification of human rights. We also highlight how these authors share some basic premises and pursue a common project, albeit in a plurality of ways and informed by different contexts. If we start with the commonality, they all refer to the Kantian tradition of philosophical criticism, but transform this legacy according to various stages in the development of Critical Theory. Regarding their differences, each author offers a unique contribution to distinctive aspects of the theory and practice of human rights. It is based on these considerations that we can talk of plural perspectives on human dignity informed by a Critical Theory of Human Rights.

1. A critical tradition in human rights

The Philosophy of Human Rights is an emerging field that has attracted the attention of many philosophers whose contributions to this area have helped to clarify the theories and practices in the worldwide promotion of human rights.[1] Within this broad framework, there are several approaches to human dignity, including religious or theological, ethical, political, and legal perspectives.[2] Many philosophical programs could be defined as representing "critical theories," are informed by diverse theoretical backgrounds, and reflect on contemporary questions concerning human rights and human dignity according to their particular contexts.[3] In this book, the reference to a Critical Theory of Human Rights – conventionally written in capital letters to allude to the Critical Theory of Society proposed by the Frankfurt School in the 1920s and 1930s – denotes an interdisciplinary method that reflects on the relationship between human rights and human dignity in Immanuel Kant's writings, considers his legacy of a secular definition of these topics, observes what influenced subsequent conceptual developments related to the German context, and discusses global contemporary issues related to these matters.[4]

Kant's views on human rights and human dignity are informed by the "critical turn" in his philosophy, which occurred in 1781 and shaped his systematic work in areas such as morality, politics, law, international relations, religion, and aesthetics. In his writings on practical philosophy, Kant defines humanity in terms of rationality, freedom, and autonomy. In his ethics, he derived basic rights and duties from the human ability to self-legislate and, thereby, he defined the concepts of human rights [*Menschenrechte*] and human dignity [*Menschenwürde*] based on the premise that the human being is an "end in itself" [*Zweck an sich selbst*].[5] However, in his legal and political writings – such as in *Toward Perpetual Peace* (1795) and in his *Doctrine of Right* (1797) – he expands these notions in order to propose a broader legal framework with different levels corresponding to a public domestic component [*staatliches Recht*], a comparative dimension involving the plurality of peoples and their juridical traditions [*Völkerrecht*], and a right to world citizenship or cosmopolitan right [*Weltbürgerrecht*] based on a universal right of humanity [*Recht der Menschheit*].[6] Kant's so-called formula of humanity in the second formulation of his categorical imperative – i.e., the demand to treat humanity as an end in itself – is, therefore, an inescapable element that informs the entirety of his practical philosophy, a principle that influences the tradition of critique inaugurated by him, and an important basis for a contemporary philosophy of human dignity and human rights.[7]

Some of these ideas were adopted by Georg Wilhelm Friedrich Hegel, although he criticized Kant's views as too abstract, formal, rigid, and disconnected from social and political reality. For Hegel, Kant was not critical enough because he refused to open reason to the dialectics of natural evolution, historical experiences, and concrete social practices. Thus, Hegel prefers to emphasize how individuals are dialectically subsumed to a family structure whose unity is based on love, a unity which is then negated when civil society supersedes both individuality and family to forge a community based on law and rights, subsequently sublated by a more general conscience of a national Spirit [*Volksgeist*] expressed in a Constitution – or, more precisely, in a law-giving system based on a particular ethos.[8] Like Kant, Hegel recognized the international and global dimensions of politics and rights. For instance, he initially saw the French Revolution not simply as a national political realization, but rather as the manifestation of an absolute free will that expressed a larger event, the Spirit of the world [*Weltgeist*] – a view he later changed due to Napoleon Bonaparte's invasion of Germany. He also developed his *Philosophy of Right*, in which an earlier version of what we now call human rights is related to the advent of civil society [*bürgerliche Gesellschaft*] and the association of self-sufficient individuals under the protection of legal institutions.[9] This legacy has been taken up later in Critical Theory, in the work of Herbert Marcuse, Theodor Adorno, and, among others, Axel Honneth.[10]

For Karl Marx, however, Hegel's stress on the bourgeoisie contradicted the revolutionary impetus, so Marx and Friedrich Engels rescued the tradition of criticism and added a radical twist to the meanings of "critique" and "dialectics." In his critique of Hegel's philosophy of right, Marx required a consideration of *real humans* in real historical conditions and identified a new collective agent for historical change: the proletarian class of workers who were treated as objects, so that the bourgeoisie could accumulate capital at the expense of natural and human exploitation. Based on this perspective, in his article on "The Jewish Question" Marx compared several bills and declarations of rights available at his time and showed that one of the problems with the Hegelian philosophy was its individualistic interpretation of natural rights.[11] This critique of bourgeois rights eventually led to Marx's most important contribution to the tradition of critique: his "critique of political economy."[12] His rather disapproving references to human rights and human dignity were framed by his critique of ideology and critique of political economy.[13]

2. The Frankfurt School and the question about human dignity

In the Critical Theory of Society developed by intellectuals affiliated with the University of Frankfurt – and therefore, identified as members of the "Frankfurt School" of philosophy and social sciences – these previous ideas were adapted to the conditions of contemporary European society and connected more directly with the concepts of human rights and human dignity. Following a typology suggested by Joel Anderson, we can identify several generations of philosophers connected to the Critical Theory of Society of the Frankfurt School, identified by their ages, mentors, contexts, and intellectual concerns.[14]

The *first generation* of critical theorists included intellectuals such as Max Horkheimer, Theodor Adorno, Herbert Marcuse, Walter Benjamin, Erich Fromm, and many others who contributed to the design of a new interdisciplinary methodology that allowed them to expand on the early considerations of Kant, Hegel, and Marx. Their innovative re-reading of the critical tradition reflected the transformations occurring in Germany and Europe at the beginning of the twentieth century. The transition from the Weimar Republic to the National Socialist dictatorship in Germany and retrocessions in the guarantees of equal rights motivated an ongoing dialogue among critical theorists, who denounced blatant violations and indirectly affirmed the importance of values that are now related to discourses on human dignity and human rights.[15]

For instance, in lectures at the University of Frankfurt around 1928, Horkheimer connected the theme of human dignity to his critique of science, thus preparing the ground for what he would later propose as a differentiation between traditional theory espoused by positivist science and the interdisciplinary social methodology of Critical Theory:

> If no other realities existed beyond the world of physics and psychology, then the ideals which had guided the early development of this society

and which justified the efforts of its individual members – be it human dignity, morality, freedom or something similar – were at best imagined or even fictitious.[16]

Horkheimer and Adorno collaborated in the writing of *Dialectics of the Enlightenment* in 1944, where they denounce the philosophical themes underlying authoritarianism, anti-Semitism, and the violation of human dignity during the dictatorship of National Socialism and World War II.[17] They also present their diagnosis that this evil has its origins in the very project of the Enlightenment. Adorno had a few but explicit references to human rights and human dignity as well, which became more poignant "after Auschwitz." In *Minima Moralia*, he writes – in his peculiar hermetic language – about the triviality and banality of insisting on doing art or philosophy as if nothing had happened.

> Something of the usurpation which dwells within all lecturing and indeed all reading aloud, has permeated the lucid construction of the periods, which reserve so much leisure for the most uncomfortable things. An unmistakable sign of latent contempt for human beings in the last advocate of human dignity is the dauntlessness with which he expresses platitudes, as if no-one dared to notice them: *"L'artist doit aimer la vie et nous montrer qu'elle est belle. Sans lui, nous en douterions."*[18]

In another aphorism of *Minima Moralia*, he states that "human dignity insisted on the right to walk a rhythm not extorted by the body through command or terror."[19] Finally, in his *Negative Dialectics*, he concludes that "in the concentration camps it was no longer an individual who died, but a specimen."[20] These statements correspond to initial elements of a "Critical Theory of Human Rights" which remained dormant, waiting for further considerations.

Although Ernst Bloch and Hannah Arendt were not part of the group involved with the Frankfurt School, they participated in this same context and developed much more explicit references to human rights and human dignity.[21] Bloch dedicated a whole publication to the concept of human dignity, showing how central it was to historical struggles against domination, oppression, and humiliation. In showing these struggles, he mapped the ongoing demand for human dignity, seeing it as the condition based upon which a right may be claimed and achieved.[22] This is very similar to Arendt's consideration on the "right to have rights." She started with the negative condition she observed during the dictatorship of National Socialism in Germany, when Jews were denied citizenship and stripped of their rights, and then noticed that the failure of nation-states in guaranteeing the rights of peoples is more prevalent that often assumed. Thus, in *The Origins of Totalitarianism* Arendt concluded that "Human dignity needs a new guarantee which can be found only in a new political principle, in a new law on earth, whose validity this time must comprehend the whole of humanity."[23] This tradition of reflection on social and political issues related to human dignity is still relevant today in a variety of contexts. Therefore, these initial elements of a "Critical Theory of Human Rights" have been rescued and advanced in a different direction by many other authors related to the tradition of Critical Theory.

3. Critical Theory of Human Rights and human dignity

The many violations of rights, the various forms of oppression, and the multiple structures of domination denounced by the first generation of critical theorists became visible at the end of World War II, when documentation about the systematic outrages against human dignity by means of crimes against humanity and the Holocaust gained wider public attention. After Auschwitz, as Adorno expressed it, a new world order began to emerge with the founding of the United Nations, restructuring of war-plagued nations, independence of colonized states, movements for civil rights, and the adoption of the *Universal Declaration of Human Rights* whose first article states that "All human beings are born free and equal in dignity and rights." This statement certainly encountered an echo in peoples subjugated by colonialism and racism, thus yielding new struggles for human rights, often based on the claim to human dignity.[24] However, only recently Critical Theory has addressed these issues more directly.[25]

A *second generation* of critical theorists, born before World War II, was formed in the shadow of these events and influenced by both the re-education process in Germany and the international events unfolding in the 1960s. This generation is best represented by the philosophies developed by Karl Otto-Apel and Jürgen Habermas. Apel reflected on his own experiences making the transition from National Socialism to Critical Theory, based on the recognition that a whole nation had fallen prey to particularist vicissitudes. In a long essay included in his book, *Discourse and Responsibility*, he reflected on his own journey as an officer during the war, who realized how a whole nation blindly followed the limited conventional morality of nationalism and negated the postconventional ethical universality proper of human rights.[26] As he also recognized that many sovereign states routinely disrespect human rights nowadays, Apel concentrated his intellectual efforts to develop a strong justification for universal ethics inspired by the Kantian tradition in practical philosophy and maintained a dialogue with Latin American philosophy.[27] Habermas reflected on the importance of human rights as early as in 1962, in his *Structural Transformation of the Public Sphere*, where he observed how a change from an aristocratic representation to a new bourgeois "public sphere" [*Öffentlichkeit*] based on the free and non-hierarchical human interactions led to a liberal state that established rational norms and laws to guarantee the "humanity" [*Humanität*] and basic rights of *bourgeois* and *citoyens*.[28] Much later, in *Theory of Communicative Action*, published in 1981, he indirectly discussed the paradigmatic transition of rights from religion and morality to law,[29] but a decade later – in *Between Facts and Norms* – he focused more directly on the role of the "citizen of the state" [*Staatsbürger*] and postulated the co-originality of human rights, popular sovereignty, and the democratic framework of a nation-state.[30] As he later defined human rights in relation to cosmopolitanism in a series of other publications, Habermas expanded his reflections on human rights and complemented the dimension of the national-state with the regional structure of the European Union and the global role of the United Nations.[31] In *The Crisis of the European Union: A Response*, he explicitly connected this multi-level understanding of human rights with a conception of human dignity.[32] Habermas's discussion of this theme is, therefore, a recent development in his philosophy. He expanded his views on the juridification of moral norms and their necessary translation into positive law to propose a significant revision to his own philosophy, arriving to the idea of a "co-originality" of human dignity as a complementary element to human rights, which has been enshrined in constitutional law in many countries. Thomas McCarthy not only represented Critical Theory in the United States, but also related these discussions to issues of racism.[33]

This leads to a *third generation* of critical theorists, born after World War II, educated during the 1970s, and represented by the contributions of Matthias Lutz-Bachmann, James Bohman, Nancy Fraser, Seyla Benhabib, Axel Honneth, and Klaus Günther, among others. Matthias Lutz-Bachmann reflects on the historical meanings of *humanity, rights*, and *law*, [34] but relies more directly on the Salamanca School and the original Kantian views on human rights, human dignity, and humanity to explore the ethical implications of these concepts in contemporary society. While presenting the original Kantian views on practical philosophy and interpreting them through the discourse-ethical lenses,[35] Lutz-Bachmann also addresses a series of challenges in world politics. In his view, addressing these challenges requires a new cosmopolitan theory explicitly based on the human rights framework established by the United Nations.[36] However, he insists that these rights are to be defined in relation to specific ethical norms based on freedom and autonomy, which are to be distinguished from the juridical and political applications derived from such norms. Bohman accompanies Lutz-Bachmann and his global approach, but starts from the premise that humanity and the plurality of rights are fundamental aspects necessary for a Critical Theory of Human Rights inspired by Kant's cosmopolitanism.[37] However, he sees that recent discussions about human rights have given much more emphasis on the meaning of *rights* than to the meaning of *human* because references to human worth, human dignity, human needs, or human capabilities are deemed too metaphysical or weak to provide a stable legal foundation for the universality of human rights. As an alternative to these positions, Bohman relies on Karl Jaspers and Hannah Arendt to insist on the importance of plurality and provide an insightful distinction between humanness and humanity as to better qualify the status of what is "human" in human rights.

Nancy Fraser complements this argument by emphasizing the need for the recognition of cultural difference and social equality. Relying on feminism and Marxism, she retrieves some key aspects of the first generation of critical theorists to argue that a mere affirmation of what is common to all humans or the simple recognition of difference is not enough, if social, economic, and political forms of justice are not addressed directly.[38] For her, this recognition of difference and addressing of injustices needs to be connected to a defense of human rights, but this requires a focus on particular human *needs* as well more than an emphasis on abstract *rights* of a supposedly common humanity. Abstract values may disregard particularities – such as gender, race, economic status, and others – that are often used to discriminate certain people as non-humans.[39] Seyla Benhabib rescues Arendt's statement, in *The Origins of Totalitarianism*, about the "right to have rights," which is interpreted not only as the right to belong to a community or to have the protection of a national state, but also the basic individual entitlement to be counted as part of humanity.[40] Recognizing that the current global political situation has led to a growing number of displaced persons, immigrants, refugees, and asylum see-kers who claim humanity but are denied political participation and social recognition, Benhabib established a dialogue involving modern Jewish think-ing, Arendt's political philosophy, the tradition of Critical Theory, and con-temporary theories – feminist, postmodern, liberal – in order to connect human rights more directly to human dignity. Thus, in books such as *The Rights of Others*, in *Another Cosmopolitanism*, and in *Dignity in Adversity*, [41] Benhabib insists on the proposition that human rights are ought to each and every individual on the basis of his or her human dignity, not necessarily due to one's national citizenship. As she focuses on more recent developments related to debates about the status of women, immigrants, and their human rights, she upholds the idea of democratic iterations and the need to affirm and reaffirm human dignity in times of adversity.

Finally, a *fourth generation* of critical theorists was born in the 1960s and 1970s, but still had the opportunity to study directly with Apel and Habermas and work under the third generation. In the present publication, this genera-tion is represented by Rainer Forst, Cristina Lafont, Eduardo Mendieta, Amos Nascimento, and Andreas Niederberger, who discuss human dignity from a variety of perspectives, mirroring their multifarious backgrounds and concerns of their time.

Niederberger's work on human rights is informed by historical research on medieval European philosophy, strong emphasis on Kantian political philo-sophy, and an effort to put Critical Theory in dialogue with important current of contemporary French and North American philosophies. These compo-nents come together in a systematic way in his work on cosmopolitanism and republicanism,[42] and his critique of conceptions of human rights as moral rights.[43] In addressing questions about human dignity, Niederberger provides some historical background to the concept of human dignity and then ques-tions whether the appeal to human dignity may be helpful to understand modernity or to provide the foundations for human rights.[44] He shows problematic and controversial aspects involved in the recent appeal to human dignity as a foundational concept.

Forst expands on the philosophies of Jürgen Habermas and John Rawls to develop a theory on "the right to justification," which is then applied to human rights.[45] In fact, the demand as well as the duty to justification is seen by him as a basic right. By extension, human rights can only be affirmed if they are reciprocal and universal, that is, if they can guarantee the same treatment for each and every human being without exemptions.[46] Similarly, Forst defends the idea that human dignity can be understood as a normative guarantee in light of a "right to justification."[47] Accordingly, he defines human dignity as the dignity of justificatory beings who have the right to reciprocal and universal responses to their concerns within different normative contexts. Lafont has written a series of texts on human rights and international law, in which she affirms the premise that human rights are possessed by all human beings simply in virtue of their humanity, but at the same time she criticizes state-centric limitations regarding the responsibilities to enforce and protect such rights. As alternative, she expands contemporary approaches to human rights by including new actors as agents of human rights practices.[48] Moreover, she considers that human dignity is already accepted as a premise in the existing human rights regime, but questions the use of this premise to justify rights for non-human actors. She points out that questions about human dignity bring to the fore very important challenges that need to be addressed by a critical theory today, especially as corporations appeal to human dignity to defend purely economic interests in profitability.[49]

Mendieta builds on these views by performing a creative combination of multiple perspectives. He takes up the European discourse ethics of Karl-Otto Apel and Habermas's discourse theory of morality, law, and politics; he then links it with the Latin American contributions of Anibal Quijano's decolonial theory and Enrique Dussel's liberation philosophy; and he also includes the North American pragmatist tradition that goes from Charles S. Peirce and W.E.B. Du Bois to Cornel West.[50] In this ambitious project, Mendieta addresses questions of cosmopolitanism, human rights, and human dignity in direct and indirect ways.[51] For instance, by proposing a "decolonial turn" in philosophy, he implicitly performs an archaeology of human rights, going back to conceptions of rights in Francisco de Vitoria and Bartolomé de Las Casas and including contemporary questions on the civil rights of Native Americans, African Americans, and Latinos in the United States. In this process, he also highlights the experiences of colonialism and oppression as an important condition that affects the understanding of human dignity in contemporary understandings of human rights. Mendieta, therefore, contributes to a Critical Theory of Human Rights by proposing a critique of human dignity in light of the coloniality of human rights violations.[52] Nascimento relates to these points in order to put Critical Theory in dialogue with other philosophies worldwide.[53] Acknowledging the importance of postmodern, poststructuralist, postcolonial, and neopragmatic approaches that insist on the recognition of contingencies in human practices, Nascimento criticizes contemporary theories of human rights that focus much more on rights and neglect the importance of a conceptualized humanity.[54] For him, the concept of human dignity serves as an entry point for a plurality of views on humanity as well as a critique of a positivistic conception of legal rights. Affirming that contemporary philosophies need to be more cognizant of a multiplicity of human experiences across cultures, Nascimento follows the critical tradition and defends a pluralist approach to human dignity.

Taking all these views into consideration, we can see not only how different approaches contribute to the evolving discussion on human dignity within a Critical Theory of Human Rights, but also observe a consistent line that serves as a guiding thread connecting all the authors in this volume. One of the challenges that all these authors attempt to address is the need to understand social and political change in relation to the transformation of global normative ideals, especially *human rights* norms. As each generation tries to address this issue in light of the transformations they observe at different historical moments, they relate questions of human dignity not only to core understandings of human rights, but also to social and political issues such as an emerging post-national constellation, the questioning of territorial sovereignty, the review of traditional arguments for war and cosmopolitan pacifism, the situation of immigrants and refugees, and the plight of individuals who are not adequately respected and protected by state-centered approaches. Based on the consideration of these facts and events, the goal of the authors in this book is threefold: first, to reconstruct modern philosophical theories that have contributed to a critical theory of human rights; second, to highlight the moral importance of *humanity* and human dignity in contrast and complementation to a mere emphasis on positive rights; and, finally, to see *human dignity* as a controversial but fruitful concept that needs to be discussed "critically," for it offers an entry point for a consideration of humanity and rights in times of globalization.

4. The justification of human rights by appealing to human dignity

The authors in this collection represent the variety of approaches mentioned above and follow on the footsteps of the *first generation* of critical theorists connected to the Frankfurt School. Jürgen Habermas is the most prominent member of the *second generation* and his views on human dignity and human rights are based on his discourse theory of morality and law. The *third generation* of critical theorists is represented here by Matthias Lutz-Bachmann, who amplifies the framework of Habermas's considerations by including concerns with globalization, cosmopolitanism, democratic theory, and religion. The other authors, related to a *fourth generation* of critical theorists – Cristina Lafont, Rainer Forst, Eduardo Mendieta, Andreas Niederberger, and Amos Nascimento – re-evaluate previous debates on human dignity considering recent theories of justice, multiculturalism, republicanism, decolonial theories, cosmopolitanism, and other topics. They offer unique perspectives on human dignity and how it relates to the justification of human rights.

In terms of format, this publication consists of this introduction and seven chapters organized in a chronological fashion, beginning with historical considerations on human dignity and modernity, the Kantian definition of human dignity, and other important authors mentioned above. Progressively, the texts advance to include more issues.

In "Human dignity as path to modernity in Ficino and Pico della Mirandola?" Andreas Niederberger shows how the concept of human dignity was introduced in the Renaissance as philosophers such as Marsilio Ficino and Giovanni Pico della Mirandola provided a transition from medieval to modern discourses. This was possible because their works related human dignity to both an ancient metaphysical ontology and a modern democratic conception of freedom. This provides the path based upon which contemporary debates on rights, politics, and ethics rest. In "Human rights and human dignity" Matthias Lutz-Bachmann argues that although human dignity can be traced to the historical background of ancient, medieval, and early modern philosophers such as Giovanni Pico della Mirandola, it is in the philosophy of the Enlightenment, especially in Immanuel Kant, that a particular human status is defined systematically in ethical and legal terms. He therefore provides a systematic summary of the concept of human dignity in Kant and briefly discusses how Kant's views can be relevant for contemporary debates in bioethics and constitutional law today. Jürgen Habermas's chapter, "The concept of human dignity and the realistic utopia of human rights," provides a systematic discussion on how human rights developed in response to specific violations of human dignity. Human rights generalize and grant to all humans the particularistic "dignities" that emerged throughout history and were once reserved to only a few. The articles in the *Universal Declaration of Human Rights* can be conceived as specifications on human dignity and their moral source, but they also serve to implement the moral values of universal egalitarianism in terms of positive law. Due to the co-originality, internal relationship, and complementarity between human dignity and human rights, we can now define the concept of human dignity in terms of full democratic citizenship.

The remaining chapters expand on these considerations and relate human dignity to different areas. In "The ground of critique" Rainer Forst argues that there are widely divergent philosophical, anthropological, and religious approaches to human dignity, but this concept can be defined normatively in terms of the moral status of the person as a reason-giving, reason-demanding, and reason-deserving being. This means that a basic moral right to justification is the ground for claiming dignity: a person should not be subjected to norms, rules, or institutions which cannot be properly justified to that person in appropriate practices of justification. Because human dignity means being an equal and respected member in the realm of subjects and authorities of justification, Critical Theory must focus on social and political demands raised in given historical contexts and evaluate how human dignity emerges within a given social order of justification. In her chapter, "Should we take the 'human' out of human rights?" Cristina Lafont proposes four steps. First, she offers a brief overview of the debate between humanist and political approaches to human rights in order to better identify the role of the concept of human dignity. Second, she indicates the key functions of the concept of human dignity and shows the problematic implications of leaving this concept undefined, especially the case of extending human rights to corporations. Third, she analyzes the dangers of granting human rights to corporations and ascribing dignity to all legal subjects. Finally, she defends that the protection of human dignity is the ultimate goal of human rights practices, which need to prioritize the fundamental interests of human beings over those of corporations. Lafont concludes that a jurisprudence of dignity offers some normative resources to explore this possibility.

In "Dignity, communicative freedom, and law" Eduardo Mendieta develops a constructivist, non-metaphysical, non-essentialist conception of human dignity by revisiting the historical accounts of human rights discussed in previous chapters. He defines four possible frameworks for discussions of this theme: first, a social tradition that ascribes honor and status; then a metaphysical view that speaks of the dignity of creation; third, a conception of human dignity in terms of freedom and autonomy as seen in Pico della Mirandola and Immanuel Kant; and finally, a relational affirmation of dignity by those who stand in opposition to torture, coloniality, and other forms of oppression. Mendieta concludes that human dignity ought to be based on the communicative or reflexive conception of freedom developed by Critical Theory. In the last chapter, "Human dignity and plurality in justifications of human rights," Amos Nascimento relies on a Kantian approach and the discourse-ethical version of a Critical Theory, but also puts these positions in dialogue with other philosophies as a way of highlighting the normative importance of plurality in the justification of human rights. He links John Tasioulas's pluralist approach to the contributions of Jürgen Habermas, Seyla Benhabib, and Rainer Forst in order to argue that a variety of perspectives on human dignity relates to a plurality of human rights and yields multiple human duties. It is by reflecting on the normativity of plurality and this horizontal chain of values that human dignity is affirmed, human duties emerge, and new human rights practices and institutions are developed.

The main relevance of the critical approach to human rights and human dignity is its intrinsically plurality at both the theoretical and practical levels. One of the current challenges brought against globalization and human rights discourses is that they impose one particular perspective as global and foundational, without paying due attention to the diversity of contemporary societies and the need to consider different claims according to their specificity and context. The different generations of critical theorists address issues that emerge in specific cultural and historical contexts and then transcend them, reflecting on matters of global concern and affirming the moral universality of the very act of claiming dignity or rights. Discussions on globalization now need to uphold this universality while recognizing the different voices that help us define more clearly what it means to be a "human" who claims "dignity" and "rights." This collection not only rescues and articulates important elements that may assist us to find answers to these challenges, but it also provides a collective and interdisciplinary approach, with critical conceptual tools to better understand and define the relationship between human rights and human dignity in the twenty-first century.

Notes

1 Maurice Cranston, *What Are Human Rights?* (London: Bodley Head, 1973) and Alan Gewirth, *Human Rights: Essays on Justification and Applications* (Chicago, IL: University of Chicago Press, 1982) are among the first contemporary philosophers working in this emerging field. More recent publications in the English-speaking world include Henry Shue, *Basic Rights* (Princeton, NJ: Princeton University Press, 1996); Brian Tierney, *The Idea of Natural Rights* (Grand Rapids, MI: Eerdmans, 1997); John Rawls, *The Law of Peoples* (Cambridge, MA: Harvard University Press, 1999); Johannes Morsink, *Universal Declaration of Human Rights: Origins, Drafting, and Intent* (Philadelphia, PA: University of Pennsylvania Press, 1999); Patrick Hayden (ed.), *The Philosophy of Human Rights* (St. Paul, MN: Paragon Press, 2001); Thomas Pogge, *World Poverty and Human Rights: Cosmopolitan Responsibilities and Reforms* (Cambridge: Polity Press, 2002); Carol Gould, *Globalizing Democracy and Human Rights* (Cambridge: Cambridge University Press, 2004); William Talbott, *Which Rights Should Be Universal?* (Oxford: Oxford University Press, 2005); James Nickel, *Making Sense of Human Rights* (Malden, MA: Blackwell, 2007); James Griffin, *On Human Rights* (Oxford: Oxford University Press, 2008); Charles Beitz, *The Idea of Human Rights* (Oxford: Oxford University Press, 2009); Samuel Moyn, *The Last Utopia: Human Rights in History* (Cambridge, MA: Harvard University Press, 2010); John Finnis, *Natural Law and Natural Rights* (Oxford: Oxford University Press, 2011); Conrado Corradetti (ed.), *Philosophical Dimensions of Human Rights* (New York, NY: Springer, 2012); Philip Alston and Ryan Goodman (eds.), *International Human Rights* (Oxford: Oxford University Press, 2013); Alan Buchanan, *The Heart of Human Rights* (Oxford: Oxford University Press, 2013); Jack Donnelly, *Universal Human Rights in Theory and Practice* (Ithaca, NY: Cornell University Press, 2002); Cindy Holder and David Reidy (eds.), *Human Rights: The Hard Questions* (Cambridge: Cambridge University Press, 2013). See also Rowan Cruft, S. Matthew Liao, and Massimo Renzo (eds.), *Philosophical Foundations of Human Rights* (Oxford: Oxford University, 2015).

2 Christopher McCrudden, "Human Dignity and Judicial Interpretation of Human Rights," *European Journal of International Law* 19, no. 4 (2008): 655–724 provides a detailed historical overview of various arguments for human dignity and their legal impact. See also Christopher McCrudden (ed.), *Understanding Human Dignity* [Proceedings of the British Academy, 192] (Oxford: Oxford University Press, 2013) and Marcus Düwell, Jens Braarvig, Roger Brownsword, and Dietmar Mieth (eds.), *The Cambridge Handbook of Human Dignity* (Cambridge: Cambridge University Press, 2014). Other publications include Thomas Hill, Jr., *Dignity and Practical Reason in Kant's Moral Theory* (Ithaca, NY: Cornell University Press, 1992); David Kretzmer and Eckart Klein (eds.), *The Concept of Human Dignity in Human Rights Discourse* (The Hague: Kluwer, 2002); Patrick Capps, *Human*

Dignity and the Foundations of International Law (Portland, OR: Hart Publishing, 2009); Oliver Sensen, *Kant on Human Dignity* (Berlin: De Gruyter, 2009); George Kateb, *Human Dignity* (Cambridge, MA: Harvard University Press, 2011); Paul Tiedemann, *Menschenwürde als Rechtsbegriff: Eine philosophische Klärung* (Berlin: Berliner Wissenschaftsverlag, 2012); Michael Rosen, *Dignity: Its History and Meaning* (Cambridge, MA: Harvard University Press, 2012); and Jeremy Waldron, *Dignity, Rank, and Rights* (Oxford: Oxford University Press, 2012).

3 In the African context, see Francis Deng, "Human Rights in the African Context," in Kwasi Wiredu (ed.), *A Companion to African Philosophy* (Malden, MA: Blackwell, 2004), 499–508; Thaddeus Metz, "*Ubuntu* as a Moral Theory and Human Rights in South Africa," *African Human Rights Law Journal* 11 (2011): 532–539 and "African Conceptions of Human Dignity," *Human Rights Review* 13 (2012): 19–37. For Asia, see Stephen Angle, *Human Rights and Chinese Thought* (Cambridge: Cambridge University Press, 2002) and the brief chapters in *The Cambridge Handbook of Human Dignity*: Jens Braarvig, "Hinduism: The Universal Self in Class Society" (chapter 15) and "Buddhism: Inner Dignity and Absolute Altruism" (chapter 16) as well as Luo An'Xian, "Human Dignity in Traditional Chinese Confucianism" (chapter 17) and Qiao Qing-Ju, "Dignity in Traditional Chinese Daoism" (chapter 18). From a Confucian and Neo-Confucian perspective, however, one should rather speak of human duties and humanness [*ren*]. See Confucius, *The Analects*, trans. Roger T. Ames and Henry Rosemont, Jr. (New York, NY: Random House, 1998); Qianfan Zhang, "Humanity or Benevolence? The Interpretation of Confucian *Ren* and Its Modern Implications," in Kam-Por Yu, Julia Tao, and Philip Ivanhoe (eds.), *Taking Confucian Ethics Seriously: Contemporary Theories and Applications* (Albany, NY: State University of New York Press, 2010), 53–72; Peimin Ni, *Confucius: The Man and the Way of Gongfu* (Lanham, MD: Rowman & Littlefield, 2016), 57–63; Stephen Angle and Justin Tiwald, *Neo-Confucianism: A Philosophical Introduction* (Cambridge: Polity, 2017); and Sangjin Han, "Confucianism and Human Rights," in Wonsuk Chang and Leah Kalmanson (eds.), *Confucianism in Context: Classic Philosophy and Contemporary Issues, East Asia and Beyond* (Albany, NY: State University of New York Press, 2010), 121–144. For Latin America, the Salamanca School is a basic reference: Francisco de Vitoria, *De Actibus Humanis/Sobre los Actos Humanos*, ed. and trans. Augusto Sarmiento [Reihe Politische Philosophie und Rechtstheorie des Mittelalters, Band 8] (Stuttgart: frommann-holzboog, 2015) and *De Indis/De jure belli*, ed. J.B. Scott (New York, NY: Wildy & Sons Ltd, 1917); Lewis Hanke, *All Mankind is One: A Study of the Disputation Between Bartolomé de Las Casas and Juan Ginés de Sepúlveda in 1550 on the Intellectual and Religious Capacity of the American Indians* (De Kalb, IL: Northern Illinois University Press, 1974); Mauricio Beauchot, "Bartolomé de Las Casas, el humanismo indígena y los derechos humanos," *VI Anuario Mexicano de Historia del Derecho* 37 (1994): 37–39; Paul Carroza, "From Conquest to Constitutions: Retrieving a Latin American Tradition in the Idea of Human Rights," *Human Rights Quarterly* 25 (2006): 281–313; and Enrique Dussel, "Las Casas, Vitoria, Suárez," in José-Manuel Barreto (ed.), *Human Rights from a Third World Perspective: Critique, History, and International Law* (Newcastle upon Tyne: Cambridge Scholars Publishing, 2013), 172–207. For Islam, see Abdullahi An-Na'im, "Human Rights in the Muslim World: Socio-Political Conditions and Scriptural Imperatives," *Harvard Human Rights Journal* 3 (1990): 13–52 and *Islam and Human Rights* (Surrey: Ashgate, 2010); Heiner Bielefeldt, "Muslim Voices in the Human Rights Debate," *Human Rights Quarterly* 17, no. 4 (1995): 587–617; and Muhammad Khan, *Human Rights in the Muslim World* (Durham, NC: Carolina Academic Press, 2003).

4 We proposed this terminology in Matthias Lutz-Bachmann and Amos Nascimento (eds.), *Human Rights, Human Dignity, and Cosmopolitan Ideals: Essays on Critical*

Theory and Human Rights (Surrey: Ashgate, 2014), 6. See also Douglas Kellner, "Critical Theory, Democracy, and Human Rights," *New Political Science* 1, no. 1 (1979): 12–18; Lars Rensmann, "Critical Theory of Human Rights," in Michael Thompson (ed.), *The Palgrave Handbook of Critical Theory* (New York, NY: Palgrave Macmillan, 2017), 631–653; and Rainer Forst, "A Critical Theory of Human Rights: Some Groundwork," in Penelope Deutscher and Cristina Lafont (eds.), *Critical Theory in Critical Times* (New York, NY: Columbia University Press, 2017), 74–88.

5 Immanuel Kant, *Groundwork of the Metaphysics of Morals*, trans. and ed. Mary J. Gregor (Cambridge: Cambridge University Press, 1996); original German in *Grundlegung zur Metaphysik der Sitten*, in *Werkausgabe*, Band VII, ed. Wilhelm Weischedel (Frankfurt a.M.: Suhrkamp, 2000).

6 Matthias Lutz-Bachmann and James Bohman (eds.), *Perpetual Peace* (Cambridge, MA: MIT Press, 1997). See also Matthias Lutz-Bachmann and James Bohman (eds.), *Frieden durch Recht. Kants Friedensidee und das Problem einer neuen Weltordnung* (Frankfurt a.M.: Suhrkamp, 1996) and Matthias Lutz-Bachmann, Hauke Brunkhorst, and Wolfgang Köhler (eds.), *Recht auf Menschenrechte: Menschenrechte, Demokratie und internationale Politik* (Frankfurt a.M.: Suhrkamp, 1999).

7 Sensen, *Kant on Human Dignity*, 202–211.

8 Georg Friedrich Hegel, *Enzyklopädie* in *Werke* (Frankfurt a.M.: Suhrkamp, 1977) Band 8, § 517. See also *Rechtsphilosophie* in *Werke*, Band 8, § 33, §§ 261–269.

9 Hegel, *Rechtsphilosophie*, § 187. See Michael Salter and Julia Shaw, "Towards a Critical Theory of Constitutional Law: Hegel's Contribution," *Journal of Law & Society* 21, no. 4 (December 1994): 464–486.

10 Herbert Marcuse, *Reason and Revolution: Hegel and the Rise of Social Theory* (London: Oxford University Press, 1941); Axel Honneth, *The Struggle for Recognition: The Moral Grammar of Social Conflicts*, trans. J. Anderson (Cambridge, MA: MIT Press, 1996), *The Pathologies of Individual Freedom: Hegel's Social Theory*, trans. L. Löb (Princeton, NJ: Princeton University Press, 2010), and *Freedom's Right: The Social Foundations of Democratic Life*, trans. Joseph Ganahl (New York, NY: Columbia University Press, 2014).

11 Karl Marx, "Zur Judenfrage," in *Marx and Engels Werke* [MEW] (Berlin: Dietz, 1980) Band 3, 70–77.

12 See Karl Marx, *Grundrisse: Einleitung zur Kritik der politischen Ökonomie – Rohentwurf* in *Marx and Engels Werke* [MEW] (Berlin: Dietz, 1980), Band 13.

13 See Georg Lohmann, "Human Dignity and Socialism," in Marcus Düwell, Jens Braarvig, Roger Brownsword, and Dietmar Mieth (eds.), *The Cambridge Handbook of Human Dignity* (Cambridge: Cambridge University Press, 2014), 126–134.

14 Joel Anderson, "The 'Third Generation' of the Frankfurt School," in *Intellectual History Newsletter* 22 (2000) at www.phil.uu.nl/~joel/research/publications/3rdGeneration.htm accessed on September 28, 2017.

15 Caren Irr, "One-Dimensional Symptoms: What Marcuse Offers a Critical Theory of Law," in Jeffrey T. Nealon and Caren Irr (eds.), *Rethinking the Frankfurt School: Alternative Legacies of Cultural Critique* (Albany, NY: State University of New York Press, 2012), 169–186. See also Geoffrey Robertson, *The Struggle for Global Justice: Crimes Against Humanity* (New York, NY: The New Press, 1999).

16 Max Horkheimer, "Einführung in der Philosophie der Gegenwart," in *Gesammelte Schriften*, vol. 10, ed. Alfred Schmidt (Frankfurt a.M.: Fischer, 1990), 170–333; here, 319–20.

17 Max Horkheimer and Theodor Adorno, *Dialectic of the Enlightenment: Philosophical Fragments*, trans. Edmund Jephcott (Palo Alto, CA: Stanford University Press, 2002).

18 Theodor Adorno, *Minima Moralia: Reflexionen aus dem beschädigten Leben (1944–1946)* (Frankfurt a.M.: Suhrkamp, 1997), Aphorism 62.

19 Ibid., Aphorism 102.
20 Theodor Adorno, *Negative Dialectics*, trans. E.B. Ashton (New York, NY: Seabury Press, 1973).
21 Robert Fine, "Debating Human Rights, Law, and Subjectivity: Arendt, Adorno, and Critical Theory," in Lars Rensmann and Samir Gandesha (eds.), *Arendt and Adorno: Political and Philosophical Investigations* (Palo Alto, CA: Stanford University Press, 2012), 154–172.
22 Ernst Bloch, *Natural Law and Human Dignity*, trans. D.J. Schmidt (Cambridge, MA: MIT Press, 1986).
23 Hannah Arendt, *The Origins of Totalitarianism* (New York, NY: Harcourt, Brace & Co., 1951), ix.
24 See McCrudden, "Human Dignity and Judicial Interpretation of Human Rights," for a detailed overview of these developments at various levels.
25 Amy Allen states that Critical Theory has remained silent on imperialism, racism and colonialism. See *The End of Progress: Decolonizing the Normative Foundations of Critical Theory* (New York, NY: Columbia University Press, 2017), 2. Exceptions to this indictment include Enrique Dussel, Karl-Otto Apel, and Thomas McCarthy.
26 Karl-Otto Apel, *Diskurs und Verantwortung: Das Problem des Übergangs zur postkonventionellen Moral* (Frankfurt a.M.: Suhrkamp, 1988), 377.
27 Karl-Otto Apel, "On the Relationship between Ethics, International Law and Politico-Military Strategy in Our Time: A Philosophical Retrospective on the Kosovo Conflict," *European Journal of Social Theory* 4, no. 1 (February 2001): 29–39 and "Die Diskursethik von der Herausforderung der Dritten Welt: Versuch einer Antwort an Enrique Dussel," in Raúl Fomet-Betancourt (ed.), *Diskursethik oder Befreiungsethik? Dokumentation des Seminars: Die Transzendentalpragmatik und die ethischen Probleme im Nord-Sud-Konflikt* (Aachen: Verlag der Augustinus-Buchhandlung, 1992), 18–21. See Enrique Dussel, *The Underside of Modernity: Apel Ricoeur, Rorty, Taylor, and the Philosophy of Liberation*, trans. Eduardo Mendieta (Atlantic Highlands, NJ: Humanities Press, 1996).
28 Jürgen Habermas, *The Structural Transformation of the Public Sphere*, trans. T. Burger (Cambridge, MA: MIT Press), 117–121.
29 Jürgen Habermas, *Theory of Communicative Action*, trans. T. McCarthy (Boston: Beacon Press, 1987), Vol. 2, 194, 257–265, 350.
30 Jürgen Habermas, *Between Facts and Norms: Contributions to a Discourse Theory of Law and Democracy*, trans. W. Rehg (Cambridge, MA: MIT Press, 1996), 456.
31 Jürgen Habermas, *The Inclusion of the Other: Studies in Political Theory*, trans. C. Cronin (Cambridge, MA: MIT Press, 1998), 210–216, 226–234; *The Postnational Constellation*, trans. M. Pensky (Cambridge, MA: MIT Press, 1998), 166; *The Divided West*, trans. C. Cronin (Cambridge: Polity, 2007), 135; and *Europe: The Faltering Project*, trans. C. Cronin (Cambridge: Polity, 2009), 96.
32 Jürgen Habermas, *The Crisis of the European Union*, trans. C. Cronin (Cambridge: Polity, 2012), 82, 92–93.
33 Thomas McCarthy, *Race, Empire, and the Idea of Human Development* (Cambridge: Cambridge University Press, 2009).
34 Matthias Lutz-Bachmann, Alexander Fidora, and Andreas Wagner (eds.), *Lex und Ius. Beiträge zur Begründung des Rechts in der Philosophie des Mittelalters und der Frühen Neuzeit* (Stuttgart: frommann-holzboog, 2010).
35 Matthias Lutz-Bachmann, *Grundkurs Philosophie. Band 7: Ethik* (Stuttgart: Reclam, 2013).
36 Lutz-Bachmann and Bohman, *Frieden durch Recht*; Lutz-Bachmann and Bohman, *Perpetual Peace*; Matthias Lutz-Bachmann and James Bohman (eds.), *Weltstaat oder Staatenwelt?* (Frankfurt a.M.: Suhrkamp, 2002).
37 James Bohman, *Democracy across Borders: From Dêmos to Demoi* (Cambridge, MA: MIT Press, 2007), 101f.

38 Nancy Fraser, *Justice Interruptus: Rethinking Key Concepts of a "Postsocialist" Age* (New York, NY: Routledge, 1996).

39 Nancy Fraser, "Social Justice in the Age of Identity Politics: Redistribution, Recognition and Participation," in Nancy Fraser and Axel Honneth, *Redistribution or Recognition? A Political-Philosophical Exchange* (London: Verso, 2003), 7–109.

40 Seyla Benhabib, *The Reluctant Modernism of Hannah Arendt* (Lanham, MD: Rowman & Littlefield, 2000).

41 Seyla Benhabib, *The Rights of Others: Aliens, Residents, and Citizens* (Cambridge: Cambridge University Press, 2004); *Another Cosmopolitanism* (Oxford: Oxford University Press, 2006); *Dignity in Adversity: Human Rights in Troubled Times* (Cambridge: Polity Press, 2011).

42 Andreas Niederberger, "Die Grenzen und Möglichkeiten kosmopolitanen Rechts in den Schriften von Hugo Grotius, Samuel von Pufendorf und Émer de Vattel," in Matthias Lutz-Bachmann, Andreas Niederberger, and Philipp Schink (eds.), *Kosmopolitanismus: Zur Geschichte und Zukunft eines umstrittenen Ideals* (Weilerswist: Velbrück, 2010), 101–121; "Recht als Grund der *res publica* und *res publica* als Grund des Rechts: Zur Theorie legitimer Herrschaft und des *ius gentium* bei Francisco de Vitoria," in Kirstin Bunge (ed.), *Die Normativität des Rechts bei Francisco de Vitoria* (Stuttgart: frommann-holzboog, 2011), 171–200; "Kant und der Streit um den Kosmopolitismus in der politischen Philosophie," in Oliver Eberl (ed.), *Transnationalisierung der Volkssouveränität: radikale Demokratie diesseits und jenseits des Staates* (Stuttgart: Franz Steiner Verlag, 2011), 295–316.

43 Andreas Niederberger, "Are Human Rights Moral Rights?" in Matthias Lutz-Bachmann and Amos Nascimento (eds.), *Human Rights, Human Dignity, and Cosmopolitan Ideals: Essays on Critical Theory and Human Rights* (Surrey: Ashgate, 2014), 75–92.

44 Andreas Niederberger, "*Esse servitutis omnis impatientem*/Man is Impatient of All Servitude: Human Dignity as a Path to Modernity in Ficino and Pico della Mirandola?" *The European Legacy: Towards New Paradigms* 20, no. 5 (2015): 513–526.

45 Rainer Forst, "The Justification of Basic Rights and the Basic Right to Justification," *Ethics* 120, no. 4 (2010): 711–740.

46 Rainer Forst, *Justification and Critique: Towards a Critical Theory of Politics* (Cambridge: Polity, 2013).

47 Rainer Forst, "The Basic Right to Justification: Toward a Constructivist Conception of Human Rights," *Constellations* 6, no. 1 (March 1999): 35–60; "The Ground of Critique: On the Concept of Human Dignity in Social Orders of Justification," in *Justification and Critique* (Cambridge: Polity, 2013); and "A Critical Theory of Human Rights: Some Groundwork."

48 Cristina Lafont, *Global Governance and Human Rights* (Amsterdam: Van Gorcum, 2012).

49 Cristina Lafont, "Should We Take the 'Human' Out of Human Rights? Human Dignity in a Corporate World," *Ethics and International Affairs* 30, no. 2 (June 2016): 233–252.

50 Eduardo Mendieta, *The Adventures of Transcendental Philosophy: Karl-Otto Apel's Semiotics and Discourse Ethics* (Lanham, MA: Rowman & Littlefield, 2003) and *Global Fragments: Latinamericanism, Globalizations, and Critical Theory* (Albany, NY: SUNY Press, 2007). See also, *Thinking from the Underside of History: Enrique Dussel's Philosophy of Liberation*, ed. Eduardo Mendieta and Linda Martín Alcoff (Lanham: Rowman & Littlefield, 2000) and *Pragmatism, Racism, Empire: Community in the Age of Empire*, ed. Eduardo Mendieta (Bloomington, IN: Indiana University Press, 2009).

51 Eduardo Mendieta, "From Imperial to Dialogical Cosmopolitanism," in Matthias Lutz-Bachmann and Amos Nascimento (eds.), *Human Rights, Human Dignity, and Cosmopolitan Ideals: Essays on Critical Theory and Human Rights* (Surrey:

Ashgate, 2014), 119–138, "World Society, Public Sphere and Cosmopolitanism," in Raúl Fornet-Betancourt, Hans Schelkshorn, and Franz Gmainer-Pranzl (eds.), *Auf dem Weg zu einer gerechten Universalität: Philosophische Grundlagen und Politische Perspektiven* (Aachen: Wissenschaftsverlag Mainz, 2013), 127–139, and "Globalization, Cosmopolitics, Decoloniality: Politics for/of the Anthropocene," in Andrew Fiala (ed.), *Bloomsbury Companion to Political Philosophy* (London: Bloomsbury, 2015), 213–221.

52 Eduardo Mendieta, "The Legal Orthopedia of Human Dignity: Thinking with Axel Honneth," in *Philosophy and Social Criticism* 40, no. 8 (Fall 2014): 799–815.

53 Amos Nascimento, *Building Cosmopolitan Communities: A Critical and Multidimensional Approach* (New York, NY: Palgrave Macmillan, 2013) and "From Plural Worldviews to Global Human Rights Discourses: On Multiculturalism, Interculturalism, and the Possibility of an Overlapping Consensus," in *Revista de Direito* 1/2 (Jul-Dec 2015): 7–26. See also Amos Nascimento (ed.), *A Matter of Discourse: Community and Communication in Contemporary Philosophies* (Aldershot: Ashgate, 1998) and Amos Nascimento and Kirsten Witte (eds.), *Grenzen der Moderne: Europa und Lateinamerika* (Frankfurt a.M.: Verlag für Interkulturelle Kommunikation, 1997).

54 Amos Nascimento, "Human Rights and the Paradigms of Cosmopolitanism: From Rights to Humanity," in Matthias Lutz-Bachmann and Amos Nascimento (eds.), *Human Rights, Human Dignity, and Cosmopolitan Ideals: Essays on Critical Theory and Human Rights* (Surrey: Ashgate, 2014), 95–117.

References

Adorno, Theodor. *Minima Moralia: Reflexionen aus dem beschädigten Leben (1944–1946)* (Frankfurt a.M.: Suhrkamp, 1997).

Adorno, Theodor. *Negative Dialectics*, trans. E.B. Ashton (New York, NY: Seabury Press, 1973).

Allen, Amy. *The End of Progress: Decolonizing the Normative Foundations of Critical Theory* (New York, NY: Columbia University Press, 2017).

Alston, Philip and Ryan Goodman (eds.). *International Human Rights* (Oxford: Oxford University Press, 2013).

An'Xian, Luo. "Human Dignity in Traditional Chinese Confucianism," in Marcus Düwell, Jens Braarvig, Roger Brownsword, and Dietmar Mieth (eds.), *The Cambridge Handbook of Human Dignity* (Cambridge: Cambridge University Press, 2014), 177–181.

Anderson, Joel. "The 'Third Generation' of the Frankfurt School," *Intellectual History Newsletter* 22 (2000) at www.phil.uu.nl/~joel/research/publications/3rdGeneration. htm accessed on September 28, 2017.

Angle, Stephen. *Human Rights and Chinese Thought* (Cambridge: Cambridge University Press, 2002).

Angle, Stephen and Justin Tiwald. *Neo-Confucianism: A Philosophical Introduction* (Cambridge: Polity, 2017).

An-Na'im, Abdullahi. *Islam and Human Rights* (Surrey: Ashgate, 2010).

An-Na'im, Abdullahi. "Human Rights in the Muslim World: Socio-Political Conditions and Scriptural Imperatives," *Harvard Human Rights Journal* 3 (1990): 13–52.

Apel, Karl-Otto. "On the Relationship between Ethics, International Law and Politico-Military Strategy in Our Time: A Philosophical Retrospective on the Kosovo Conflict," *European Journal of Social Theory* 4, no. 1 (February 2001): 29–39.

Apel, Karl-Otto. "Die Diskursethik von der Herausforderung der Dritten Welt: Versuch einer Antwort an Enrique Dussel," in Raúl Fornet-Betancourt (ed.), *Diskursethik oder Befreiungsethik? Dokumentation des Seminars: Die Transzendentalpragmatik und die ethischen Probleme im Nord-Sud-Konflikt* (Aachen: Verlag der Augustinus-Buchhandlung, 1992), 18–21.

Apel, Karl-Otto. *Diskurs und Verantwortung: Das Problem des Übergangs zur postkonventionellen Moral* (Frankfurt a.M.: Suhrkamp, 1988).

Arendt, Hannah. *The Origins of Totalitarianism* (New York, NY: Harcourt, Brace & Co., 1951).

Beauchot, Mauricio. "Bartolomé de Las Casas, el humanismo indígena y los derechos humanos," *VI Anuario Mexicano de Historia del Derecho* 37 (1994): 37–39.

Beitz, Charles. *The Idea of Human Rights* (Oxford: Oxford University Press, 2009).

Benhabib, Seyla. *Dignity in Adversity: Human Rights in Troubled Times* (Cambridge: Polity Press, 2011).

Benhabib, Seyla. *Another Cosmopolitanism* (Oxford: Oxford University Press, 2006).

Benhabib, Seyla. *The Rights of Others: Aliens, Residents, and Citizens* (Cambridge: Cambridge University Press, 2004).

Benhabib, Seyla. *The Reluctant Modernism of Hannah Arendt* (Lanham, MD: Rowman & Littlefield, 2000).

Bielefeldt, Heiner. "Muslim Voices in the Human Rights Debate," *Human Rights Quarterly* 17, No. 4 (1995): 587–617.

Bloch, Ernst. *Natural Law and Human Dignity*, trans. D.J. Schmidt (Cambridge, MA: MIT Press, 1986).

Bohman, James. *Democracy across Borders: From Dêmos to Demoi* (Cambridge, MA: MIT Press, 2007).

Braarvig, Jens. "Buddhism: Inner Dignity and Absolute Altruism," in Marcus Düwell, Jens Braarvig, Roger Brownsword, and Dietmar Mieth (eds.), *The Cambridge Handbook of Human Dignity* (Cambridge: Cambridge University Press, 2014), 170–176.

Braarvig, Jens. "Hinduism: The Universal Self in Class Society," in Marcus Düwell, Jens Braarvig, Roger Brownsword, and Dietmar Mieth (eds.), *The Cambridge Handbook of Human Dignity* (Cambridge: Cambridge University Press, 2014), 165–169.

Buchanan, Alan. *The Heart of Human Rights* (Oxford: Oxford University Press, 2013).

Capps, Patrick. *Human Dignity and the Foundations of International Law* (Portland, OR: Hart Publishing, 2009).

Carroza, Paul. "From Conquest to Constitutions: Retrieving a Latin American Tradition in the Idea of Human Rights," *Human Rights Quarterly* 25 (2006): 281–313.

Confucius. *The Analects*, trans. Roger T. Ames and Henry Rosemont, Jr. (New York, NY: Random House, 1998).

Corradetti, Conrado (ed.). *Philosophical Dimensions of Human Rights* (New York, NY: Springer, 2012).

Cranston, Maurice. *What Are Human Rights?* (London: Bodley Head, 1973).

Cruft, Rowan, S. Matthew Liao and Massimo Renzo (eds.). *Philosophical Foundations of Human Rights* (Oxford: Oxford University Press, 2015).

Deng, Francis. "Human Rights in the African Context," in Kwasi Wiredu (ed.), *A Companion to African Philosophy* (Malden, MA: Blackwell, 2004), 499–508.

Donnelly, Jack. *Universal Human Rights in Theory and Practice* (Ithaca, NY: Cornell University Press, 2002).

Dussel, Enrique. "Las Casas, Vitoria, Suárez," in José-Manuel Barreto (ed.), *Human Rights from a Third World Perspective: Critique, History, and International Law* (Newcastle upon Tyne: Cambridge Scholars Publishing, 2013), 172–207.

Dussel, Enrique. *The Underside of Modernity: Apel Ricoeur, Rorty, Taylor, and the Philosophy of Liberation*, trans. Eduardo Mendieta (Atlantic Highlands, NJ: Humanities Press, 1996).

Düwell, Marcus, Jens Braarvig, Roger Brownsword, and Dietmar Mieth (eds.). *The Cambridge Handbook of Human Dignity* (Cambridge: Cambridge University Press, 2014).

Fine, Robert. "Debating Human Rights, Law, and Subjectivity: Arendt, Adorno, and Critical Theory," in Lars Rensmann and Samir Gandesha (eds.), *Arendt and Adorno: Political and Philosophical Investigations* (Palo Alto, CA: Stanford University Press, 2012), 154–172.

Finnis, John. *Natural Law and Natural Rights* (Oxford: Oxford University Press, 2011).

Forst, Rainer. "A Critical Theory of Human Rights: Some Groundwork," in Penelope Deutscher and Cristina Lafont (eds.), *Critical Theory in Critical Times* (New York, NY: Columbia University Press, 2017), 74–88.

Forst, Rainer. "The Ground of Critique: On the Concept of Human Dignity in Social Orders of Justification," in *Justification and Critique* (Cambridge: Polity, 2013), 95–108.

Forst, Rainer. *Justification and Critique: Towards a Critical Theory of Politics* (Cambridge: Polity, 2013).

Forst, Rainer. "The Justification of Basic Rights and the Basic Right to Justification," *Ethics* 120, No. 4 (2010): 711–740.

Forst, Rainer. "The Basic Right to Justification: Toward a Constructivist Conception of Human Rights," *Constellations* 6, no. 1 (March 1999): 35–60.

Francisco de Vitoria. *De Actibus Humanis/Sobre los Actos Humanos*, ed. and trans. Augusto Sarmiento [Reihe Politische Philosophie und Rechtstheorie des Mittelalters, Band 8] (Stuttgart: frommann-holzboog, 2015).

Francisco de Vitoria. *De Indis/De jure belli*, ed. J.B. Scott (New York, NY: Wildy & Sons Ltd, 1917).

Fraser, Nancy. "Social Justice in the Age of Identity Politics: Redistribution, Recognition and Participation," in Nancy Fraser and Axel Honneth, *Redistribution or Recognition? A Political-Philosophical Exchange* (London: Verso, 2003), 7–109.

Fraser, Nancy. *Justice Interruptus: Rethinking Key Concepts of a "Postsocialist" Age* (New York, NY: Routledge, 1996).

Gewirth, Alan. *Human Rights: Essays on Justification and Applications* (Chicago, IL: University of Chicago Press, 1982).

Gould, Carol. *Globalizing Democracy and Human Rights* (Cambridge: Cambridge University Press, 2004).

Griffin, James. *On Human Rights* (Oxford: Oxford University Press, 2008).

Habermas, Jürgen. *The Crisis of the European Union*, trans. C. Cronin (Cambridge: Polity, 2012).

Habermas, Jürgen. *Europe: The Faltering Project*, trans. C. Cronin (Cambridge: Polity, 2009).

Habermas, Jürgen. *The Divided West*, trans. C. Cronin (Cambridge: Polity, 2007).

Habermas, Jürgen. *The Inclusion of the Other: Studies in Political Theory*, trans. C. Cronin (Cambridge, MA: MIT Press, 1998).

Habermas, Jürgen. *The Postnational Constellation*, trans. M. Pensky (Cambridge, MA: MIT Press, 1998).

Habermas, Jürgen. *Between Facts and Norms: Contributions to a Discourse Theory of Law and Democracy*, trans. W. Rehg (Cambridge, MA: MIT Press, 1996).

Habermas, Jürgen. *The Structural Transformation of the Public Sphere*, trans. T. Burger (Cambridge, MA: MIT Press, 1989).

Habermas, Jürgen. *Theory of Communicative Action*, trans. T. McCarthy (Boston, MA: Beacon Press, 1987), Vol. 2.

Han, Sangjin. "Confucianism and Human Rights," in Wonsuk Chang and Leah Kalmanson (eds.), *Confucianism in Context: Classic Philosophy and Contemporary Issues, East Asia and Beyond* (Albany, NY: State University of New York Press, 2010), 121–144.

Hanke, Lewis. *All Mankind is One: A Study of the Disputation Between Bartolomé de Las Casas and Juan Ginés de Sepúlveda in 1550 on the Intellectual and Religious Capacity of the American Indians* (De Kalb, IL: Northern Illinois University Press, 1974).

Hayden, Patrick (ed.). *The Philosophy of Human Rights* (St. Paul, MN: Paragon Press, 2001).

Hegel, Georg Wilhelm Friedrich. *Werke* (Frankfurt a.M.: Suhrkamp, 1977).

Hill Jr., Thomas. *Dignity and Practical Reason in Kant's Moral Theory* (Ithaca, NY: Cornell University Press, 1992).

Holder, Cindy and David Reidy (eds.). *Human Rights: The Hard Questions* (Cambridge: Cambridge University Press, 2013).

Honneth, Axel. *Freedom's Right: The Social Foundations of Democratic Life*, trans. Joseph Ganahl (New York, NY: Columbia University Press, 2014).

Honneth, Axel. *The Pathologies of Individual Freedom: Hegel's Social Theory*, trans. L. Löb (Princeton, NJ: Princeton University Press, 2010).

Honneth, Axel. *The Struggle for Recognition: The Moral Grammar of Social Conflicts*, trans. J. Anderson (Cambridge, MA: MIT Press, 1996).

Horkheimer, Max. "The Emancipation of Philosophy from Science" [Lectures from the 1920s] in Max Horkheimer, *Gesammelte Schriften*, Vol. 10, ed. Alfred Schmidt (Frankfurt a.M.: Fischer, 1990), 169–419.

Horkheimer, Max and Theodor Adorno. *Dialectic of the Enlightenment: Philosophical Fragments*, trans. Edmund Jephcott (Palo Alto, CA: Stanford University Press, 2002).

Irr, Caren. "One-Dimensional Symptoms: What Marcuse Offers a Critical Theory of Law," in Jeffrey T. Nealon and Caren Irr (eds.), *Rethinking the Frankfurt School: Alternative Legacies of Cultural Critique* (Albany, NY: State University of New York Press, 2012), 169–186.

Kant, Immanuel. *Groundwork of the Metaphysics of Morals*, trans. and ed. Mary J. Gregor (Cambridge: Cambridge University Press, 1996); originally in German as *Grundlegung zur Metaphysik der Sitten*, in *Werkausgabe*, Band VII, ed. Wilhelm Weischedel (Frankfurt a.M.: Suhrkamp, 2000).

Kateb, George. *Human Dignity* (Cambridge, MA: Harvard University Press, 2011).

Kellner, Douglas. "Critical Theory, Democracy, and Human Rights," *New Political Science* 1, no. 1 (1979): 12–18.

Khan, Muhammad. *Human Rights in the Muslim World* (Durham, NC: Carolina Academic Press, 2003).

Kretzmer, David and Eckart Klein (eds.). *The Concept of Human Dignity in Human Rights Discourse* (The Hague: Kluwer, 2002).

Lafont, Cristina. "Should We Take the 'Human' Out of Human Rights? Human Dignity in a Corporate World," *Ethics and International Affairs* 30, no. 2 (June 2016): 233–252.

Lafont, Cristina. *Global Governance and Human Rights* (Amsterdam: Van Gorcum, 2012).

Lohmann, Georg. "Human Dignity and Socialism," in Marcus Düwell, Jens Braarvig, Roger Brownsword, and Dietmar Mieth (eds.), *The Cambridge Handbook of Human Dignity* (Cambridge: Cambridge University Press, 2014), 126–134.

Lutz-Bachmann, Matthias. *Grundkurs Philosophie. Band 7: Ethik* (Stuttgart: Reclam, 2013).

Lutz-Bachmann, Matthias and James Bohman (eds.). *Weltstaat oder Staatenwelt?* (Frankfurt a.M.: Suhrkamp, 2002).

Lutz-Bachmann, Matthias and James Bohman (eds.) *Perpetual Peace* (Cambridge, MA: MIT Press, 1997).

Lutz-Bachmann, Matthias and James Bohman (eds.) *Frieden durch Recht. Kants Friedensidee und das Problem einer neuen Weltordnung* (Frankfurt a.M.: Suhrkamp, 1996).

Lutz-Bachmann, Matthias and Amos Nascimento (eds.). *Human Rights, Human Dignity, and Cosmopolitan Ideals: Essays on Critical Theory and Human Rights* (Surrey: Ashgate, 2014 [new edition, London: Routledge, 2016]).

Lutz-Bachmann, Matthias, Hauke Brunkhorst, and Wolfgang Köhler (eds.). *Recht auf Menschenrechte: Menschenrechte, Demokratie und internationale Politik* (Frankfurt a.M.: Suhrkamp, 1999).

Lutz-Bachmann, Matthias, Alexander Fidora, and Andreas Wagner (eds.). *Lex und Ius: Beiträge zur Begründung des Rechts in der Philosophie des Mittelalters und der Frühen Neuzeit* (Stuttgart: frommann-holzboog, 2010).

Marcuse. Herbert. *Reason and Revolution: Hegel and the Rise of Social Theory* (London: Oxford University Press, 1941).

Marx, Karl. "Zur Judenfrage," in *Marx and Engels Werke* [MEW] (Berlin: Dietz, 1980) Band 3, 70–77.

Marx, Karl. *Grundrisse: Einleitung zur Kritik der politischen Ökonomie – Rohentwurf* in *Marx and Engels Werke* [MEW] (Berlin: Dietz, 1980), Band 13.

McCarthy, Thomas. *Race, Empire, and the Idea of Human Development* (Cambridge: Cambridge University Press, 2009).

McCrudden, Christopher (ed.). *Understanding Human Dignity* [*Proceedings of the British Academy, 192*] (Oxford: Oxford University Press, 2013).

McCrudden, Christopher. "Human Dignity and Judicial Interpretation of Human Rights," *European Journal of International Law* 19, no. 4 (2008): 655–724.

Mendieta, Eduardo. "Globalization, Cosmopolitics, Decoloniality: Politics for/of the Anthropocene," in Andrew Fiala (ed.), *Bloomsbury Companion to Political Philosophy* (London: Bloomsbury, 2015), 213–221.

Mendieta, Eduardo. "From Imperial to Dialogical Cosmopolitanism," in Matthias Lutz-Bachmann and Amos Nascimento (eds.), *Human Rights, Human Dignity, and Cosmopolitan Ideals: Essays on Critical Theory and Human Rights* (Surrey: Ashgate, 2014), 119–138.

Mendieta, Eduardo. "The Legal Orthopedia of Human Dignity: Thinking with Axel Honneth," *Philosophy and Social Criticism* 40, no. 8 (Fall 2014): 799–815.

Mendieta, Eduardo. "World Society, Public Sphere and Cosmopolitanism," in Raúl Fornet-Betancourt, Hans Schelkshorn, and Franz Gmainer-Pranzl (eds.), *Auf dem*

Weg zu einer gerechten Universalität: Philosophische Grundlagen und Politische Perspektiven (Aachen: Wissenschaftsverlag Mainz, 2013), 127–139.

Mendieta, Eduardo. *Global Fragments: Latinamericanism, Globalizations, and Critical Theory* (Albany, NY: SUNY Press, 2007).

Mendieta, Eduardo. *The Adventures of Transcendental Philosophy: Karl-Otto Apel's Semiotics and Discourse Ethics* (Lanham, MA: Rowman & Littlefield, 2003).

Mendieta, Eduardo (ed.). *Pragmatism, Racism, Empire: Community in the Age of Empire* (Bloomington, IN: Indiana University Press, 2009).

Mendieta, Eduardo and Linda Martín Alcoff (eds.). *Thinking from the Underside of History: Enrique Dussel's Philosophy of Liberation* (Lanham: Rowman & Littlefield, 2000).

Metz, Thaddeus. "African Conceptions of Human Dignity," *Human Rights Review* 13 (2012): 19–37.

Metz, Thaddeus. "*Ubuntu* as a Moral Theory and Human Rights in South Africa," *African Human Rights Law Journal* 11 (2011): 532–539.

Morsink, Johannes. *Universal Declaration of Human Rights: Origins, Drafting, and Intent* (Philadelphia, PA: University of Pennsylvania Press, 1999).

Moyn, Samuel. *The Last Utopia: Human Rights in History* (Cambridge, MA: Harvard University Press, 2010).

Nascimento, Amos. "From Plural Worldviews to Global Human Rights Discourses: On Multiculturalism, Interculturalism, and the Possibility of an Overlapping Consensus," *Revista de Direito* 1/2 (Jul-Dec 2015): 7–26.

Nascimento, Amos. "Human Rights and the Paradigms of Cosmopolitanism: From Rights to Humanity," in Matthias Lutz-Bachmann and Amos Nascimento (eds.), *Human Rights, Human Dignity, and Cosmopolitan Ideals: Essays on Critical Theory and Human Rights* (Surrey: Ashgate, 2014), 95–117.

Nascimento, Amos. *Building Cosmopolitan Communities: A Critical and Multidimensional Approach* (New York, NY: Palgrave Macmillan, 2013).

Nascimento, Amos (ed.). *A Matter of Discourse: Community and Communication in Contemporary Philosophies* (Aldershot: Ashgate, 1998).

Nascimento, Amos and Kirsten Witte (eds.). *Grenzen der Moderne: Europa und Lateinamerika* (Frankfurt a.M.: Verlag für Interkulturelle Kommunikation, 1997).

Ni, Peimin. *Confucius: The Man and the Way of Gongfu* (Lanham, MD: Rowman & Littlefield, 2016).

Nickel, James. *Making Sense of Human Rights* (Malden, MA: Blackwell, 2007).

Niederberger, Andreas. "Esse servitutis omnis impatientem/Man is Impatient of All Servitude: Human Dignity as a Path to Modernity in Ficino and Pico della Mirandola?" *The European Legacy: Towards New Paradigms* 20, no. 5 (2015): 513–526.

Niederberger, Andreas. "Are Human Rights Moral Rights?" in Matthias Lutz-Bachmann and Amos Nascimento (eds.), *Human Rights, Human Dignity, and Cosmopolitan Ideals: Essays on Critical Theory and Human Rights* (Surrey: Ashgate, 2014), 75–92.

Niederberger, Andreas. "Kant und der Streit um den Kosmopolitismus in der politischen Philosophie," in Oliver Eberl (ed.), *Transnationalisierung der Volkssouveränität: radikale Demokratie diesseits und jenseits des Staates* (Stuttgart: Franz Steiner Verlag, 2011), 295–316.

Niederberger, Andreas. "Recht als Grund der *res publica* und *res publica* als Grund des Rechts: Zur Theorie legitimer Herrschaft und des *ius gentium* bei Francisco de Vitoria," in Kristin Bunge (ed.), *Die Normativität des Rechts bei Francisco de Vitoria* (Stuttgart: frommann-holzboog, 2011), 171–200.

Niederberger, Andreas. "Die Grenzen und Möglichkeiten kosmopolitanen Rechts in den Schriften von Hugo Grotius, Samuel von Pufendorf und Émer de Vattel," in Matthias Lutz-Bachmann, Andreas Niederberger, and Philipp Schink (eds.), *Kosmopolitanismus: Zur Geschichte und Zukunft eines umstrittenen Ideals* (Weilerswist: Velbrück, 2010), 101–121.

Pogge, Thomas. *World Poverty and Human Rights: Cosmopolitan Responsibilities and Reforms* (Cambridge: Polity Press, 2002).

Qing-Ju, Qiao. "Dignity in Traditional Chinese Daoism," in Marcus Düwell, Jens Braarvig, Roger Brownsword, and Dietmar Mieth (eds.), *The Cambridge Handbook of Human Dignity* (Cambridge: Cambridge University Press, 2014), 182–187.

Rawls, John. *The Law of Peoples* (Cambridge, MA: Harvard University Press, 1999).

Rensmann, Lars. "Critical Theory of Human Rights," in Michael Thompson (ed.), *The Palgrave Handbook of Critical Theory* (New York, NY: Palgrave Macmillan, 2017), 631–653.

Robertson, Geoffrey. *The Struggle for Global Justice: Crimes Against Humanity* (New York, NY: The New Press, 1999).

Rosen, Michael. *Dignity: Its History and Meaning* (Cambridge, MA: Harvard University Press, 2012).

Salter, Michael and Julia Shaw. "Towards a Critical Theory of Constitutional Law: Hegel's Contribution," *Journal of Law & Society* 21, no. 4 (December 1994): 464–486.

Sensen, Oliver. *Kant on Human Dignity* (Berlin: De Gruyter, 2009).

Shue, Henry. *Basic Rights* (Princeton, NJ: Princeton University Press, 1996).

Talbott, William. *Which Rights Should Be Universal?* (Oxford: Oxford University Press, 2005).

Tiedemann, Paul. *Menschenwürde als Rechtsbegriff: Eine philosophische Klärung* (Berlin: Berliner Wissenschaftsverlag, 2012).

Tierney, Brian. *The Idea of Natural Rights* (Grand Rapids, MI: Eerdmans, 1997).

Waldron, Jeremy. *Dignity, Rank, and Rights* (Oxford: Oxford University Press, 2012).

Zhang, Qianfan. "Humanity or Benevolence? The Interpretation of Confucian *Ren* and Its Modern Implications," in Kam-Por Yu, Julia Tao, and Philip Ivanhoe (eds.), *Taking Confucian Ethics Seriously: Contemporary Theories and Applications* (Albany, NY: State University of New York Press, 2010), 53–72.

2 Human dignity as a path to modernity in Ficino and Pico della Mirandola?

Andreas Niederberger

In the course of the twentieth century, human dignity became a major point of reference in the debate about rights, politics, and ethics. The UN declarations and covenants on human rights consider "freedom, justice and peace in the world" to be founded on the "recognition of the inherent dignity and of the equal and inalienable rights of all members of the human family."[1] National constitutions, prominently in Germany and Israel, attribute a preeminent role to human dignity, which has resulted in strong forms of judicial review in both countries.[2] And in political and ethical debates on the use of genetic diagnostics or genetic engineering the question of their compatibility with human dignity is often applied as an important moral standard.[3] At the same time there is no consensus on the meaning of human dignity and some even think that it is redundant and can be reduced to other moral standards, like autonomy. It is only agreed that human dignity comes simply with the humanity of human beings (i.e., it does not depend on any special achievement, position, or form of life) and that it imposes strict obligations on second and third parties or even on entire legal and political systems.[4]

Human dignity seems to be tied to both modern and premodern aspects of politics and ethics: It looks modern since it emphasizes the foundational role of mere humanness or equal individuality detaching the rights and the political or moral status of persons from any specific cosmological, social, or communitarian function or their position in a theological order. It also seems related, however, to the premodern idea of a given, probably even ontological, "moral" universe (the idea of the goodness of each human being) creating values and obligations beyond social contracts and the requirements for right, that is, reasonable and mutually justifiable standards of coexistence and interaction. Especially this second dimension stops many from referring to human dignity, because one could understand such a reference, first, as defending a problematic moral realism or Platonism and, second, as authorizing political decisions based not on democratic legitimacy, but on moral expertise or even ultimately arbitrary interpretations of legal documents.[5]

This ambiguity of the modern legal, political, and ethical concept of human dignity suggests that we should reconsider its history and especially its role among some of the Renaissance writers who are commonly seen as originators of the modern concept.[6] Such a reconsideration can serve two purposes. On the one hand, it can contribute to a better understanding of the contemporary concept of human dignity by highlighting some of the ideas that led to its current status. On the other hand, it is also interesting to re-evaluate the "modernity" of some of the writers of the fifteenth and sixteenth centuries, because for many the "discovery" of human dignity in Renaissance philosophy is one of its main path-breaking achievements on the way to modernity. But if human dignity is an ambiguous concept (i.e., a concept that merges modern and premodern aspects), one might wonder which aspects of the concept the Renaissance thinkers developed or established.

Critics of the thesis that it was the Renaissance thinkers' concept of human dignity that paved the way to modernity have argued that for these thinkers human dignity primarily expresses a relation to other beings, namely, that human beings are superior especially to animals. Human dignity, thus, is no inherent property of human beings, but depends on the existence of other beings lacking certain capacities. Moreover, these critics have pointed out that in the relevant texts human dignity lays no direct moral obligations on others, but rather leads to obligations toward oneself. On this view, human dignity does not refer to the absolute value of the individual person – which in turn implies that the central role of individuals in modern times is, if at all, only contingently related to the Renaissance idea of human dignity.[7]

Opposing this view, Paul Oskar Kristeller, though aware of at least some of these difficulties, still defends the modernity thesis. He argues that we should understand the idea of human dignity in Renaissance philosophy (in Petrarch, Ficino, Pico, and Pomponazzi) as the way to modernity in three respects. First it moved the focus away from the theological role of human beings to humanity as such, to human beings in their "natural" appearance in the world. Second, possibly by comparing human beings to other animals, it initiated the removal of human beings from the "chain of being." For Pico della Mirandola, for example, Kristeller argues, human beings no longer have a "determined nature and ... fixed place in the hierarchy of beings,"[8] so that the comparison is one between fundamentally different kinds of beings. Human beings are superior to other animals because they differ in their "ontological status" and not simply because they are higher in the hierarchy of beings. They are thus able to relate themselves to all other beings, which, third, leads to the idea of individuality as the "self-fashioning" of one's existence and the duty to "self-fashion" it (i.e., human beings cannot simply conceive of themselves as having a natural or assigned "purpose" or role anymore). To sum up Kristeller's view: at least some of the Renaissance ideas on human dignity are modern, because they liberate human beings from mere subjection to the "history of being" and open up the space for individual responsibility for one's own life. Neither ontology nor community prescribe or should prescribe how one should lead one's life.[9]

While embracing Kristeller's emphasis on the particular ontological understanding of human beings in thinkers like Ficino and Pico, I contend that it is not "modern" because it liberates human beings from the "history of being," from the expectations and the pressure of the community, or because it opens the world to some kind of creative individualism. The case of Pico will show that the prominent role of liberty can even result in tying dignity to specific achievements and deserts. The particular ontological understanding is modern because it views individuals as rational beings whose rationality can only be exercised by them. It is, thus, a liberation to being rational beings. This assumes that each and every person has dignity, which, in turn, entails duties in regard to other persons, and which – mediated by many additional thoughts – leads to the ideas of modern rights and democracy.

While several Renaissance writers discuss human dignity in various treatises and texts, the study of all these contributions to the discourse on human dignity, especially its relationship to medieval philosophy and its role in the changing religious, social and cultural contexts of the fifteenth and sixteenth centuries, has only just begun.[10] In the following I will not attempt a general survey of all the positions and ideas on human dignity,[11] but will focus on Marsilio Ficino (1433–99) and Giovanni Pico della Mirandola (1463–94). These are not only the most prominent Renaissance writers on the subject but are also among the most challenging. They combine ideas of human particularity with strongly Platonic views of the coherence and order of beings. The question thus is how Ficino and Pico can assert that being is the overarching, divinely ordained realm of goodness and at the same time that human beings differ in ontological status from other beings, which undermines the idea of one coherent and continuous realm of being and confers on human beings a particular dignity. In the last part of this chapter, I will return to the question of these authors' modernity and offer an interpretation of their contribution to the development of the concept of human dignity as part of its revised understanding today.

1. Ficino's Platonic theology, complexities of ontology, and human dignity

Any study of human dignity in Ficino and Pico must start by noting that *dignitas* is not a key term in their texts. In the eighteen books of Ficino's major work, the *Theologia Platonica de Immortalitate Animorum* (1469–74), *dignitas* is used less than fifteen times and some of the usages are even in quotations from other authors, namely Plato.[12] And Pico della Mirandola's *Oratio de hominis dignitate* (1486) is famously considered an important text on human dignity because of its title and not because the term appears in the text. Moreover, the semantic field of *dignitas* is quite wide, making it difficult to assume that one can pin down a univocal meaning in these texts to gain a precise understanding of their concept(s) of human dignity. In some passages, *dignitas* just means value or higher value, whereas in others it denotes something more complex. Ficino's and Pico's concept of human dignity must be read with the methodological premise that it is not strictly tied to the term (*hominis*) *dignitas*, though their concept must at least be compatible with the existing use of the term in the texts.

In his *Theologia Platonica* Ficino offers two perspectives on how human beings come close(r) to God or the highest being (the highest good for human beings)[13]: in the first he analyses – often following Plato and other Neo-Platonists – the similarity/dissimilarity of the faculties and capabilities of human beings compared to those of higher beings like angels or even God. Here Ficino mainly describes the purposes and abilities of the human body and human soul from an objective or ontological point of view. He presents an *exitus-reditus* scheme, which, on the one hand, explains how the world proceeded from God, and, on the other hand, shows how the proximity to the origin of being depends on the degree to which material beings are or become less and less material. Human beings are "composite" beings, which is why they can achieve a higher position than they would naturally have done by developing their more ideal parts (especially their soul).

The second perspective, in contrast, sounds like a contribution to the *studia humanitatis* as it was known from less Platonic authors, those who were less interested in a coherent and continuous view of being. Here Ficino presents observations on human beings in real social and political contexts and interprets them as expressions of human nature. In his observations, often related to quite material actions and behaviors and thus unlike the ideal detachment of the soul from the body, human beings seem to act as if they were themselves gods:

> We have ... declared that man is forever striving to rule over himself and over all others, men and beasts; that he is impatient of all servitude; that even if he is compelled to serve, he hates his master in that to serve is contrary to [his] nature. But he strives resolutely in everything to achieve mastery and is ashamed to be overcome in even the smallest matters and the most frivolous games as being counter to man's natural dignity ... Thus man wants neither a superior nor an equal, nor does he suffer anything to thrive outside his dominion. [But] this condition is God's alone. Thus, man seeks the divine condition ... Finally, all men want the same thing, and if they hope to attain it in the future they will proceed as though they are going to lay claim to divinity as their right.[14]

Platonists and Neo-Platonists traditionally favored a life of contemplation over an active or a political life. They often suggested that the (God-)given hierarchy of being implied the need to subject oneself to this hierarchy and to attempt to assimilate oneself to God by leaving material existence with its practical necessities and the limitations of the human body behind. Ficino himself takes this view (not only directly but self-reflectively by pointing out that "all Platonists" share it) in many chapters of the *Platonic Theology*, where he advocates contemplation as the way to unite human beings with God.[15] In his commentary on Plato's *Symposium* (1469), for example, he explains that the difference between good and bad love does not depend on the actions or practical attitudes of the lovers but on the effects their love has for approximating the divine ideal and/or on their enjoyment of bodily pleasures.[16]

A person's mode of behavior toward others, in contrast, as stated in the quotation above, shows that Ficino holds that one can see man's approximation to God (also) in his refusal to subject himself to others or to a pre-given order. Human beings assimilate themselves to God in their practical aspiration to be masters and not subjects, and in doing so they even claim a right (*ius*) to divinity. Ficino ties human dignity (and indeed here he uses the term *hominis dignitas*) to this practical attitude of refusing subjugation to anyone or of being ruled by somebody or something else. Human dignity thus seems to consist in being in a position where one decides on one's own existence and on the order of things and persons surrounding one.

Yet how can these two ways of approximating God or the highest human perfection go together? How can one come closer to God both by accepting the hierarchy of being and by trying to elevate oneself through contemplation above worldly preoccupations,[17] and simultaneously by claiming an un-dominated, active position in the world, that is, by claiming to be god in the world and for the world? How can human beings be said to have a "soul [which] has been endowed with such dignity that it has been granted in a way an infinite power of understanding and of willing"?[18] Ficino is quite careful in delimiting the negative and positive aspects in one's claim to have a right to divinity. He does not simply argue that human beings approximate God by claiming the right to a kind of voluntarist or arbitrary liberty with respect to their existence and the existence of those who depend or could depend on them. Some elements of such voluntarism emerge in a passage, where Ficino describes human operations as competing with "nature," but the description immediately following also indicates the limits of this voluntarism:

> Men by contrast are the inventors of numberless arts that they pursue at their own choosing. Evidence is the fact that individual men practice many of the arts and they develop and become more skilled as a result of daily practice; and what is marvelous is that human arts make on their own whatever nature itself makes: it is as if we were not her slaves but her rivals ... Man's power is very like the power of divine nature, since man rules himself through himself, that is, through his own counsel and art: uncircumscribed by the limits of corporeal nature, he emulates the individual work of higher nature. He needs the help of lower nature far less than the animals to the extent that he has been allotted fewer protections for his body than the brutes; and he has used his own resources to grow his own food, and to make his own clothes, coverings, dwellings, furnishings, and arms. Since he therefore supports himself by his own ability, he supports himself more lavishly than nature herself supports the beasts.[19]

Human beings rival nature and because of this they are not strictly determined by anything pre-given (if by nature we mean the necessity and determination that are independent of the will of those who are part of it). But the aim of this rivalry is still to achieve a state in which human beings can subsist and flourish – and this means that they can subsist and flourish better than or at least as well as they would have with the "support" of nature alone. Human beings thus imitate nature and its way of functioning, yet they do not create a second "un-natural" world with wholly different laws and conditions. They act "as if they were not nature's slaves," which means that they remain its slaves in the sense that they must meet the same goals as nature. Human beings will still have to be provided with the "natural" resources for their survival and to continue their existence as a species. Men can choose different means to attain these resources and can even develop arts, knowledge and techniques with which to produce them in different ways than nature produces them, or they can resort to different resources and, in this sense, human beings do not have to subject themselves to nature. But they are not in a position to simply decree or defy the fulfillment of their vital needs: they must set up a "second" or "other" nature.

What are the consequences of this double structure of in- or under-determination and of necessity for Ficino's understanding of human dignity? Human dignity consists in being oneself the rational being who does the right things for survival and flourishing.[20] Human beings refuse to be dominated by others because they claim to be sufficiently rational to understand what is necessary and best for them and capable of taking the actions required by their initial insights. Human dignity thus does not express a "positive" desire for individualism, for a domain that one can regard as one's own, where one may take idiosyncratic decisions and where one is a "small scale sovereign" (in the words of H.L.A. Hart), but rather it expresses the negative claim that others should not pretend to know better what is right and good for oneself, or be in a position to make decisions that are more rational than one's own decisions. This anti-paternalism, which goes far beyond the medieval acknowledgment of human beings' *liberum arbitrium*,[21] opens up the possibility to develop other ways to meet one's goals and the option to set different goals for oneself – but these are effects of one's claim to dignity and not the reason for or the purpose of this claim.

2. Pico della Mirandola on human dignity: between liberty and desert

Studies on the work of Ficino's disciple Pico della Mirandola[22] have stressed his search for unity in the manifold forms of being, thinking, and discourse.[23] Unlike other Neo-Platonists he rejected the "simple" option of turning away from the diversity of beings in the world to (mystically) contemplate God's or the highest being's oneness and simplicity. For Pico the diversity and complexity of beings, thinking, and discourse express the power and nature of the highest unity. The original "unity" was powerful enough to produce the existing multiplicity, and now this multiplicity has the task of reaching a new kind of unity without simply returning to its original unity. As a result, the new unity must be grasped through an understanding of the diversity in its unifying aspects (without reducing it to its common origin). Pico thus searches for new ways of viewing the unity in and of the different beings and realms of being, or in and of the seeming contradictions between texts, authors, and schools. These ways should lead one to apprehend the highest unity as the unity and peaceful coexistence of all beings, thoughts, and ideas in their heterogeneity.[24]

This recognition that diversity and unity belong together and that unity exists in the diversity itself leads to a new appreciation of humanity and of man's cognitive faculties in two respects. First, the very existence of human beings is an important expression of unity in diversity, since what is distinctive about human beings is that they have no fixed essence and are open to many forms of life, but are also capable of achieving some kind of unity in their life. Human beings are, as Pico writes, taking up Fragment 106 of the Chaldaean Oracles, "animal[s] of diverse, multiform, and destructible nature."[25] Like Ficino, who stressed the human duty to overcome corporeal nature by detaching the soul and its divine, unitary aspects from the physical body, Pico assumes the same obligation as the starting point from which humans must develop their life – which ideally is a life of pure contemplation:

> If you see a man given over to his belly and crawling upon the ground, it is a bush not a man that you see. If you see anyone blinded by the illusions of his empty and Calypso-like imagination, seized by the desire of scratching, and delivered over to the senses, it is a brute not a man that you see. If you come upon a philosopher winnowing out all things by right reason, he is a heavenly not an earthly animal. If you come upon a pure contemplator, ignorant of the body, banished to the inner-most places of the mind, he is not an earthly, not a heavenly animal; he more superbly is a divinity clothed with human flesh.[26]

Thus, being human does not in itself determine what kind of being one is: human beings can lead the life of a plant, an animal, a rational being, or God. Their being as such is open to all these possibilities. Like Ficino, Pico thus reinforces the in- or under-determination of human beings, their ontological "liberty," suggesting that being human consists in a variety of potentialities that require finding some unity that is neither given, nor obvious in any single life.

But Pico does not limit his description of human beings to these external relations to other beings or to their objective integration into the realm of beings. He, second, also points out that humans' cognitive faculties have a particularly strong ability to detect and bring about unity in diversity. These faculties can synthesize the diversity of the given, but most of all they can detect viewpoints or principles that enable human beings to find the compatibility and at best the necessity of seeming contradictions and mutually exclusive phenomena. From these viewpoints, the phenomena do not simply appear as defective in their seeming lack of unity. Rather, it becomes clear as to why their diversity, or even exclusiveness, serve the end of establishing a true or higher unity.[27] And this is why philosophy is the most important achievement of humanity, since for Pico it is the perpetual questioning and opening up of seemingly fixed insights and oppositions. Philosophy teaches us to take fresh looks at phenomena and to debate and discover each time anew their points of convergence, while simultaneously being an active exercise of the philosopher's highest human faculties.[28]

This double reflection on the human being and human faculties leads Pico to an important distinction between the theoretical and practical faculties. By virtue of the former, human beings can at most understand why the contradictions are necessary, as for instance when natural philosophy explains that tensions and struggles among animals are expressions of the particular unity of nature, or when in theology humans contemplate the highest form of unity in God. With respect to their own "nature," in contrast, human beings can achieve a different kind of unity that is not primarily the object of understanding and contemplation but of practical decisions, which unity is therefore the object of moral philosophy and not of natural philosophy or theology.[29] Since the starting points of both natural and moral philosophy are similar, whether for understanding the fights among animals or the tensions among sentiments and penchants, moral philosophy will also use those faculties that enable the detection of unity within diversity. But whereas natural philosophy will have to accept the necessity of diversity and contradictions as constitutive principles of nature's unity, moral philosophy can teach human beings how to transcend that state so as to achieve the higher unity that resembles God's unity.[30]

How are these thoughts on diversity and unity and the particularity of human faculties related to Pico's concept of human dignity? As mentioned before, Pico emphasizes much more strongly than Ficino the under-determination and liberty of human beings in their initial state. Because of this under-determination and liberty human beings must use their will to strive and activate their cognitive faculties for realizing a certain form of life and the will itself is a necessary factor for the level and kind of unity a human being will achieve. This emphasis on the will and its exercise has led some to argue that Pico presents a two-tiered concept of human dignity. On the first level, human dignity consists in the fact of human liberty with regard to their will and being, which gives them a higher value than other beings. However, on a second level, human beings only "deserve" this higher value, if they use their liberty in the right way by choosing a contemplative or at least rational form of life. Thus, in contrast to Ficino, one would have to assert that for Pico "real" or full dignity is the result of a person's good life and that it commands others to act respectfully towards that person only if she achieves a dignified life.[31]

It might be true that the ultimate goal of Pico's work is to argue for a specific form of dignified life. But does this mean that one only "deserves" the conditions for such a life if one makes the right use of these conditions? One way to reject this "conditionality" of dignity is to point out that liberty has independent value for Pico, which becomes clear, for instance, when one looks at his view on the Fall of Man.[32] The problem with this interpretation is that one ends up weighing different values (i.e., the value of a dignified life is higher than that of an undignified life, but the value of an undignified life is still higher than that of an imposed form of life or of non-existence, etc.). It would already be difficult to understand why, given the teleological structure of human existence, liberty as such should have value (which would call for a different kind of justification than that offered by moral teleology). But at least the weighing of values would lead to a hierarchy of human beings and not (necessarily) imply that what is required is a state where one is not subject to another person because of their equal dignity.

Pico, like Ficino, certainly thinks that human beings can arrive at the right form of life only if they choose it themselves, and thus on this point he shares Ficino's anti-paternalism. But whereas for Ficino human dignity primarily consists in this negative claim of not being dominated by others,[33] it is less clear what Pico's anti-paternalism entails for others, given his much stronger emphasis on voluntarism and on singular unities that are found and achieved each time by one person.[34] It thus seems right to say that Pico's concept of dignity primarily applies to the person leading the dignified life. This person will claim recognition of her dignity from others only after having taken the right decisions, not before. Ficino, in contrast, is much more interested in the consequences of dignity for the relationship between human beings.

3. How modern are Ficino's and Pico's concepts of dignity?

As thinkers Ficino and Pico were obviously not modern in their Neo-Platonic approaches to being, goodness, and reason. They had not yet overcome the theologico-metaphysical view of the world and of knowledge that conceived the categories and forms of our cognition as real, though at least partially immaterial entities. In this respect, one must acknowledge that they were even less modern than the medieval Aristotelians who in their "second beginning of metaphysics"[35] marginalized the role of philosophical theology and concentrated on ontology as a science of being as being. These medieval Aristotelians, like Albert the Great, Thomas Aquinas and others, thought of metaphysics or ontology as a science that provided them with the concepts and categories necessary to understand the most general properties and aspects of individual beings – a science that supplemented the other sciences of different realms of being rather than a science that encompassed and integrated the other sciences. Ficino and Pico, in contrast, despite their views of the diversity and partial indeterminacy of being and thought (still) operated within the framework of one "unitary science," which ultimately subsumed all particular bodies of knowledge under the highest form of contemplation. This is decidedly a premodern view of science and of the role of philosophy with respect to other sciences and forms of knowledge.

However, their concepts of human dignity are clearly closer to modernity than those of medieval philosophers. And one can even say that in some respects especially Ficino's concept of dignity is more modern than those presented by some twentieth- and twenty-first-century writers who see human dignity as the expression of the presumable fact that human beings are good in themselves. Given their Neo-Platonic understanding of science and philosophy, one could expect Ficino and Pico to offer a concept of human dignity that ties dignity either to the particular position of human beings in the hierarchy of being, to the specific cognitive abilities of human beings, or to the intrinsic goodness of their being. All these points are important in their general philosophical approach, but with respect to human dignity they take a different stand. Starting from the anti-paternalist insight that human beings are "naturally" free and able to make the right choices for their own lives themselves, both Ficino and Pico argue that human dignity relates to the ability of human beings to understand what is rational or good and to act accordingly.

Traditionally, Pico has been seen as the more modern of the two Renaissance philosophers, mainly because of his emphasis on human liberty and indeterminacy. This may seem to prefigure the modern idea of individual liberty, which eventually – so runs the typical story of modernity – lead to individual rights, the claim to individual domains of free choice, and individual responsibility for one's own life.[36] On the basis of my reconstruction of Pico's concept of human dignity, this view is in need of further clarification. First, one would still have to find in his texts an appreciation of liberty that does not depend on its teleological function for achieving a life of contemplation. Most of Pico's arguments on the value of liberty show that freedom is necessary if one is to reach the highest kind of unity in one's life. This, in turn, means that liberty could lose its value if persons lead the wrong or a less ideal life. Second, even if one could find a different justification of liberty in Pico's texts, this would still not mean that it is one of the concepts of liberty that later became important for modern morality, law, and politics. These modern concepts are not simply based on the recognition or the esteem of the liberty of each and every human being, but there are very different normative and non-normative, positive and negative or instrumental and non-instrumental concepts of liberty, which are more or less important for modernity. To be a modern thinker it is not enough to stress liberty – the Ancients also had their ideas of liberty as Benjamin Constant already noted in his famous lecture in 1819.[37]

If one brackets the too simplistic assumption or presumption that any defense of liberty is modern, Ficino's negative claim to human dignity as nondomination is the more modern concept, first because it is not strictly tied to the assumption that human beings or their liberty are intrinsically good and, second, because it implies that second and third parties will have to respect this dignity absolutely. If human beings are beings who only live rationally, if they live rationally by themselves, then this excludes almost all external interventions in their exercise of reason. "Almost all" because there might be situations where persons are so mistaken about what is right and good for them that interventions are necessary and admissible to ensure that these persons maintain their abilities to exercise their own rationality (even in such cases one could not exercise rationality for them, but only guarantee that they do not act in a way that fully undermined their rational abilities). This is exactly the shared aspect common to all contemporary understandings of human dignity in social and political contexts. This dignity is violated when some second or third party undermines the capacity of a person to relate to others as a member of the human species or as an equal within a given political or social context. In such a violation of dignity the victim can no longer understand her doings or her situation as the exercise of her abilities, which is why she can no longer stand up for her actions and the life she leads.[38]

But Pico's view of dignity is not unimportant for modernity – and it is not unimportant in its presumably premodern part: dignity obviously still has much to do with the way human beings relate to themselves and their lives. Thus, people can lead an "undignified" life that makes it impossible for them to relate to themselves in a way that is required for relating to others as equals or as members of the same species. Without self-respect, which is probably a better term for this aspect of dignity, human beings would very likely not be able to stand up to others and claim their respect for their own humanness.

But even though human dignity consists of these two aspects – of one's relation to oneself and to others – one should not reverse the order of obligations. Seen in negative terms – and this is the main conclusion of my interpretation of Ficino – the obligation not to dominate others, which is entailed by their (possible) dignity, is more fundamental than their or one's own obligation to lead a life of self-respect. In other words, the non-existence of self-respect can never be a reason to dominate another person.

Notes

1 One can find the exact same formulation in the Preambles of the Universal Declaration of Human Rights, the International Covenant on Civil and Political Rights, the International Covenant on Economic, Social and Cultural Rights and other UN documents. Further UN declarations refer to the "dignity and worth of the human person" (e.g., the Declaration on the Elimination of Discrimination against Women).

2 See Ernst Benda, "The Protection of Human Dignity (Article 1 of the Basic Law)," *SMU Law Review* 53 (2000): 443–456; Izhak Englard, "Human Dignity: From Antiquity to Modern Israel's Constitutional Framework," *Cardozo Law Review* 21, no. 5–6 (2000): 1903–1927. Even the US Supreme Court has referred to "human dignity" especially with regard to free choices concerning one's life and freedom of expression. See Michael J. Meyer and William A. Parent (eds.), *The Constitution of Rights: Human Dignity and American Values* (Ithaca, NY: Cornell University Press, 1992), and Maxine D. Goodman, "Human Dignity in Supreme Court Constitutional Jurisprudence," *Nebraska Law Review* 84, no. 3 (2005–6): 740–794.

3 See, for example, Nikolaus Knoepffler, Dagmar Schipanski, and Stefan Lorenz Sorgner (eds.), *Humanbiotechnology as Social Challenge* (Aldershot: Ashgate, 2007).

4 General bibliographies on human dignity are provided by Bjorn Haferkamp, "The Concept of Human Dignity: An Annotated Bibliography," in *Sanctity of Life and Human Dignity*, ed. Kurt Bayertz (Dordrecht: Kluwer, 1996), 275–291, and George Kateb, *Human Dignity* (Cambridge, MA: Belknap Press, 2011).

5 See Christopher McCrudden, "Human Dignity and Judicial Interpretation of Human Rights," *European Journal of International Law* 19, no. 4 (2008): 655–724. For a defense of the "metaphysical" aspect of human dignity, see Michael Rosen, *Dignity: Its History and Meaning* (Cambridge, MA: Harvard University Press, 2012), 144–156.

6 As an alternative view, one could also consider Ancient Rome, the Jewish tradition, or medieval Christian thought as the origin of a legal concept of dignity. See Teresa Iglesias, "Bedrock Truths and the Dignity of the Individual," *Logos: A Journal of Catholic Thought and Culture* 4, no. 1 (2001): 111–134, and Stéphanie Hennette-Vauchez, "A Human *dignitas*? Remnants of the Ancient Legal Concept in Contemporary Dignity Jurisprudence," *International Journal of Constitutional Law* 9, no. 1 (2011): 32–57. On this Roman and Christian background, see also Jeremy Waldron, "Dignity and Rank," *European Journal of Sociology* 48, no. 2 (2007): 201–237, and Jürgen Habermas, "The Concept of Human Dignity and the Realistic Utopia for Human Rights," *Metaphilosophy* 41, no. 4 (July 2010): 464–480.

7 See, for example, Oliver Sensen, "Human Dignity in Historical Perspective: The Contemporary and Traditional Paradigms," *European Journal of Political Theory* 10, no. 1 (2011): 71–91.

8 Paul Oskar Kristeller, *Renaissance Thought and Its Sources* (New York: Columbia University, 1979), 175.

9 Kristeller, *Renaissance Thought and Its Sources*, 180–181.

10 See, for example, Amos Edelheit, "Human Will, Human Dignity, and Freedom: A Study of Giorgio Benigno Salviati's Early Discussion of the Will, Urbino 1474–1482," *Vivarium* 46, no. 1 (2008): 82–114.

11 This implies that there will be no direct discussion of the texts defending human dignity against Pope Innocent III's suggestion of the *miseria hominis*. The most notorious example of this discussion is Giannozzo Manetti's *De Dignitate et excellentia hominis* (1452; reprint edited by Elizabeth R. Leonard, Padova: Antenore, 1975). Implicit references to this discussion can be found in the idea of human dignity as the result of the *studia humanitatis*.

12 The use of *dignitas* in a quotation from Plato is interesting in itself, since the term does not have a clear corresponding term in Greek. But *dignitas* served as the translation for the Greek word "αξίωμα" (*axioma*). See, on the history of the translation of Greek words with the Latin term *dignitas*, Ramsay MacMullen, "The Power of the Roman Empire," *Historia. Zeitschrift für Alte Geschichte* 55, Heft 4 (2006): 471–481.

13 This chapter will obviously not present a general study on the whole work of Ficino but concentrate on the narrow question of his understanding of human dignity. Important publications on Ficino's philosophy include Michael J.B. Allen, *Plato's Third Eye: Studies in Marsilio Ficino's Metaphysics and its Sources* (Aldershot: Ashgate, 1995); Michael J.B. Allen, Valery Rees, and Martin Davies (eds.), *Marsilio Ficino: His Theology, His Philosophy, His Legacy* (Leiden: Brill, 2002); Matthias Bloch and Burkhard Mojsisch (eds.), *Potentiale des menschlichen Geistes: Freiheit und Kreativität, praktische Aspekte der Philosophie Marsilio Ficinos (1433–1499)* (Stuttgart: Steiner, 2003); Stephen Clucas, Peter J. Forshaw, and Valery Rees (eds.), *Laus Platonici Philosophi: Marsilio Ficino and his Influence* (Leiden: Brill, 2011); Paul Oskar Kristeller, *The Philosophy of Marsilio Ficino*

(New York: Columbia University Press, 1943); Maria Christine Leitgeb, Stéphanie Toussaint, and Herbert Bannert (eds.), *Platon, Plotin, und Marsilio Ficino: Studien zu den Vorläufern und zur Rezeption des Florentiner Neuplatonismus* (Vienna: Verlag der Österreichischen Akademie der Wissenschaften, 2009). In a more general study one would also have to discuss how revelation and philosophical theology are related in Ficino's work. See on this issue Michael J.B. Allen, "At Variance: Marsilio Ficino, Platonism, and Heresy," in Douglas Hedley and Sarah Hutton (eds.), *Platonism at the Origins of Modernity: Studies on Platonism and Early Modern Philosophy* (Dordrecht: Springer, 2008), 31–44; Ardis B. Collins, *The Secular Is Sacred: Platonism and Thomism in Ficino's Platonic Theology* (The Hague: Nijhoff, 1974); Amos Edelheit, *Ficino, Pico, and Savonarola: The Evolution of Humanist Theology 1461/2–1498* (Leiden: Brill, 2008).

14 "Diximus etiam hominem semper contendere ut et sibi ipsi ceteris cunctis tum hominibus tum bestiis dominetur. Esse servitutis omnis impatientem. Qui etiam si servire cogatur, odit dominum, utpote qui serviat contra naturam. Superare autem obnixe qualibet in re contendit, pudetque vel in rebus minimis ludisque levissimis superari, tamquam id sit contra naturalem hominis dignitatem … Ita nec superiorem vult homo nec parem, neque patitur superesse aliquid ab imperio eius exclusum. Solius dei hic status est. Statum igitur quaerit divinum … Denique omnes idem affectant, et si successurum sperarent, aggrederentur quasi iure suo vindicent sibi divinitatem." Marsilio Ficino, *Platonic Theology, Vol. 4., Books XII–XIV* (Cambridge, MA: Harvard University Press, 2004), 249/51 viz. 248/50 (bk. 14, chap. 4).

15 "And all Platonists support the view that, in the contemplation of rational principles, the divine reason is 'touched' by a substantial, not just by an imaginary, touching of the mind; and that the unity proper to the mind is joined to God, the unity of all things, in a manner beyond our conception. Plato often confirms this in the *Phaedrus* and the *Epinomis* and elsewhere, and particularly when he says in the *Phaedrus* that the contemplator of things divine is set apart from other men and totally purified, and that he cleaves to God and is filled with God; and in the *Epinomis*, that the rational soul, made perfect by contemplation, emerges wholly unified in the presence of the divine unity." "Et Platonici omnes probant in rationibus contemplandis divinam rationem tactu quodam mentis substantiali potius quam imaginario tangi, unitatemque mentis propriam deo rerum omnium unitati modo quodam inaestimabili copulari. Quod Plato in *Phaedro* et in *Epinomide* et alibi saepe confirmat, praesertim quando in *Phaedro* divinorum ait contemplatorem a reliquis segregari, purgari prorsus, haerere deo, impleri deo et in *Epinomide* animum contemplatione perfectum penes divinam unitatem unum prorsus evadere" (4.28/29; bk. 12, chap. 2).

16 Marsilio Ficino, *De amore / Über die Liebe oder Platons Gastmahl* (Hamburg: Meiner, 2004). Similarly, in his discussion of justice Ficino argues that human virtue is only a small contribution compared to God's justice. Justice, here, seems to depend on contemplating "that whatever happens eventually leads to the good" (*ut quaecumque contingunt, in bonum denique perducatur*) (4.324/25; bk. 14, chap. 10).

17 See on this also the following passage: "Yet why are we not aware of the wondrous spectacle of that divine mind which is ours? Perhaps it is either because, given that we are continually used to seeing it, we have lost the habit of admiring and noticing it, or because the intermediary faculties of the soul, the reason, and the phantasy, being for the most part more involved in life's daily affairs, do not clearly view the works of the divine mind." "Verum cur non animadvertimus tam mirabile nostrae illius divinae mentis spectaculum? Forsitan quia propter continuam spectandi consuetudinem admirari et animadvertere desuevimus, aut quia mediae vires animae, ratio videlicet et phantasia, cum sint ut plurimum ad negotia vitae procliviores, mentis illius opera non clare persentiunt" (4.50/52 viz. 51; bk. 12, chap. 4).

18 "humanus animus tanta est dignitate donatus ut concessa sibi fuerit infinita quodammodo virtus intellegendi ac volendi." Marsilio Ficino, *Platonic Theology, Vol. 2, Books V–VIII* (Cambridge, MA: Harvard University Press, 2002), 368/69; bk. 8, chap. 15.

19 "Contra homines artium innumerabilium inventores sunt, quas suo exsequuntur arbitrio. Quod significatur ex eo quod singuli multas exercent artes, mutant, et diuturno usu fiunt solertiores, et quod mirabile est, humanae artes fabricant per se ipsas quaecumque fabricat ipsa natura, quasi non servi simus naturae, sed aemuli ... Similis ergo ferme vis hominis est naturae divinae, quandoquidem homo per se ipsum, id est per suum consilium atque artem, regit se ipsum a corporalis naturae limitibus minime circumscriptum, et singula naturae altioris opera aemulatur. Et tanto minus quam bruta naturae inferioris eget subsidio, quanto pauciora corporis munimenta sortitus est a natura quam bruta, sed ipsemet illa sua copia construit alimenta, vestes, stramenta, habitacula, suppellectilia, arma. Ideo cum ipse sua facultate se fulciat, fulcit uberius quam bestias ipsa natura" (4.169/71 viz. 168/70; bk. 13, chap. 3).

20 This is an unspecific use of "rationality," which includes both the sense of "instrumental rationality" (choosing the right/best means for given ends) and of a broader concept of reason, which also relates to final ends. Obviously, this second meaning of rationality is more important in many passages of the *Platonic Theology*, but in the preceding quotation Ficino also seems to have in view a narrower concept of instrumental rationality.

21 Relevant authors here are, among others, Thomas Aquinas, John Duns Scotus, and William of Ockham.

22 For a comprehensive list of publications on Pico see Leonardo Quaquarelli and Zita Zanardi, *Pichiana: Bibliografia delle edizioni e degli studi* (Florence: Olschki, 2005). See also the documentation of English publications at www.mvdougherty.com/pico.htm (accessed on September 4, 2017).

23 See with many references to other important research on Pico, Oliver W. Lembcke, "Die Würde des Menschen, frei zu sein. Zum Vermächtnis der *Oratio de hominis dignitate* Picos della Mirandola," in Rolf Gröschner, Stephan Kirste, and Oliver W. Lembcke (eds.), *Des Menschen Würde – entdeckt und erfunden im Humanismus der italienischen Renaissance* (Tübingen: Mohr Siebeck, 2008), 159–186.

24 On the relationship between unity and peace in Pico, see Paul Richard Blum, "Eintracht und Religion bei Giovanni Pico della Mirandola," in Norbert Brieskorn and Markus Riedenauer (eds.), *Suche nach Frieden: Politische Ethik in der frühen Neuzeit II* (Stuttgart: Kohlhammer, 2002), 29–46.

25 Giovanni Pico della Mirandola, *On the Dignity of Man*, in *On the Dignity of Man / On Being and the One / Heptaplus* (Indianapolis, IN: Hackett, 1998), 6. "Id est homo, variae ac multiformis et desultoriae naturae animal." Pico della Mirandola, *De hominis dignitate / Über die Würde des Menschen* (Stuttgart: Reclam, 2009), 12. See also the new English translation and commentary of the *Oratio* in *Pico della Mirandola – Oration on the Dignity of Man: A New Translation and Commentary*, ed. Francesco Borghesi, Michael Papio, and Massimo Riva (Cambridge: Cambridge University Press, 2012).

26 Pico, *On the Dignity*, 6. "Si quem enim videris deditum ventri humi serpentem hominem, frutex est, non homo, quem vides; si quem in phantasiae quasi Calypsus vanis praestigiis caecutientem et subscalpenti delinitum illecebra sensibus mancipatum, brutum est, non homo, quem vides; si recta philosophum ratione omnia discernentem, hunc venereris: caeleste est animal, non terrenum; si purum contemplatorem corporis nescium, in penetralia mentis relegatum: hic non terrenum, non caeleste animal, hic augustius est numen humana carne circumvestitum" (*De hominis*, 10–12).

27 This part of Pico's thought has led many to consider him as a major precursor of modern idealism (especially Hegel) and its conception of dialectics.

28 "Philosophy herself has taught me to weigh things rather by my own conscience than by the judgments of others, and to consider not so much whether I should be badly spoken of as whether I myself should say or do anything bad" (*On the Dignity*, 18); "Docuit me ipsa philosophia a propria potius conscientia quam ab externis pendere iudiciis cogitareque semper non tam ne male audiam quam ne quid male vel dicam ipse vel agam" (*De hominis*, 40).

29 "Indeed, fathers, there is multiple discord in us, and we have severe, intestine, and more than civil wars at home: if we are unwilling to have these wars, if we will strive for that peace which so lifts us up to the heights that we are made to stand among the exalted of the lord, moral philosophy alone will still those wars in us, will bring calm successfully" (*On the Dignity*, 10–11); "Multiplex profecto, patres, in nobis discordia; gravia et intestina domi habemus et plus quam civilia bella. Quae si noluerimus, si illam affectaverimus pacem, quae in sublime ita nos tollat, ut inter excelsos domini statuamur, sola in nobis compescet prorsus et sedabit philosophia moralis" (*De hominis*, 22).

30 See Pico, *On the Dignity*, 11–12; *De hominis*, 22–24.

31 See on this reading of Pico, Eckhard Keßler, "Menschenwürde in der Renaissance," in Anne Siegetsleitner and Nikolaus Knoepffler (eds.), *Menschenwürde im interkulturellen Dialog* (Freiburg: Alber, 2005), 41–66.

32 Compare this interpretation with Lembcke, "Die Würde des Menschen," 177.

33 See on the distinction between "positive" and "negative" freedom the crucial and highly problematic essay by Isaiah Berlin, "Two Concepts of Liberty," in *Four Essays on Liberty* (Oxford: Oxford University Press, 1969), 118–172. On the understanding of "non-domination" as a third (or different negative) concept of freedom, see Philip Pettit, *Republicanism: A Theory of Freedom and Government* (Oxford: Oxford University Press, 1997), and in a more historical perspective Quentin Skinner, *Liberty Before Liberalism* (Cambridge: Cambridge University Press, 1998).

34 See for example the following passage from Pico's *On the Dignity*: "But why all this? In order for us to understand that, after having been born in this state so that we may be what we will to be, then, since we are held in honor, we ought to take particular care that no one may say against us that we do not have knowledge, similar to brutes and mindless beasts of burden" (7; translation modified). "Sed quorsum haec? ut intellegamus, postquam hac nati sumus condicione, ut id sumus, quod esse volumus, curare hoc potissimum debere nos, ut illud quidem in nos non dicatur, cum in honore essemus, non cognovisse similes factos brutis et iumentis insipientibus" (*De hominis*, 12).

35 See on this reconstruction of late medieval metaphysics Ludger Honnefelder, "Der zweite Anfang der Metaphysik. Voraussetzungen, Ansätze und Folgen der Wiederbegründung der Metaphysik im 13./14. Jahrhundert," in Jan P. Beckmann et al. (eds.), *Philosophie im Mittelalter. Entwicklungslinien und Paradigmen* (Hamburg: Meiner, 1987), 165–186.

36 "Pico's oration might seem to open a relatively clear path toward the use of dignity we find in modern human rights documents. 'Dignity' goes from being a matter of the elevated status of a few persons in a particular society to being a feature of human beings in general, closely connected with their capacity for self-determination" (Rosen, *Dignity*, 15).

37 Benjamin Constant, "De la liberté des Anciens comparée à celle des Modernes," in *Écrits politiques* (Paris: Gallimard, 1997), 589–619.

38 See, on such views of human dignity in the contemporary philosophical debate, Peter Schaber, *Instrumentalisierung und Würde* (Paderborn: Mentis, 2010).

References

Allen, Michael J.B. "At Variance: Marsilio Ficino, Platonism, and Heresy," in Douglas Hedley and Sarah Hutton (eds.), *Platonism at the Origins of Modernity: Studies on Platonism and Early Modern Philosophy* (Dordrecht: Springer, 2008), 31–44.

Allen, Michael J.B. *Plato's Third Eye: Studies in Marsilio Ficino's Metaphysics and its Sources* (Aldershot: Ashgate, 1995).

Allen, Michael J.B., Valery Rees, and Martin Davies (eds.). *Marsilio Ficino: His Theology, His Philosophy, His Legacy* (Leiden: Brill, 2002).

Benda, Ernst. "The Protection of Human Dignity (Article 1 of the Basic Law)," *SMU Law Review* 53 (2000): 443–456.

Berlin, Isaiah. *Four Essays on Liberty* (Oxford: Oxford University Press, 1969).

Bloch, Matthias and Burkhard Mojsisch (eds.). *Potentiale des menschlichen Geistes: Freiheit und Kreativität, praktische Aspekte der Philosophie Marsilio Ficinos (1433–1499)* (Stuttgart: Steiner, 2003).

Blum, Paul Richard. "Eintracht und Religion bei Giovanni Pico della Mirandola," in Norbert Brieskorn and Markus Riedenauer (eds.), *Suche nach Frieden: Politische Ethik in der frühen Neuzeit II* (Stuttgart: Kohlhammer, 2002), 29–46.

Clucas, Stephen, Peter J. Forshaw, and Valery Rees (eds.). *Laus Platonici Philosophi: Marsilio Ficino and his Influence* (Leiden: Brill, 2011).

Collins, Ardis B. *The Secular Is Sacred: Platonism and Thomism in Ficino's Platonic Theology* (The Hague: Nijhoff, 1974).

Constant, Benjamin. "De la liberté des Anciens comparée à celle des Modernes," in *Écrits politiques* (Paris: Gallimard, 1997), 589–619.

Edelheit, Amos. "Human Will, Human Dignity, and Freedom: A Study of Giorgio Benigno Salviati's Early Discussion of the Will, Urbino 1474–1482," *Vivarium* 46, no. 1 (2008): 82–114.

Edelheit, Amos. *Ficino, Pico, and Savonarola: The Evolution of Humanist Theology 1461/2–1498* (Leiden: Brill, 2008).

Englard, Izhak. "Human Dignity: From Antiquity to Modern Israel's Constitutional Framework," *Cardozo Law Review* 21, no. 5–6 (2000): 1903–1927.

Ficino, Marsilio. *De amore / Über die Liebe oder Platons Gastmahl* (Hamburg: Meiner, 2004).

Ficino, Marsilio. *Platonic Theology, Vol. 4., Books XII–XIV* (Cambridge, MA: Harvard University Press, 2004).

Ficino, Marsilio. *Platonic Theology, Vol. 2, Books V–VIII* (Cambridge, MA: Harvard University Press, 2002).

Goodman, Maxine D. "Human Dignity in Supreme Court Constitutional Jurisprudence," *Nebraska Law Review* 84, no. 3 (2005–6): 740–794.

Habermas, Jürgen. "The Concept of Human Dignity and the Realistic Utopia for Human Rights," *Metaphilosophy* 41, no. 4 (July 2010): 464–480.

Haferkamp, Bjorn. "The Concept of Human Dignity: An Annotated Bibliography," in Kurt Bayertz (ed.), *Sanctity of Life and Human Dignity* (Dordrecht: Kluwer, 1996), 275–291.

Hennette-Vauchez, Stéphanie. "A Human *dignitas*? Remnants of the Ancient Legal Concept in Contemporary Dignity Jurisprudence," *International Journal of Constitutional Law* 9, no. 1 (2011): 32–57.

Honnefelder, Ludger. "Der zweite Anfang der Metaphysik. Voraussetzungen, Ansätze und Folgen der Wiederbegründung der Metaphysik im 13./14. Jahrhundert," in Jan P. Beckmann, Ludger Honnefelder, Gangolf Schrimpf, and Georg Wieland (eds.), *Philosophie im Mittelalter. Entwicklungslinien und Paradigmen* (Hamburg: Meiner, 1987), 165–186.

Iglesias, Teresa. "Bedrock Truths and the Dignity of the Individual," *Logos: A Journal of Catholic Thought and Culture* 4, no. 1 (2001): 111–134.

Kateb, George. *Human Dignity* (Cambridge, MA: Belknap Press, 2011).

Keßler, Eckhard. "Menschenwürde in der Renaissance," in Anne Siegetsleitner and Nikolaus Knoepffler (eds.), *Menschenwürde im interkulturellen Dialog* (Freiburg: Alber, 2005), 41–66.

Knoepffler, Nikolaus, Dagmar Schipanski, and Stefan Lorenz Sorgner (eds.). *Human-biotechnology as Social Challenge* (Aldershot: Ashgate, 2007).

Kristeller, Paul Oskar. *Renaissance Thought and Its Sources* (New York: Columbia University Press, 1979).

Kristeller, Paul Oskar. *The Philosophy of Marsilio Ficino* (New York: Columbia University Press, 1943).

Leitgeb, Maria Christine, Stéphanie Toussaint, and Herbert Bannert (eds.). *Platon, Plotin, und Marsilio Ficino: Studien zu den Vorläufern und zur Rezeption des Florentiner Neuplatonismus* (Vienna: Verlag der Österreichischen Akademie der Wissenschaften, 2009).

Lembcke, Oliver W. "Die Würde des Menschen, frei zu sein. Zum Vermächtnis der Oratio de hominis dignitate Picos della Mirandola," in Rolf Gröschner, Stephan Kirste, and Oliver W. Lembcke (eds.), *Des Menschen Würde – entdeckt und erfunden im Humanismus der italienischen Renaissance* (Tübingen: Mohr Siebeck, 2008), 159–186.

MacMullen, Ramsay. "The Power of the Roman Empire," *Historia. Zeitschrift für Alte Geschichte* 55, Heft 4 (2006): 471–481.

Manetti, Giannozzo. *De Dignitate et excellentia hominis* (1452), reprint edited by Elizabeth R. Leonard (Padova: Antenore, 1975).

McCrudden, Christopher. "Human Dignity and Judicial Interpretation of Human Rights," *European Journal of International Law* 19, no. 4 (2008): 655–724.

Meyer, Michael J. and William A. Parent (eds.). *The Constitution of Rights: Human Dignity and American Values* (Ithaca, NY: Cornell University Press, 1992).

Pettit, Philip. *Republicanism: A Theory of Freedom and Government* (Oxford: Oxford University Press, 1997).

Pico della Mirandola, Giovanni. *Pico della Mirandola – Oration on the Dignity of Man: A New Translation and Commentary*, ed. Francesco Borghesi, Michael Papio, and Massimo Riva (Cambridge: Cambridge University Press, 2012).

Pico della Mirandola, Giovanni. *De hominis dignitate / Über die Würde des Menschen* (Stuttgart: Reclam, 2009).

Pico della Mirandola, Giovanni. *On the Dignity of Man*, in *On the Dignity of Man / On Being and the One / Heptaplus* (Indianapolis, IN: Hackett, 1998).

Quaquarelli, Leonardo and Zita Zanardi. *Pichiana: Bibliografia delle edizioni e degli studi* (Florence: Olschki, 2005).

Rosen, Michael. *Dignity: Its History and Meaning* (Cambridge, MA: Harvard University Press, 2012).

Schaber, Peter. *Instrumentalisierung und Würde* (Paderborn: Mentis, 2010).

Sensen, Oliver. "Human Dignity in Historical Perspective: The Contemporary and Traditional Paradigms," *European Journal of Political Theory* 10, no. 1 (2011): 71–91.

Skinner, Quentin. *Liberty Before Liberalism* (Cambridge: Cambridge University Press, 1998).

Waldron, Jeremy. "Dignity and Rank," *European Journal of Sociology* 48, no. 2 (2007): 201–237.

3 Human rights and human dignity

Matthias Lutz-Bachmann

It is not a discovery of Enlightenment philosophy that humans have a particular status in the order of nature which distinguishes them from other creatures. Already in ancient philosophy one sees this special place given to humans, based on the assumption that humans are endowed with reason – as Cicero affirms – and, therefore, justified in their "priority" or "dignity" (from the Latin, *dignitas*)[1] over all other creatures. In Early Christianity, many theologians such as Theophilus of Antioch, Origen of Alexandria, Gregory of Nyssa in the East as well as Lactantius, Ambrose or Augustine in the West praised the nature of humans as dignified by God through incarnation and the resurrection of Christ. In the Middle Ages, authors such as Thomas Aquinas qualified the ontological status of the human person as inherently dignified through reason and the special biological constitution.[2] In the Renaissance and Early Modernity, philosophers as well as theologians or writers like Petrarch, Pico della Mirandola or Erasmus spoke in consonance with these aforementioned traditions, reaffirming the continuity of this perspective, according to which the property of reason and freedom of will is what characterizes the "likeness" of the human person to God. This "likeness" grants "dignity" to humans vis-à-vis the whole order of God's creation – as a gift or natural endowment that is, at the same time, a moral commission. It is only in the philosophy of Immanuel Kant that we encounter a first systematic philosophical concept of human dignity that considers dignity as a normative principle with equal importance and implications for both ethics and legal theory.

In my contribution to this volume I would like to (1) initially provide a systematic summary of the guiding idea represented by the concept of human dignity in Kant, and then (2) briefly discuss the question about which insights from Kant's philosophical contribution are systematically important, so that (3) some important conclusions can be drawn which are relevant for contemporary debates in bioethics and constitutional law (3).

1. The concept of human dignity in Kant

The definition of "dignity" presented by Kant in his first ethical text published in 1785, *The Groundwork of the Metaphysics of Morals*, is widely known and frequently cited both in philosophy and law: "In the kingdom of ends everything has either price or dignity. Whatever has a price, can be replaced by something else, reported as equivalent; whatever, on the contrary, is elevated above all price and therefore admits of no equivalent, has dignity."[3] Kant defines dignity as a general and, therefore, not merely relative but "intrinsic value" that should be the "condition" under which "something can be only an end in itself" [*Zweck an sich selbst*].[4] Now, for Kant it is only under the presuppositions of morality that a rational being can have "an end in itself." Therefore, for him, only humanity has "dignity" because humans are capable of living an ethical life [*Sittlichkeit*], which means that each and every human exercises morality by virtue of his or her practical reason and deserves to be elevated above any price on the basis of his or her membership in humanity.

Humans possess autonomy based on practical reason, i.e., the ability to self-legislate as a moral subject. This is considered by Kant as the "reason for the dignity of the human nature and any other rational nature."[5] This is also in agreement with his famous third formulation of the categorical imperative, which has been received in the form of the so-called "object formula" [*Objektformel*] of his doctrine of constitutional law: "Act in such a way that you always treat the humanity in your own person or in the person of any other as an end in itself and never merely as means."[6]

While these formulations by Kant enjoy a certain notoriety outside the narrower technical circle of philosophy, discussions on this theme have given less attention to the consequences that Kant has extracted from them for the systematic development of his mature moral and legal doctrines. As shown in the Doctrine of Virtue of the *Metaphysics of Morals* published in 1797, Kant understands human dignity not primarily as a general kind of precedence, award or privilege, as was then held traditionally, but rather in the strict sense of a normative obligation that every human owes to himself or herself as well as to all other humans. In this sense, Kant writes: "Only a human can be regarded as a person, i.e., as the subject of a moral and practical reason, and be elevated above all";[7] because the moral and practical reason commands us to never consider a human as means, to neither regard a human as a means for any purpose pursued by other humans nor lower oneself to a level of degradation in which one becomes the means to pursue the goals of one's own determination. Rather, it is always necessary to consider a human as an "end in itself." According to Kant, this is the core of the commandment for normative ascription of dignity to humans.

For Kant, humans "possess," in this sense, a "dignity" [an absolute intrinsic value] that requires recognition and respect from all other humans, so that all other humans are owed the same respect. "The humanity in his person is the object of respect that he can demand of any other human."[8] Conversely, practical reason simultaneously requires from us an absolute respect to all other people as free and equal beings. In this postulate, the demand is that every human being should necessarily recognize not only the others in their dignity as well as never deny his or her own dignity, but also always act "with the awareness of the sublimity of his moral disposition [which is already included in the concept of Virtue]."[9] And Kant adds: "This self-estimation is a duty of man to himself."[10] The obligation is not given to humans in a heteronomous way, but it springs from the human's autonomous practical use of reason. As a duty toward oneself, human dignity is therefore articulated as a higher principle of morality while as a duty toward all other humans it has the character of a higher legal principle.

An equally innovative potential for ethics and law is developed in Kant's mature views on human dignity and presented in arguments that rely neither on the perspective of theoretical reason [*Vernunft*] or intellectual understanding [*Verstand*] nor on the perspective of a natural or social ontology, but rather on the perspective of practical reason. In practical reason, the human self-awareness is articulated as the awareness of a free acting being who asks himself or herself (as well as others) about the justifying reasons for his or her (as well as others') actions, which is why each and every human has an intrinsic value or dignity, according to Kant; because only someone who can act according to his or her own rational insights can be designated by Kant as a being who represents "an end in itself." On the one hand, the dignity of humans is based on their nature as beings capable of performing free actions and making use of practical reason. We can also refer to this as the specific capability to use reason with regard to intentions and actions. On the other hand, the specific dignity of humans becomes an uncircumventable [*unhintergehbares*] principle that is morally obligatory and worked out abstractly in ethical and legal theories, but becomes more visible only in the context of human action.

This occurs more specifically in two ways: first, in the knowledge that humans, as beings with dignity, have an intrinsic obligation toward morality and self-esteem, which becomes evident in the very subjective activity of asking for justifiable or reasonable grounds for one's own actions. Humans can be fair to their own subjective freedom by obeying the autonomous rules of one's practical reasoning. Second, this occurs through acknowledging that each human being has the obligation to respect all other persons as being equal and free beings. This insight leads to the obligation to submit oneself to an external rule, defined by Kant as "Right" [*Recht*], for the purpose of achieving intersubjective freedom together with the other human beings. "Right," Kant writes, "is therefore the sum of the conditions under which the voluntary choice of one can be harmonized with the voluntary choices of others in accordance with a universal law of freedom."[11] Kant demands two things from law: on the one hand, that it be necessarily equipped to apply sanctions in order to preserve the external freedom of people in their intersubjective actions,[12] and on the other that it emerges simultaneously from the "combined will"[13] of all those affected by law. Kant relates the system of "rights" [*System des "Rechts"*] with the right to external freedom that is innate and original to every human being, who should be able to be independent from the arbitrariness of any other human being "as long as" this external freedom "can coexist with each other's freedom according to a general law."[14] For Kant, this innate right to freedom is realizable only as inter-subjective freedom and similarly presupposes the "innate equality"[15] of all legal subjects in the sense of a reciprocal independence of all human beings from each other, which shows itself in the fact that no one will be subjected to an alien will. As it is known, this demand for a rational right [*Vernunftrecht*] is spelled out by Kant in republican terms, in the form of a democratic legal system. Thereby he does not remain limited to a juridical system internal to a state [*innerstaatlichen*], but rather sketches a right to peace among people [*Völkerfriedensrecht*] and a right to world citizenship [*Weltbürgerrecht*].[16]

In summary, it can be said that Kant's claims about "dignity" as the view of the human *as* human – that is, as a being who is member of humanity, capable of freedom, and obligated to morality and to legal relationships arising from one's own rational insight – contains two dimensions: both a moral duty towards oneself, whose detailed elaboration is the task of Kant's moral doctrine, as well as a legal-moral commitment [*rechtsmoralische Pflicht*] toward all others with whom human beings interact, a task whose elaboration is the responsibility of the legal doctrine.

Ethics and legal theory therefore rely on the principle of human dignity in order to make two different duties explicit, both of which are connected in the concept of the human as a moral species and based on the natural capacity to use of practical reason. At the same time, it is of substantive importance for the debates on issues related to bioethics and constitutional law, that Kant does not include the "conditions for the realization of the human existence" or the "good life" as an unconditional legal obligation that can be possibly imposed by a political community upon its members, even with the use of coercion. Rather he refers only to the "initial conditions" that make it possible for humans "to become humans and to live a human existence."[17] This task is seen in our contemporary legal systems, particularly in regard to the first generation of human rights and basic rights, which are fundamentally for-mulated in the form of a negative defensive right and not in the form of a positive right to certain guarantees or fulfilments.

2. Kant's philosophical contribution

What follows from the contributions of Kant's practical philosophy? What are the implications of his moral philosophy and his legal theory for our debates on the meaning and importance of the principle of human dignity? In the next sections I consider three central aspects related to new debates on bioethics and constitutional norms.

Semantic ambiguities

Already at the level of the linguistic use of the term "human dignity," Kant's considerations offer a valuable contribution that helps us overcome the semantic ambiguities that characterize the use of the term in the history of philosophy and continue to this day. Among these ambiguities I include the confusion by many authors in the legal literature, who are confronted with the necessary interpretation of the first article of the German Constitution [*Grundgesetz*]. The famous dictum of Theodor Heuss about the dignity of the human being as "a non-interpreted thesis"[18] or Erhard Denninger's plea for an interpretation of the term "human dignity" as a constitutionally desired "empty formula"[19] are consequences of the problematic ambiguity and lack of clarity on the linguistic-semantic level on the meaning of the term. However, this can be avoided by using Kant's argument. With this argument, we can avoid an inflationary use of this fundamental article on human dignity in the German Constitution, an inflation that can be observed in many public debates and obviously serves to misuse the term as a way to justify arbitrary interests or intentions. Using the semantic clarification in the Kantian sense, it is possible to reject the understanding of dignity in the sense of a mere granting of preeminence to human beings, avoid a supposed prejudice based on speciesism, and refuse a merely subjective preference.

On the reflection and justification of practical philosophy

At the level of the disciplinary classification of human dignity as a theme, Kant's contribution is useful to this date because he makes it evident that the concept of human dignity belongs in the context of the reflection and justification of practical philosophy. Thus, this concept neither presupposes a specific ontology or natural doctrine nor can it be derived from a more descriptive theory of nature or society. The concept of human dignity requires neither religion-based assumptions about nature or humans nor theological axioms. But even if it were true that Kant is arguing in favor of a pure philosophical concept of human dignity, his arguments do not exclude additional theological perspectives about the human; thus, his views may even have an integrative effect on inter-religious and intercultural matters. Because it is conceived as a principle of practical philosophy, Kant's concept of human dignity is concurrently capable of being related to the contemporary debates about non-reductionist theories of action and society as well as to modern theories of law. With regard to the assumptions of contemporary naturalistic theories of the mind, however, the argumentative situation of Kant's theory is not different from other theories in ethics and law. The naturalistic theories would have to demonstrate – by means of a reduction to a pure deterministic explanation of mind and body activities – that an exclusive conception of human reasoning and acting is inadequate. These proposals are weak since their descriptions of the human being suffer from a deep performative self-contradiction as well as from a methodological misunderstanding of the limits of their own explanatory competence.

Human dignity as a normative principle

Finally, it turns out that Kant's contribution to the *foundation of human dignity as a normative principle* for autonomous ethics and for a doctrine of law built upon the primacy of intersubjective freedom is systematically compelling and viable. Considered as a principle or axiom of practical philosophy which formulates a basic insight and demand for both the moral philosophy as well as the legal doctrine, the human dignity principle has a double function. First, it makes the foundations of a philosophical theory of morality and law more explicit, as we could see in Kant, by demonstrating the unconditional validity of one's claim to freedom and to be an end in itself. Second, the principle of human dignity provides a verification criterion through which it is indeed impossible to deduce an ethical or legal maxim in a positive way, but we can probably determine negatively which action or legal maxims are in contradiction to the command of practical reason. In light of this second function of the principle of human dignity as a command of reason – which should not contradict any action rule, otherwise it would not be morally or legally legitimate – it is also possible to introduce some questions related to today's debates on bioethics and constitutional law, for these questions are waiting for clarification and require public discussion as well as reasonable decisions. However, this presupposes that the principle of human dignity should remain detached from any attempt at weighing conceptions of the Good [*Güterabwägung*] or evaluating consequences [*Folgeabschätzung*], so that we can ascribe an "unconditional," action-related and, therefore, practical validity to this principle.

3. Contemporary implications for the debates in bioethics and constitutional law

Whoever ignores this axiomatic or primary-theoretical status of the human dignity-principle, becomes entangled in inextricable logical contradictions with considerable practical consequences. An example of such an argument can be seen in Bernhard Schlink. In his contribution to *Spiegel*[20] he had mentioned that human-dignity would be "overwhelmed" in case it was not considered according to a "logic of weighing" [*Logik der Abwägung*] that would compare it with other goods such as the protection of life. This argument makes it clear that the author is not familiar with Kant's important differentiation between a first practical principle in the sense of an unconditional postulate and other practical demands or maxims that can neither be deduced materially from the first principle nor contradict it. If we take into consideration the very example given by Schlink about the open discussion whether the general prohibition against torture should be maintained in the case of a horrendous kidnapping, at the very least one should not miss the point that this case is not a matter of weighing between the "dignity of the kidnapped" against the "dignity of the kidnapper," as Schlink puts it, but rather a matter of considering the rights to life and integrity as negative rights defending the people against state violence. Yet, it would be a mistake to disregard the difference between the principle of human dignity on the one hand and the negative right of defense in the German Constitution on the other hand, and to confound both levels – a mistake that Schlink in fact commits – because such a procedure would also lead to confusion in the case of issues related to the bioethical debate. This confusion is only avoidable – at least theoretically – by means of the Kantian insights already mentioned.

Another example of a non-compelling way of dealing with the principle of human dignity as the highest legal principle can also be found in the highly regarded commentary and interpretation of basic rights by Matthias Herdegen.[21] On the one hand, he recognizes that the guarantee of human dignity has the highest rank due to its position "at the top of the part on basic rights of the [German] Constitution [*Grundgesetz*] ... with the consecutive connection between human dignity clause and the commitment to human rights";[22] but on the other hand, he defends the notion of "absolute dominance"[23] of the principle of dignity with respect to the basic rights in the articles that follow from it and advocates a "differentiation" according to "type and level of the claim to dignity" in the sense of a "situational concretization of the demands for respect that follow from dignity."[24] This interpretation of the function of the human dignity principle has many important consequences and follows Herdegen's interpretation of human dignity as a subjective basic right to be weighed on an individual basis and in relation to other competing basic rights. However, in so doing, Herdegen also dissolves the principled status of human dignity worked out by Kant.[25] This argumentation leads to a problematic consequence, based upon which he clearly relativizes the claim that the human dignity principle grounds an unconditional ban on torture.[26] The modal and quantitative weighing of the claim to dignity also leads him to the thesis defending "increased standards of dignity ... for the mentally or physically handicapped persons"[27] as well as to a relativizing of the claim for the dignity of embryos. For embryos, Herdegen proposes to make the protection of their dignity dependent on the status of their physical development. In the case of in vitro produced embryos, this implies that they should be awarded a kind of dignity that is different from the dignity of embryos after a successful implantation.[28]

Herdegen undermines his argument with a categorical mistake similar to the one committed by Bernhard Schlink. From the perspective of an inter-pretation of the human dignity principle as a first practical axiom or as an unconditionally valid principle for ethics and law, any modal or quantitative modification is erroneous. The principle of human dignity, which formulates the principles of freedom and equality of all human beings, precedes all basic rights and this means that it provides the theoretical justification for such rights. Wherever it is limited or weighted situationally against other goods, first it loses its justification status and second it loses its important function as a negative criterion for the evaluation of the admissibility of individual action rules or maxims. Human dignity is "inviolable" only if it can be neither modal nor final, neither quantitatively nor qualitatively weighed and limited. This same limitation on the practice of weighing does not apply to the supplementary statements related to human rights or basic rights; rather, the inherent nature of these rights allows them to issue an unconditional injunction against anyone, especially against state power, but not according to a situational claim or in a way that legally and positively binds all people to a mandatory guarantee.

In this sense, it is possible to say that a negative right to life is grounded on human dignity. Human dignity has the form of a necessarily and unconditionally valid prohibition to impair the right to life of another human being; but from this it does not follow that we have either a positive commandment to preserve a person's life at any cost or an absolute "right to life" which must be enforced against others by force – even if this means that their right to life would be affected. However, this negative right to life must also be granted to all human beings who have been generated "in vitro." From this right, however, no "right to implantation" can be derived. For all the reasons above, the ethical-legal weighing of different possibilities of affirming the fundamental right to the protection of life should not be confused with the attempt to subsume the "principle of human dignity" to the logic of weighing.

Translated by Amos Nascimento

Notes

1 Cicero, *De officiis* [*On Duties*, Loeb Classical Library, Vol. 30] (Cambridge, MA: Harvard University Press, 1913), I.
2 See Thomas Aquinas, *Summa Theologiae* [*Summa Theologica*] (Chambersburg, PA: The Aquinas Institute, 2012), I, q. 91 or II–II, q. 113.
3 Immanuel Kant, *Groundwork of the Metaphysics of Morals*, translated and edited by Mary J. Gregor (Cambridge: Cambridge University Press, 1996); original German citation from *Grundlegung zur Metaphysik der Sitten*, in *Werkausgabe*, Band VII, edited by Wilhelm Weischedel (Frankfurt a.M.: Suhrkamp, 2000), BA 77.
4 Ibid., BA 78.
5 Ibid., BA 79.
6 Ibid., BA 66f.
7 Immanuel Kant, *Metaphysics of Morals*, Doctrine of Virtue; translated and edited by Mary J. Gregor (Cambridge: Cambridge University Press, 1996), 353–604; original German citation from *Metaphysik der Sitten*, in *Werkausgabe*, Band VIII, ed. Wilhelm Weischedel (Frankfurt a.M.: Suhrkamp, 2000), Tugendlehre § 11, A 93.
8 Ibid., A 94.
9 Ibid.
10 Ibid., loc. cit.
11 Ibid., Doctrine of Right, § B, A 33 B 34.
12 Ibid., § 8, AB 35.
13 Ibid., § 46, A 165 B 195.
14 Ibid., The Division of the Doctrine of Right, AB 45.
15 Ibid.
16 Matthias Lutz-Bachmann and James Bohman (eds.), *Frieden durch Recht. Kants Friedensidee und das Problem einer neuen Weltordnung* (Frankfurt a.M.:

Suhrkamp, 1996); see Matthias Lutz-Bachmann and Amos Nascimento (eds.), *Human Rights, Human Dignity, and Cosmopolitan Ideals* (Surrey: Ashgate, 2014).

17 Otfried Höffe, "Menschenwürde als ethisches Prinzip," in Otfried Höffe, Ludger Honnefelder, Josef Isensee and Paul Kirchhoff (eds.), *Gentechnik und Menschenwürde* (Köln: DuMont, 2002), 133; Matthias Lutz-Bachmann and James Bohman (eds.), *Frieden durch Recht. Kants Friedensidee und das Problem einer neuen Weltordnung* (Frankfurt a.M.: Suhrkamp, 1996); Hauke Brunkhorst, Wolfgang R. Köhler, and Matthias Lutz-Bachmann (eds.), *Recht auf Menschenrechte* (Frankfurt a.M.: Suhrkamp, 1999); Matthias Lutz-Bachmann and James Bohman (eds.), *Weltstaat oder Staatenwelt? Für und wider die Idee einer Weltrepublik* (Frankfurt a. M.: Suhrkamp, 2002). See Matthias Lutz-Bachmann and Amos Nascimento (eds.), *Human Rights, Human Dignity, and Cosmopolitan Ideals* (Surrey: Ashgate, 2014).

18 See Klaus-Berto Doemming, Werner Füsslein and Werner Matz, *Entstehungsgeschichte der Artikel des Grundgesetzes* (Tübingen: Mohr [Siebeck], 1951), 49.

19 Erhard Denninger, *Staatsrecht. Einführung in die Grundprobleme des Verfassungsrechts der Bundesrepublik Deutschland* (Reinbek: Rowohlt, 1973), 26.

20 Bernhard Schlink, "Die überforderte Menschenwürde," *Der Spiegel* 51 (December 15, 2003): 50–54.

21 Matthias Herdegen, "Kommentierung von Art. 1 Abs. 1 GG und Abs. 3 GG," in Theodor Maunz and Günter Düring (eds.), *Grundgesetzkommentar*, Lfg. 44 (München: Beck, 2005).

22 Ibid., 12.

23 Ibid., 15.

24 Ibid., 19.

25 See on this, ibid., 18, among others.

26 See ibid., 28, 31 and 33.

27 Ibid., 36.

28 See ibid., 40–43.

References

Aquinas, Thomas. *Summa Theologiae* [*Summa Theologica*] (Chambersburg, PA: The Aquinas Institute, 2012).

Brunkhorst, Hauke, Wolfgang R. Köhler and Matthias Lutz-Bachmann (eds.). *Recht auf Menschenrechte* (Frankfurt a.M.: Suhrkamp, 1999).

Cicero. *De officiis* (*On Duties*) [Loeb Classical Library, Vol. 30] (Cambridge, MA: Harvard University Press, 1913).

Denninger, Erhard. *Staatsrecht. Einführung in die Grundprobleme des Verfassungsrechts der Bundesrepublik Deutschland* (Reinbek: Rowohlt, 1973).

Doemming, Klaus-Berto, Werner Füsslein and Werner Matz. *Entstehungsgeschichte der Artikel des Grundgesetzes* (Tübingen: Mohr [Siebeck], 1951).

Herdegen, Matthias. "Kommentierung von Art. 1 Abs. 1 GG und Abs. 3 GG," in Theodor Maunz and Günter Düring (eds.), *Grundgesetzkommentar*, Lfg. 44 (München: Beck, 2005).

Höffe, Otfried. "Menschenwürde als ethisches Prinzip," in Otfried Höffe, Ludger Honnefelder, Josef Isensee and Paul Kirchhof (eds.), *Gentechnik und Menschenwürde* (Köln: DuMont, 2002), 119–144.

Kant, Immanuel. *Groundwork of the Metaphysics of Morals*, translated and edited by Mary J. Gregor (Cambridge: Cambridge University Press, 1996), 37–108; original German as *Grundlegung zur Metaphysik der Sitten*, in *Werkausgabe*, Band VII, edited by Wilhelm Weischedel (Frankfurt a.M.: Suhrkamp, 2000).

Kant, Immanuel. *Metaphysics of Morals*, translated and edited by Mary J. Gregor (Cambridge: Cambridge University Press, 1996), 353–604; original German as *Metaphysik der Sitten*, in *Werkausgabe*, Band VIII, edited by Wilhelm Weischedel (Frankfurt a.M.: Suhrkamp, 2000).

Lutz-Bachmann, Matthias. "Menschen sind Personen," *Information Philosophie* 3 (August 2001): 16–20.

Lutz-Bachmann, Matthias and James Bohman (eds.). *Frieden durch Recht. Kants Friedensidee und das Problem einer neuen Weltordnung* (Frankfurt a.M.: Suhrkamp, 1996).

Lutz-Bachmann, Matthias and James Bohman (eds.). *Weltstaat oder Staatenwelt? Für und wider die Idee einer Weltrepublik* (Frankfurt a.M.: Suhrkamp, 2002).

Lutz-Bachmann, Matthias and Amos Nascimento (eds.). *Human Rights, Human Dignity, and Cosmopolitan Ideals: Essays on Critical Theory and Human Rights* (Surrey: Ashgate, 2014).

Schlink, Bernhard. "Die überforderte Menschenwürde," *Der Spiegel* 51 (December 15, 2003): 50–54.

4 The concept of human dignity and the realistic utopia of human rights

Jürgen Habermas

Article 1 of the Universal Declaration of Human Rights, which was adopted by the United Nations on December 10, 1948, begins with the statement: "All human beings are born free and equal in dignity and rights."[1] The preamble also speaks of human dignity and human rights in the same breath. It reaffirms the "faith in fundamental rights, in the dignity and worth of the human person."[2] The Basic Law of the Federal Republic of Germany, which was enacted some sixty years ago, begins with a section on basic rights. Article 1 of this section opens with the statement: "Human dignity is inviolable." Prior to this, similar formulations appeared in three of the five German state constitutions enacted between 1946 and 1949. Nowadays human dignity also features prominently in human rights discourse and in judicial decision-making.[3]

The inviolability of human dignity commanded the attention of the German public in 2006 when the Federal Constitutional Court declared the "Aviation Security Act" to be unconstitutional. At the time, the Parliament was thinking of the "9/11" scenario – in other words, the terrorist attack on the Twin Towers of the World Trade Center; the intention of the bill was to authorize the armed forces in such a situation to shoot down a passenger aircraft which had been transformed into missiles in order to avert the threat to an indeterminately large number of people on the ground. According to the court, however, the killing of the passengers by agencies of the state would be unconstitutional. It argued that the duty of the state (according to Art. 2.2 of the Basic Law)[4] to protect the lives of the potential victims of a terrorist attack is secondary to the duty to respect the human dignity of the passengers: "with their lives being disposed of unilaterally by the state, the persons on board the aircraft ... are denied the value which is due to a human being for his or her own sake."[5] These words of the court unmistakably echo Kant's categorical imperative. The respect for the dignity of every person forbids the state to dispose of any individual merely as a means to another end, even if that end be to save the lives of many other people.

It is an interesting fact that it was only after the end of World War II that the philosophical concept of human dignity, which already existed in antiquity and acquired its current canonical expression in Kant, found its way into texts of international law and recent national constitutions that came into force in the postwar period. Only during the past decades has it also played a central role in international jurisdiction. By contrast, the notion of human dignity featured as a legal concept neither in the classical human rights declarations of the eighteenth century nor in the codifications of the nineteenth century.[6] Why did the notion of "human rights" find its way into the law so much earlier than that of "human dignity"? To be sure, the founding documents of United Nations, which make the connection between human rights and human dignity explicit, were clearly a response to the mass crimes committed under the Nazi regime and to the massacres of World War II. Does this also account for the prominent place accorded human dignity in the German, Italian, and Japanese postwar constitutions, hence in the constitutions of the successor regimes of the authors of this twentieth-century moral catastrophe and their allies? Does the idea of *human rights* become, as it were, retrospectively morally charged – and possibly over-charged – with the concept of *human dignity* only against the historical background of the Holocaust?

The recent career of the concept of "human dignity" in constitutional and international legal discussions tends to support this idea. There is just one exception from the mid-nineteenth century. In the negotiations over the abolition of the death penalty and of corporal punishment in §139 of the German Constitution of March 1849, we find the statement: "A free people must respect human dignity even in the case of a criminal."[7] However, this constitution, which was the product of the first bourgeois revolution in Germany, did not come into force. One way or the other, the temporal dislocation between the history of *human rights* dating back to the seventeenth century and the relatively recent currency of the concept of *human dignity* in codifications of national and international law and in the administration of justice over the past half-century remains a striking fact.

Contrary to the assumption that the concept of human rights became morally charged by that of human dignity only in retrospect, I would like to defend the thesis that a close conceptual connection existed, if at first only implicit, from the very beginning. The origin of human rights has always been resistance to despotism, oppression, and humiliation. Today nobody can utter these venerable articles – for example, the proposition: "No one shall be subjected to torture or to cruel, inhuman or degrading treatment or punishment" (Article 5 of the Universal Declaration) – without hearing the echo of the outcry of countless tortured and murdered human creatures that resonates in them. The appeal to human rights feeds off the outrage of the humiliated at the violation of their human dignity. If this forms the starting point, traces of a conceptual connection between human dignity and human rights should be evident early on in the development of law itself. Thus we face the question of whether "human dignity" signifies a substantive normative concept from which human rights can be deduced by specifying the conditions under which they are violated. Or is the expression merely an empty formula which summarizes a catalogue of individual, disparate, and unrelated human rights?

I will present some legal reasons in support of the claim that "human dignity" is not merely a classificatory expression, an empty placeholder, as it were, which lumps a multiplicity of different phenomena together but the moral "source"[8] from which all of the basic rights derive their sustenance (1). I will go on to present a systematic analysis, in the guise of a conceptual history, of the catalytic role played by the concept of dignity in the construction of human rights out of rational morality and the form of law. Finally, the origin of human rights in the moral notion of human dignity explains the explosive political force of a concrete utopia which I would like to defend against the blanket dismissal of human rights (Carl Schmitt), on the one hand, and against more recent attempts to blunt their radical thrust, on the other (3).

1

Because of their abstract character, basic rights need to be spelled out in concrete terms in each particular case. In the process, lawmakers and judges often arrive at different results in different cultural contexts; today this is apparent for example in the regulation of controversial ethical issues such as euthanasia, abortion, and genetic enhancement. Equally uncontroversial is that, because of this need for interpretation, universal legal concepts facilitate negotiated compromises. Thus, appealing to the concept of human dignity undoubtedly made it easier to reach an overlapping consensus among parties from different cultures at the founding of the United Nations, for example, and more generally when negotiating human rights agreements and international legal conventions: "Everyone could agree that human dignity was central, but not why or how."[9]

In spite of this observation, the juridical meaning of human dignity is not exhausted by its function as a smokescreen for disguising more profound differences. The fact that the concept of human dignity can also occasionally facilitate compromises when specifying and extending human rights by neutralizing unbridgeable differences cannot explain its belated emergence *as* a legal concept. I would like to show that changing historical conditions have merely thematized and made us aware of something that was inscribed in human rights implicitly from the outset – namely, the normative substance of the equal dignity of every human being which human rights only spell out. Thus judges appeal to the protection of human dignity, for example, when the unforeseen risks of new invasive technologies lead them to introduce a right to informational autonomy. The Federal Constitutional Court in Germany took a similar line in its groundbreaking decision of February 9, 2010 on the assessment of benefits entitlements in accordance to SGB II (Second Book of the Code of Social Law), section 20, paragraph 2 (unemployment benefit II).[10] It took this occasion to "derive" a basic right to a minimum income from Article 1 of the German Basic Law that enables the beneficiaries (and their children) to enjoy an appropriate "participation in social, cultural, and political life."[11]

The experience of the violation of human dignity fulfills an inventive function in many cases, be it in view of the unbearable social conditions and the marginalization of impoverished social classes; or in view of the unequal treatment of women and men in the workplace; or of discrimination against foreigners and against cultural, linguistic, religious, and racial minorities; or in view of the ordeal of young women from immigrant families who have to liberate themselves from the violence of a traditional code of honor; or in view of the brutal expulsion of illegal immigrants and asylum seekers. In the light of such specific challenges, *different* aspects of the meaning of human dignity acquire urgency and relevance in each case. These features of human dignity specified and actualized on different occasions can then lead both to a more complete exhaustion of the normative substance of existing civil rights and to the discovery and construction of *new* ones.[12] Through this process the background intuition of humiliation forces its way first into the consciousness of suffering individuals and then into the legal texts, where it finds conceptual articulation and elaboration.

The 1919 Constitution of the German Reich, which pioneered the introduction of social rights, provides an example of this incremental development. In Article 151 the text speaks of "achieving a dignified life for everyone." Here the concept of human dignity remains concealed behind the adjectival use of a colloquial expression; but as early as 1944 the International Labour Organization (ILO) employs the rhetoric of human dignity without qualification in a similar context.[13] Moreover, just a few years later Article 22 of the Universal Declaration of Human Rights already calls for guarantees of economic, social, and cultural rights, so that every individual can live under conditions which are "indispensable for his dignity and the free development of his personality."[14] Since then we speak of successive "generations" of human rights. The heuristic function of human dignity is the key to the logical interconnections between these four categories of rights. Only *in collaboration* with each other can basic rights fulfill the moral promise to respect the human dignity of every person *equally*.[15]

The *liberal rights*, which crystallize around the inviolability and security of the person, around free commerce, and around the unhindered exercise of religion, are designed to prevent the intrusion of the state into the private sphere. They constitute, together with the *democratic rights of participation*, the package of so-called classical civil rights. In fact, however, the citizens have equal opportunities to make use of these rights only when they simultaneously enjoy guarantees of a sufficient level of independence in their private and economic lives and when they are able to form their personal identities in the cultural environment of their choice. Experiences of exclusion, suffering, and discrimination teach us that classical civil rights acquire "equal value" (Rawls) for all citizens only when they are supplemented by *social and cultural rights*. The claims to an appropriate share in the prosperity and culture of society as a whole place narrow limits on the scope for shifting *systemic* costs and risks onto the shoulders of individuals. These claims set constraints on the increase of in social inequality and forbid the exclusion of entire groups from social and cultural life as a whole. Thus policies such as those which have predominated in recent decades not only in the United States and Great Britain but also in continental Europe, and indeed throughout the world – i.e., ones which pretend to be able to secure an autonomous life for citizens *primarily* through guarantees of economic liberties – tend to destroy the balance between the different categories of basic rights. Human dignity, which is one and the same everywhere and for everyone, grounds the *indivisibility* of the all categories of human rights.

This development also explains the prominent role played by this concept in the administration of justice. The more deeply civil rights suffuse the legal system as a whole, the more often their influence extends beyond the vertical relation between individual citizens and the state and permeates the horizontal relations among individuals and groups. The result is an increase in the frequency of collisions that call for a balancing of competing claims founded upon basic rights.[16] A justified decision in such hard cases often becomes possible only by appealing to a violation of human dignity whose *absolute* validity grounds a claim to priority. In judicial discourse, therefore, the role of this concept is far from that of a vague placeholder for a missing conception of human rights. "Human dignity" performs the function of a seismograph that registers what is constitutive for a democratic legal order – namely, just those rights that the citizens of a political community must grant themselves if they are to be able to respect one another as members of a voluntary association of free and equal persons. The guarantee of these human rights gives rise to the status of citizens who have a claim as subjects of equal rights to be respected in their human dignity.

After two hundred years of modern constitutional history, we have a better grasp of what distinguished this development from the beginning: human dignity forms the "portal" through which the egalitarian-universalistic substance of morality is imported into law. The idea of human dignity is the conceptual hinge which connects the morality of equal respect for everyone with positive law and democratic lawmaking in such a way that their interplay could give rise to a political order founded upon human rights, given suitable historical conditions. To be sure, the classical human rights declarations, when they speak of "inborn" or "inalienable" rights, of "inherent" or "natural" rights, or of "*droits inalién-ables et sacrés*," betray their religious and metaphysical origins ("We hold these truths to be self-evident, that all men are endowed … with certain unalienable rights"). In the secular state, however, such predicates function primarily as placeholders; they remind us of the mode of a *generally acceptable justification* whose epistemic dimension is *beyond state control*. Moreover, the Founding Fathers recognized that human rights, notwithstanding their purely moral justification, are in need of a democratic "Declaration" and that they must be specified and implemented within an established political community.

Because the moral promise of equal respect for everybody is supposed to be cashed out in legal currency, human rights exhibit a Janus face turned simultaneously to morality and to law.[17] Notwithstanding their exclusively moral *content*, they have the *form* of positive, enforceable subjective rights that guarantee specific liberties and claims. They are designed to be *spelled out in concrete terms* through democratic legislation, to be *specified* from case to case in adjudication, and to be *enforced* with public sanctions. Thus, human rights circumscribe precisely that and only that part of an enlightened morality which can be translated into the medium of coercive law and become political reality in the robust shape of effective civil rights.[18]

2

In this entirely new category of rights, two elements are reunited that had first become separated in the course of the disintegration of Christian natural law, and then began to develop in opposite directions. The result of this differentiation was, on the one side, the internalized, rationally justified morality anchored in the individual conscience, which in Kant withdraws entirely into the transcendental domain; and on the other side, the coercive, positive, enacted law that served absolutist rulers or the traditional assemblies of estates as an instrument for constructing the institutions of the modern state and a market society. The concept of human rights is a product of an improbable synthesis of these two elements. *"Human dignity" served as a conceptual hinge in establishing this connection.* The learned concept of human dignity was itself transformed in the course of this synthesis. An important role is clearly also played by those colloquial notions of social dignity which had become associated with particular statuses in the stratified societies of medieval and early modern Europe.[19] Admittedly, the hypothesis which I am going to develop calls for more research, both in terms of conceptual history and of the history of European revolutions.

Here I would like to highlight just two aspects with a view to the genealogy of human rights: on the one hand, the mediating function of "human dignity" in the shift of perspective from moral duties to legal claims (a), and, on the other hand, the paradoxical generalization of a concept of dignity that was originally geared not to any equal distribution of dignity but to *status differences* (b).

(a)

The modern doctrines of morality and law which are based on human reason alone share the concepts of individual autonomy and equal respect for everyone. This common foundation of morality and law often obscures the decisive difference that, whereas morality imposes *duties* that pervade all spheres of action without exception, modern law creates *domains* of private choice for the pursuit of an individual life of one's own. Under the revolutionary premise that everything is legally permitted which is not explicitly prohibited, subjective rights rather than duties constitute the starting point for the construction of modern legal systems. The guiding principle for Hobbes, and for modern law generally, is that all persons are allowed to act or to refrain from acting as they wish within the confines of the law. Actors take a different perspective when, instead of *following* moral injunctions, they make use of their rights. A person in a *moral relation* asks herself what she owes to another person independently of her social relation to him – how well she knows him, how he behaves, and what she might expect from him. People who stand in a *legal relation* to one another are concerned about potential *claims* they expect others to *make* on them. In a legal community, the first person acquires obligations as a result of claims that a second person makes on her.[20]

Take the case of a police officer who wants to extort a confession from a suspect through the illegal threat of torture. In his role as moral person, this threat alone, not to speak of the actual infliction of the pain, would be sufficient to give him a bad conscience, quite apart from the behavior of the offender. By contrast, a legal relation is actualized between the police officer who is acting illegally and the individual under interrogation only when *the latter* defends herself and takes legal action to obtain her rights (or a public prosecutor acts in her place). Naturally, in both cases the person threatened is a source of normative claims that are violated by torture. However, the fact that the actions in question violate morality is all that is required to give an offender a bad conscience, whereas the legal relation which is objectively violated remains latent until a claim is raised that actualizes it.

Thus Klaus Günther sees in the "transition from reciprocal moral obligations to reciprocally established and accorded rights"[21] an act of "self-authorization to self-determination." The *transition from morality to law* calls for a shift from symmetrically intertwined perspectives of respect and esteem for the autonomy *of the other* to raising claims to recognition for *one's own autonomy* by the other. The morally enjoined *concern* for the vulnerable other is replaced by the self-confident *demand* for legal recognition as a self-determined subject who "lives, feels, and acts in accordance with his or her own judgment."[22] The recognition *claimed* by citizens reaches beyond the reciprocal moral recognition of responsible subjects; it has the concrete meaning of the respect *demanded* for a status that is *deserved*, and as such it is infused with the connotations of the "dignity" which was associated in the past with membership in socially respected corporate bodies.

(b)

The concrete concept of dignity or of "social honor" belongs to the world of hierarchically ordered traditional societies. In those societies a person could derive his dignity and self-respect, for example, from the code of honor of the nobility, from the ethos of trade guilds or professions, or from the corporative spirit of universities. When these *status-dependent* dignities, which occur in the plural, coalesce into the *universal* dignity of human beings, this new, abstract dignity sheds the particular characteristics of a corporative ethos. At the same time, however, the universalized dignity which accrues to all persons equally preserves the connotation of a *self-respect* which depends on *social recognition*. As such a form of social dignity, human dignity also requires anchoring in a social status, that is, membership in an organized community in space and time. But in this case, the status must be an equal one for everybody. Thus the concept of human dignity transfers the content of a morality of equal respect for everyone to the status order of citizens who derive their self-respect from the fact that they are recognized by all other citizens as *subjects of equal actionable rights.*

It is not unimportant in this context that this status can be established only within the framework of a constitutional state that never arises of its own accord. Rather, this framework must be *created* by the citizens themselves *using the means of positive law* and must be protected and developed under historically changing conditions. As a modern *legal* concept, human dignity is associated with the status that citizens assume in the *self-created* political order. As addressees, citizens can come to enjoy the rights that protect their human dignity only by first uniting as authors of the democratic undertaking of establishing and maintaining a political order based on human rights.[23] In view of such a community of self-legislating citizens the dignity conferred by the status of democratic citizenship is nourished by the republican appreciation of this democratic achievement and a corresponding orientation to the public good. This is reminiscent of the meaning that the ancient Romans associated with the word *dignitas,* namely, the prestige of statesmen and officeholders who have served the *res publica.* Of course, the distinction of the few outstanding "dignitaries" and notabilities contrasts with the dignity guaranteed to *all* citizens *equally* by the constitutional state.

Jeremy Waldron draws attention to the paradoxical fact that the egalitarian concept of human dignity is the result of a generalization of particularistic dignities which must not entirely lose the connotation of "fine distinctions": "Once associated with hierarchical differentiation of rank and status, 'dignity' now conveys the idea that all human persons belong to the same rank and that the rank is a very high one indeed."[24] Waldron understands this generalization process in such a way that all citizens now acquire the highest rank possible, for example that which was once reserved for the nobility. But does this capture the meaning of the equal dignity of every human being? Even the direct precursors of the concept of human dignity in Greek philosophy, above all in the Stoics and in Roman humanism (for example, with Cicero), do not form a semantic bridge to the egalitarian meaning of the modern concept. That same period developed well a *collective* notion of *dignitas humana,* but it was explained in terms of a distinguished ontological status of human beings in the cosmos, of the particular rank enjoyed by human beings vis-à-vis "lower" forms of life in virtue of species-specific faculties such as reason and reflection. The superior value of the species might justify some kind of species protection but not the inviolability of the dignity of the individual person as a source of normative claims.

Two decisive stages in the genealogy of the concept are still missing. First, universalization must be followed by individualization. The issue is the *worth of the individual* in the horizontal relations between human beings, not the status of "human beings" in the vertical relation to God or to "lower" creatures on the evolutionary scale. Second, the relative superiority of humanity and its members must be replaced by the absolute worth of any person. The issue is the *unique worth* of each person. These two steps were taken in Europe when ideas from the Judeo-Christian tradition were appropriated by philosophy, a process which I would like to address briefly.[25]

A close connection was already drawn between *dignitas* and *persona* in antiquity; but it was only in the medieval discussions of human beings' creation in the likeness to God that the individual person became liberated from its set of social roles. Everyone must face the Last Judgment as an irreplaceable and unique person. Another stage in the conceptual history of individualization is represented by the approaches in Spanish scholasticism which sought to distinguish subjective rights from the objective system of natural law.[26] However, the key parameters were set by the moralization of the understanding of individual freedom in Hugo Grotius and Samuel Pufendorf. Kant radicalized this understanding into a deontological concept of autonomy; however, the price paid for the radicality of this concept was a disembodied status of the free will in the transcendental "kingdom of ends." Freedom on this conception consists in the capacity to give oneself reasonable laws and to follow them, reflecting generalizable values and interests. The relationship of rational beings to each other is determined by the reciprocal recognition of the universally legislating will of each person, where each individual should "treat himself and all others *never merely as means* but always *at the same time as ends in themselves.*"[27]

This categorical imperative defines the limits of a domain which must remain absolutely beyond the disposition of others. The "infinite dignity" of each person consists in his claim that all others should respect the inviolability of this domain of free will. Yet the concept of "human dignity" does not acquire any systematic importance in Kant; the complete burden of justification is instead borne by the moral-philosophical explanation of autonomy: "Autonomy is therefore the ground of the dignity of human nature and of every rational nature."[28] Before we can understand what "human dignity" means we have to make sense of the "kingdom of ends."[29] In the *Doctrine of Right*, Kant introduces human rights – or rather the "sole" right to which everyone can lay claim in virtue of his humanity – by direct reference to the freedom of each "insofar as it can coexist with the freedom of every other in accordance with a universal law."[30] In Kant, too, human rights derive their moral content, which they spell out in the language of positive laws, from a universalistic and individualistic conception of human dignity. However, the latter is assimilated to an intelligible freedom beyond space and time, and loses precisely those connotations of status which qualify it as the conceptual link between morality and human rights in the first place. Thus the point of the legal character of human rights gets lost, namely, that they protect a human dignity that derives its connotations of self-respect and social recognition from a status in space and time – that of democratic citizenship.[31]

We have gathered together three elements from the perspective of conceptual history, namely, a highly normalized concept of human dignity, the recollection of a traditional understanding of social dignity and, with the emergence of modern law, the self-confident attitude of the legal person who makes claims against other legal persons. We would now have to make the transition from conceptual history to social and political history in order to render at least plausible the dynamic through which the contents of rational morality merged with the form of positive law through a generalization of the originally status-bound "dignity" into "human dignity." On this I would like to present something which is more an illustrative example than a cast-iron historical proof. The process of claiming and enforcing rights was seldom a peaceful matter. Human rights are the product of violent and at times of revolutionary struggles for recognition.[32] We can form a retrospective conception of the militant situation in which the three conceptual elements might have become connected with each other in the minds of the first freedom fighters (let us say, the Levellers). Historical experiences of humiliation and degradation, which were already interpreted in the light of an egalitarian Christian understanding of human dignity, represented one motive for resistance. But now the political outrage could find expression in the language of positive law as the self-confident demand for universal rights. Perhaps this was already connected, recollecting the familiar concept of dignity associated with rank, with the expectation that such basic rights would justify a status of citizens who recognize each other as subjects of equal rights.

3

The militant origin can only partially explain the polemical character which human rights have retained to this day. It is also the fact that they are morally charged that lends these state-sanctioned rights their unsaturated character. This character explains why a provocative tension found its way into modern societies with the two late eighteenth-century constitutional revolutions. Of course, in the social realm there is always and everywhere a difference between norms and actual behavior; however, the unprecedented event of a constitution-making practice gave rise to an entirely different, utopian gap in the temporal dimension. On the one hand, human rights could acquire the quality of enforceable rights only within a particular political community – that is, within a nation-state. On the other hand, the universalistic claim to validity of human rights which points beyond all national boundaries could be redeemed only within an inclusive worldwide political community.[33] This contradiction would find a reasonable solution only in a constitutionalized world society (which would not therefore necessarily have the characteristics of a world republic).[34] From the outset, a tension and inclusion has existed between human rights and established civil rights which under favorable historical conditions can trigger a "mutually reinforcing dynamic" (Lutz Wingert).

This is not to suggest a self-propelling dynamic. Increasing the protection of human rights within nation-states, or impelling the global spread of human rights beyond national boundaries, has never been possible without social movements and political struggles, without dauntless resistance to oppression and degradation. The struggle to implement human rights continues today in our own countries, as well as, for example, in Iran and China, in parts of Africa, or in Russia, Bosnia or Kosovo. Whenever an asylum seeker is deported at an airport behind closed doors, whenever a ship carrying refugees capsizes on the crossing from Libya to the Italian island of Lampedusa, whenever a shot is fired at the border fence between the United States and Mexico, we, the citizens of the West, confront one more troubling question. The first human rights declaration set a standard which inspires refugees, people who have been thrust into misery, and those who have been ostracized and insulted, a standard which can give them the assurance that their suffering is not a natural destiny. The translation of the first human right into positive law gave rise to a *legal duty* to realize exacting moral requirements which has become engraved into the collective memory of humanity.

Human rights constitute a *realistic* utopia insofar as they no longer project deceptive images of a social utopia that guarantees collective happiness but anchor the ideal of a just society in the institutions of constitutional states themselves.[35] Of course, this context-transcending idea of justice also introduces a problematic tension into social and political reality. Even apart from the merely symbolic force of human rights in those "façade democracies" we find in South America and elsewhere,[36] the human rights policy of United Nations reveals the contradiction between the spreading rhetoric of human rights, on the one side, and their misuse to legitimize the usual power politics, on the other. To be sure, the UN General Assembly promotes *the codification of human rights in international law*, for example by enacting human rights covenants. The *institutionalization* of human rights has also made progress – with the procedure of the individual petition, with the periodic reports on the human rights situation in particular countries, and above all with the creation of international courts such as the European Court of Human Rights, various war crimes tribunals, and the International Criminal Court. Most spectacular of all are the humanitarian interventions authorized by the UN Security Council in the name of the international community, sometimes even against the will of sovereign governments. However, these cases in particular reveal the problematic nature of the attempt to promote a world order which is institutionalized for the present only in fragmentary ways. For what is worse than the failure of legitimate attempts is their ambiguity, which brings the moral standards themselves into disrepute.[37]

One need only recall the highly selective and short-sighted decisions of a nonrepresentative and far from impartial Security Council, or the half-hearted and incompetent implementation of interventions that had been authorized – and their catastrophic failure (Somalia, Rwanda, Darfur). These police operations continue to be conducted like wars in which the military write off the death and suffering of innocent civilians as "collateral damage" (Kosovo). The intervening powers have yet to demonstrate in a single case that they are capable of marshalling the necessary energy and stamina for state-building – in other words, for reconstructing the destroyed or dilapidated infrastructure in the pacified regions (Afghanistan). When human rights policy becomes a mere fig leaf and vehicle for imposing major power interests, when the superpower flouts the UN Charter and arrogates a right of intervention, and when it conducts an invasion in violation of humanitarian international law and justifies this in the name of universal values, this reinforces the suspicion that the program of human rights *consists* its imperialist misuse.[38]

The tension between idea and reality which was imported into reality itself as soon as human rights were translated into positive law confronts us today with the challenge to think and act realistically without betraying the utopian impulse. This ambivalence can lead us all too easily into the temptation either to take an idealistic, but non-committal, way with the exacting moral requirements, or to adopt the cynical pose of the so-called realists. Since it is no longer realistic to follow Carl Schmitt in entirely rejecting the program of human rights, whose subversive force has in the meantime permeated the pores of *all* regions throughout the world, today "realism" exhibits a different aspect. The direct unmasking critique is being replaced by a mild, deflationary one. This new minimalism relaxes the claim of human rights by cutting them off from their essential moral thrust, namely the protection of the equal dignity of every human being.

Following John Rawls, Kenneth Baynes contrasts this approach as a "political" conception of human rights[39] with natural law notions of "inherent" rights which every person is supposed to possess by his very human nature: "Human rights are understood as conditions for inclusion in a political community."[40] I agree with that. The problematic move is the next one which effaces the moral meaning of this inclusion, namely, that everyone is respected in his human dignity as a subject of equal rights. Caution is certainly required in view of the disastrous failures of human rights policy. However, the latter do not provide sufficient reason for stripping human rights themselves of their moral surplus and restricting the focus of the topic of human rights from the beginning to questions of *international* politics.[41] This minimalism forgets that the still-persisting tensions between universal human rights and particular civil rights *at the domestic level* provide normative reason for the international dynamic.[42] If we ignore this connection, the global spread of human rights requires a separate justification. This is provided by the argument that, in international relations, moral obligations between states (and citizens) first arise out of the growing systemic interconnectedness of an increasingly interdependent world society.[43] From this perspective, claims to inclusion arise first out of reciprocal dependencies in *factually* established interactions.[44] This argument has a certain explanatory force for the empirical question of how a responsiveness develops in our affluent societies to the legitimate claims of marginalized and underprivileged sections of the population who want to be included in liberal social conditions. However, these normative claims themselves are grounded in universalistic moral notions that have long since gained entry into the human and civil rights of democratic constitutions through the status-bound idea of human dignity. Only this *internal* connection between human dignity and human rights gives rise to the explosive fusion of moral contents with the medium of law in which the construction of just political orders must be performed.

This investing of the law with a moral charge is a legacy of the constitutional revolutions of the eighteenth century. To neutralize this tension would be to abandon the dynamic understanding that makes the citizens of our own, halfway liberal societies open to an ever more exhaustive realization of existing rights and to the ever-present acute danger of their erosion.

Notes

1 The first sentence of the preamble calls at the same time for recognition of the "inherent dignity" and "equal and inalienable rights of all members of the human family."
2 "[T]he peoples of the United Nations have in the Charter reaffirmed their faith in fundamental human rights, in the dignity and worth of the human person."
3 Erhard Denninger, "Der Menschenwürdesatz im Grundgesetz und seine Entwicklung in der Verfassungsrechsprechung," in Franz-Josef Peine and Heinrich A. Wolf (eds.), *Nachdenken über Eigentum: Festschrift für Alexander von Brünneck* (Baden-Baden: Nomos, 2011), 397–411.
4 "Every person has the right to life and physical integrity."
5 BverfG, 1 BvR 357/05 vom 15.02.2006, Absatz-Nr. 124. (English translation: www.bundesverfassungsgericht.de/entscheidungen/rs20060215_1bvr035705en.html.) On the judgment, see J.v. Bernstorff, "Luftsicherheitsgesetz und Menschenwürde – Zum unbedingten Vorrang staatlicher Achtungspflichten im Anwendungsbereich von Art 1 GG," *Der Staat* 47 (2008): 21–40.
6 See Christopher McCrudden, "Human Dignity and Judicial Interpretation of Human Rights," *The European Journal of International Law* 19 (2008): 655–724.
7 Denninger, "Der Menschenwürdesatz im Grundgesetz," 397.
8 "The inviolability of the dignity of the person is the source of all basic rights," is how it is put, for example, in Article 14, paragraph 2, of the Constitution of the Free State of Saxony of 1992.
9 McCrudden, "Human Dignity," 678. The author speaks in this connection (719ff.) of "domesticating and contextualizing human rights."
10 BVerfG, 1 BvL 1/09 of 9 February 2010. English translation available online: www.bundesverfassungsgericht.de/entscheidungen/ls2020209_1bvl000109en.html (accessed October 11, 2011).
11 Ibid., paragraph 135.
12 McCrudden, speaks of similar cases of "justifying the creation of new, and the extension of existing rights" in "Human Dignity," 721.
13 Paragraph 2a of the declaration concerning the aims and purposes of the International Labour Organization, adopted on May 10, 1944 in Philadelphia, states that: "all human beings, irrespective of race, creed or sex, have the right to pursue both the material well-being and their spiritual development in conditions of freedom and dignity, of economic security and equal opportunity."

14 "Everyone, as a member of society, has the right to social security and is entitled to realization, through national effort and international co-operation and in accordance with the organization and resources of each State, of the economic, social and cultural rights indispensable for his dignity and the free development of his personality."

15 Gerhard Lohmann, "Die Menschenrechte: unteilbar und gleichgewichtig? Eine Skizze," in Georg Lohmann, Stefan Gosepath, Arn Pollmann, Claudia Mahler, and Norman Weiß, *Die Menschenrechte: unteilbar und gleichgewichtig? [Studien zu Grund- und Menschenrechten* 11] (Potsdam: Universitätsverlag Potsdam, 2005), 5–20.

16 The discussion concerning the so-called horizontal effect [*Drittwirkung*] of basic rights, which has been conducted in Europe over the past half-century, has recently also found an echo in the United States; see S. Gardbaum, "The Horizontal Effect of Constitutional Rights," *Michigan Law Review* 102 (2003): 399–495.

17 Gerhard Lohmann, "Menschenrechte zwischen Moral und Recht," in Stefan Gosepath and Gerhard Lohmann (eds.), *Philosophie der Menschenrechte* (Frankfurt a.M.: Suhrkamp, 1998), 62–95.

18 I do not think that this reflection requires me to revise my original introduction of the system of rights in Jürgen Habermas, *Between Facts and Norms* (Cambridge, MA: MIT Press, 1996), ch. 3; see also "Constitutional Democracy: A Paradoxical Union of Contradictory Principles?" in *Times of Transitions*, trans. Ciaran Cronin and Max Pensky (Cambridge: Polity, 2006), 113–128. Human rights differ from moral rights, among other things, in virtue of the fact that they are geared to being institutionalized, and thus have to be produced, for which purpose they require a shared democratic process, whereas people who act morally regard themselves without further qualification as subjects who are *inherently* embedded in a network of moral duties and rights; see Jeffrey Flynn, "Habermas on Human Rights: Law, Morality, and International Dialogue," *Social Theory and Practice* 29, no. 3 (2003): 431–457. However, at the time I failed to take account of two things. On the one hand, the cumulative experiences of violated dignity constitute a source of moral motivations for the historically unprecedented constitution-making practices at the close of the eighteenth century; on the other hand, the status-creating notion of social recognition of the dignity of the other forms a conceptual bridge between the moral content of the equal recognition of everyone and the legal form of human rights. Here I leave open whether the shift in attention to these states of affairs has further consequences for my deflationary reading of the discourse principle "D" in the justification of the basic rights; see my controversy with the objections of Karl-Otto Apel in "On the Architectonics of Discursive Differentiation," in *Between Naturalism and Religion* (Cambridge: Polity, 2008), 77–97.

19 On the emergence of the legal concept of human dignity through the generalization of status-bound dignity, see Jeremy Waldron, "Dignity and Rank," *European Journal of Sociology* 48 (2007): 201–237.

20 Lohmann, "Menschenrechte," 66, writes on this: "A moral right counts as justified when a corresponding moral duty exists that itself counts as justified, a legal right when it is part of a positive legal order that can claim legitimacy as a whole."

21 Lohmann, ibid., 87, seems to misunderstand this transition as one from traditional to enlightened morality.

22 Klaus Günther, "Menschenrechte zwischen Staaten und Dritten: Vom vertikalen zum horizontalen Verständnis der Menschenrechte?" in Nicole Deitelhoff and Jens Steffek (eds.), *Was bleibt vom Staat? Demokratie, Recht und Verfassung im globalen Zeitalter* (Frankfurt a.M.: Campus, 2009), here 275f.

23 Therefore human rights are not opposed to democracy but are co-original with it. The relation between the two is one of mutual presupposition: human rights make possible the democratic process, without which they themselves could not be

enacted and concretized within the framework of the civil rights-based constitutional state. K. Günther, "Liberale und diskurstheoretische Deutungen der Menschenrechte," in W. Brugger, U. Neumann, and St. Kirste (eds.), *Rechtsphilosophie im 21. Jahrhundert* (Frankfurt a.M.: Suhrkamp, 2008), 338–359.

24 Waldron, "Dignity and Rank," 201.

25 On the theological background of the concept of human rights, see the analysis of history of ideas in Tine Stein, *Himmlische Quellen und irdisches Recht* (Frankfurt a.M.: Campus, 2007), in particular ch. 7. Also Walter Huber, *Gerechtigkeit und Recht. Grundlagen einer christlichen Rechtsethik* (Gütersloh: Chr. Kaiser, 1996), 222–286.

26 Ernst-Wilhelm Böckenförde, *Geschichte der Rechts- und Staatsphilosophie. Antike und Mittelalter* (Tübingen: Mohr Siebeck, 2006).

27 Immanuel Kant, *Groundwork of the Metaphysics of Morals*, ed. and trans. M. Gregor (Cambridge: Cambirdge University Press, 1998), 41 (4:433).

28 Ibid., 43 (4:436).

29 Ibid., 42 (4:434): "In the kingdom of ends everything has either a *price* or a *dignity.* What has a price can be replaced by something else as its *equivalent*; what on the other hand is raised above all price and therefore admits of no equivalent has a dignity."

30 Immanuel Kant, *The Metaphysics of Morals*, ed. and trans. M. Gregor (Cambridge: Cambridge University Press, 1996), 30 (6:237).

31 On the premises of Kant's own theory, such a "mediation" between the transcendental realm of freedom and the phenomenal realm of necessity is neither necessary nor possible. But once the character of the free will is detranscendentalized (as it is in the theory of communicative action), the distance between morality and law has to be bridged. This is precisely what is achieved by the status-dependent concept of human dignity.

32 See Axel Honneth, *The Struggle for Recognition: Moral Grammar of Social Conflicts*, trans. Joel Anderson (Cambridge: Polity, 1996).

33 Albrecht Wellmer, "Menschenrechte und Demokratie," in Stefan Gosepath and Gerhard Lohmann (eds.), *Philosophie der Menschenrechte* (Frankfurt a.M.: Suhrkamp, 1998), 265–291; for an astute analysis of the implications of the lack of congruence between human and civil rights for the "aliens" living in a constitutional state, see Erhard Denninger, "'Die Rechte der Anderen': Menschenrechte und Bürgerrechte im Widerstreit," *Kritische Justiz* 3 (2009): 226–238.

34 On this, see my texts "Remarks on Legitimation through Human Rights" in *The Postnational Constellation: Political Essays*, trans. Max Pensky (Cambridge: Polity, 2004), 113–129; "Does the Constitutionalization of International Law Still Have a Chance?", in *The Divided West* (Cambridge: Polity, 2006), 115–193, and "The Constitutionalization of International Law and the Legitimation Problems of a Constitution for World Society," in *Europe, the Faltering Project* (Cambridge: Polity, 2009), 109–130. The contradiction between civil and human rights cannot be resolved exclusively through the global spread of constitutional states combined with the "right to have rights" demanded by Hannah Arendt (with the situation of the displaced persons at the end of World War II in mind) because classical international law leaves international relations in a "state of nature." The need for coordination in world society which has arisen in the meantime could be satisfied only by a "cosmopolitan juridical condition" (in the contemporary, revised Kantian sense).

In this context I must clear up a serious misunderstanding in the introduction to the special issue *Symposium on Human Rights: Origins, Violations, and Rectifications* (vol. 40, no. 1 [2009], 2) of the journal *Metaphilosophy* (and in Andreas Føllesdal's article "Universal Human Rights as a Shared Political Identity: Necessary? Sufficient? Impossible?" in ibid., 78–91, at 85ff.). I am, of course, a long-standing defender of the thesis that the collective identity of democratic political communities can be extended beyond the borders of nation-states, and I by no means share the reservations harbored by liberal nationalists in this regard. In developing my plea for a multilevel global constitutional system, I have offered different reasons for the thesis that a world government is neither necessary nor feasible.

35 Ernst Bloch, *Natural Law and Human Dignity* (Cambridge, MA: MIT Press, 1987).

36 Marcelo Neves, "The Symbolic Forms of Human Rights," *Philosophy and Social Criticism* 33 (2007): 411–444.

37 Moreover, the currently prevailing "gubernatorial human rights policy" is eroding the connection between human rights and democracy; on this, see Klaus Günther, "Menschenrechte zwischen Staaten und Dritten," in connection with Ingeborg Maus, "Menschenrechte als Ermächtigungsnormen internationaler Politik," in Hauke Brunkhorst, W.R. Köhler, and Matthias Lutz-Bachmann (eds.), *Recht auf Menschenrechte* (Frankfurt a.M.: Suhrkamp, 1999), 276–291. On this trend see also Klaus Günther, "Von der gubernativen zur deliberativen Menschenrechtspolitik: Die Definition und Fortentwicklung der Menschenrechte als Akt kollektiver Selbstbestimmung" in Gret Haller, Klaus Günther, and Ulfrid Neumann (eds.), *Menschenrechte und Volkssouveranität in Europa: Gerichte als Vormund der Demokratie?* (Frankfurt a.M.: Campus, 2011), 45–60.

38 Carl Schmitt was the first to formulate this suspicion explicitly. See Carl Schmitt, *War/Non-War? A Dilemma*, ed., trans. and preface by Simona Draghici (Corvallis, OR: Plutarch Press, 2004), originally in German as *Die Wendung zum diskriminierenden Kriegsbegriff* (1938), 2nd edition (Berlin: Duncker und Humblot, 1988). See also *Das international-rechtliche Verbrechen des Angriffskrieges und der Grundsatz "Nullum crimen, nullapoena sine lege"* (1945), edited with notes and an afterword by Helmuth Quaritsch (Berlin: Duncker und Humblot, 1994). Schmitt denounced human rights above all as the ideology that incriminates war as a legitimate means for resolving international conflicts. He already made the pacifist ideal of Wilsonian peace policy responsible for the fact "that the distinction between just and unjust wars is giving rise to an ever deeper and sharper, ever more 'total' distinction between friend and foe" (*War/Non-War*, 50). In the brutish domain of international relations, he argued, the moralization of enemies constitutes a disastrous method for obscuring one's own interests, for the attacker barricades himself behind the apparently transparent façade of a purportedly rational, because humanitarian, abolition of war. The critique of a "moralization" of law in the name of human rights is otiose, however, because it misses the point, namely the transposition of moral contents into the medium of coercive law. Insofar as the prohibition of war actually leads to the legal domestication of international relations, the distinction between "just" and "unjust" wars, whether based on natural law or religion, is superseded by "legal" wars which must then assume the form of global police measures. On this, see Klaus Günther, "Kampf gegen das Böse?" *Kritische Justiz* 27 (1994): 135–157.

39 Kenneth Baynes, "Toward a Political Conception of Human Rights," *Philosophy and Social Criticism* 35 (2009): 371–390.

40 Kenneth Baynes, "Discourse Ethics and the Political Conception of Human Rights," *Ethics and Global Policy* 2/1 (2009): 1–21, 6.

41 Baynes, "Discourse Ethics," 7: "Human rights are understood primarily as international norms that aim to protect fundamental human interests and/or secure for individuals the opportunity to participate as members in political society."

42 For critique of this minimalist position, see Rainer Forst, "The Justification of Human Rights and the Basic Right to Justification: A Reflexive Approach," *Ethics* 120 (2010): 711–740. There he writes: "It is generally misleading to emphasize the political-legal function of such rights within international law (or political practice)

of providing reasons for a politics of legitimate intervention. For this is to put the cart before the horse. We first need to construct (or find) a justifiable set of human rights that a legitimate political authority has to respect and guarantee, and then we will ask what kinds of legal structures are required at the international level to oversee this and help to ensure that political authority is exercised in that way" (726). That said, the narrow view on international relations outlined suggests the notion of a paternalistic export of human rights which the West confers on the rest of the world.

43 Joshua Cohen, "Minimalism about Human Rights: The Most We Can Hope For?" *The Journal of Political Philosophy* 12 (2004): 190–213.

44 Baynes, "Toward a Political Conception of Human Rights," 382: "Rights and corresponding duties are created by the special relationship that individuals stand in to one another, rather than as claims individuals have simply in virtue of their humanity."

References

Baynes, Kenneth. "Discourse Ethics and the Political Conception of Human Rights," *Ethics and Global Policy* 2/1 (2009): 1–21.

Baynes, Kenneth. "Toward a Political Conception of Human Rights," *Philosophy and Social Criticism* 35 (2009): 371–390.

Bernstorff, J.v. "Luftsicherheitsgesetz und Menschenwürde – Zum unbedingten Vorrang staatlicher Achtungspflichten im Anwendungsbereich von Art 1 GG," *Der Staat* 47 (2008): 21–40.

Bloch, Ernst. *Natural Law and Human Dignity* (Cambridge, MA: MIT Press, 1987).

Böckenförde, Ernst-Wilhelm. *Geschichte der Rechts- und Staatsphilosophie. Antike und Mittelalter* (Tübingen: Mohr Siebeck, 2006).

Bundesverfassungsgericht (BverfG). 1 BvL 1/09 of 09.02.2010. (English translation available online: www.bundesverfassungsgericht.de/entscheidungen/ls2020209_1bvl0 00109en.html).

Bundesverfassungsgericht (BverfG) (BverfG), 1 BvR 357/05 vom 15.02.2006, *Absatz-Nr. 124. (English translation available online*: www.bundesverfassungsgericht.de/entschei dungen/rs20060215_1bvr035705en.html).

Cohen, Joshua. "Minimalism about Human Right: The Most We Can Hope For?" *The Journal of Political Philosophy* 12 (2004): 190–213.

Denninger, Erhard. "Der Menschenwürdesatz im Grundgesetz und seine Entwicklung in der Verfassungsrechsprechung," in Franz-Josef Peine and Heinrich A. Wolf (eds.), *Nachdenken über Eigentum: Festschrift für Alexander von Brünneck* (Baden-Baden: Nomos, 2011), 397–411.

Denninger, Erhard. "'Die Rechte der Anderen': Menschenrechte und Bürgerrechte im Widerstreit," *Kritische Justiz* 3 (2009): 226–238.

Flynn, Jeffrey. "Habermas on Human Rights: Law, Morality, and International Dialogue," *Social Theory and Practice* 29, no. 3 (2003): 431–457.

Føllesdal, Andreas. "Universal Human Rights as a Shared Political Identity: Necessary? Sufficient? Impossible?" *Metaphilosophy* 40, no. 1 (2009): 78–91 [Special issue, *Symposium on Human Rights: Origins, Violations, and Rectifications*].

Forst, Rainer. "The Justification of Human Rights and the Basic Right to Justification: A Reflexive Approach," *Ethics* 120 (2010): 711–740.

Gardbaum, S. "The Horizontal Effect of Constitutional Rights," *Michigan Law Review* 102 (2003): 399–495.

Günther, Klaus. "Von der gubernativen zur deliberativen Menschenrechtspolitik: Die Definition und Fortentwicklung der Menschenrechte als Akt kollektiver Selbstbestimmung," in Gret Haller, Klaus Günther, and Ulfrid Neumann (eds.), *Menschenrechte und Volkssouveranität in Europa: Gerichte als Vormund der Demokratie?* (Frankfurt a.M.: Campus, 2011), 45–50.

Günther, Klaus. Menschenrechte zwischen Staaten und Dritten: Vom vertikalen zum horizontalen Verständnis der Menschenrechte?" in Nicole Deitelhoff and Jens Steffek (eds.), *Was bleibt vom Staat? Demokratie, Recht und Verfassung im globalen Zeitalter* (Frankfurt a.M.: Campus, 2009), 259–280.

Günther, Klaus. Liberale und diskurstheoretische Deutungen der Menschenrechte," in W. Brugger, U. Neumann, and St. Kirste (eds.), *Rechtsphilosophie im 21. Jahrhundert* (Frankfurt a.M.: Suhrkamp, 2008), 338–359.

Günther, Klaus. "Kampf gegen das Bose?" *Kritische Justiz* 27 (1994): 135–157.

Habermas, Jürgen. "The Constitutionalization of International Law and the Legitimation Problems of a Constitution for World Society," in *Europe, the Faltering Project* (Cambridge: Polity, 2009), 109–130.

Habermas, Jürgen. "On the Architectonics of Discursive Differentiation," in *Between Naturalism and Religion* (Cambridge: Polity, 2008), 77–97.

Habermas, Jürgen. "Constitutional Democracy: A Paradoxical Union of Contradictory Principles?" in *Times of Transitions*, trans. Ciaran Cronin and Max Pensky (Cambridge: Polity, 2006), 113–128.

Habermas, Jürgen. "Does the Constitutionalization of International Law Still Have a Chance?" in *The Divided West* (Cambridge: Polity, 2006), 115–193.

Habermas, Jürgen. "Remarks on Legitimation through Human Rights," in *The Postnational Constellation: Political Essays*, trans. Max Pensky (Cambridge: Polity, 2004), 113–129.

Habermas, Jürgen. *Between Facts and Norms* (Cambridge, MA: MIT Press, 1996).

Honneth, Axel. *The Struggle for Recognition: Moral Grammar of Social Conflicts*, trans. Joel Anderson (Cambridge: Polity, 1996).

Huber, Walter. *Gerechtigkeit und Recht. Grundlagen einer christlichen Rechtsethik* (Gütersloh: Chr. Kaiser, 1996).

Kant, Immanuel. *Groundwork of the Metaphysics of Morals*, ed. and trans. M. Gregor (Cambridge: Cambridge University Press, 1998).

Kant, Immanuel. *The Metaphysics of Morals*, ed. and trans. M. Gregor (Cambridge: Cambridge University Press, 1996).

Lohmann, Gerhard. "Die Menschenrechte: unteilbar und gleichgewichtig? Eine Skizze", in Georg Lohmann, Stefan Gosepath, Arn Pollmann, Claudia Mahler, and Norman Weiß, *Die Menschenrechte: unteilbar und gleichgewichtig?* [Studien zu Grund- und Menschenrechten 11] (Potsdam: Universitätsverlag Potsdam, 2005), 5–20.

Lohmann, Gerhard. "Menschenrechte zwischen Moral und Recht," in Stefan Gosepath and G. Lohmann (eds.), *Philosophie der Menschenrechte* (Frankfurt a.M.: Suhrkamp, 1998), 62–95.

Maus, Ingeborg. "Menschenrechte als Ermächtigungsnormen internationaler Politik," in Hauke Brunkhorst, W.R. Köhler, and Matthias Lutz-Bachmann (eds.), *Recht auf Menschenrechte* (Frankfurt a.M.: Suhrkamp, 1999), 276–291.

McCrudden, Christopher. "Human Dignity and Judicial Interpretation of Human Rights," *The European Journal of International Law* 19 (2008): 655–724.

Neves, Marcelo. "The Symbolic Forms of Human Rights," *Philosophy and Social Criticism* 33 (2007): 411–444.

Schmitt, Carl. *War/Non-War? A Dilemma*, ed., trans. and preface by Simona Draghici (Corvallis, OR: Plutarch Press, 2004), originally in German as *Die Wendung zum diskriminierenden Kriegssbegriff* (1938), 2nd edition (Berlin: Duncker und Humblot, 1988).

Schmitt, Carl. *Das international-rechtliche Verbrechen des Angriffskrieges und der Grundsatz "Nullum crimen, nullapoena sine lege"* (1945), edited with notes and an afterword by Helmuth Quaritsch (Berlin: Duncker und Humblot, 1994).

Stein, Tine. *Himmlische Quellen und irdisches Recht* (Frankfurt a.M.: Campus, 2007).

Waldron, Jeremy. "Dignity and Rank," *European Journal of Sociology/Archive Européenne de Sociologie* 48 (2007): 201–237.

Wellmer, Albrecht. "Menschenrechte und Demokratie," in Stefan Gosepath and Gerhard Lohmann (eds.), *Philosophie der Menschenrechte* (Frankfurt a.M.: Suhrkamp, 1998), 265–291.

5 The ground of critique

On the concept of human dignity in social orders of justification

Rainer Forst

1

Ernst Bloch pointed out in a particularly emphatic way that the concept of human dignity featured centrally in historical struggles against different forms of unjustified rule, i.e., domination – to which one must add that it continues to do so to the present day. The "upright gait," putting an end to humiliation and insult: this is the most powerful demand, in both political and rhetorical terms, that a "human rights-based" claim expresses. It marks the emergence of a radical, context-transcending reference point immanent to social conflicts which raises fundamental questions concerning the customary opposition between immanent and transcendent criticism. For within the idiom of demanding respect for human dignity, a right is invoked "here and now," in a particular, context-specific form, which at its core is owed to every human being as a person. Thus, Bloch is in one respect correct when he asserts that human rights are not a natural "birthright" but must be achieved through struggle;[1] but in another respect this struggle can develop its social power only if it has a firm and in a certain sense "absolute" normative anchor. Properly understood, it becomes apparent that these social conflicts always affect "two worlds": the social reality, on the one hand, which is criticized in part or radically in the light of an ideal normative dimension, on the other. For those who engage in this criticism there is no doubt that the normative dimension is no less real than the reality to which they refuse to resign themselves. Those who critically transcend reality always also live elsewhere.[2]

From the perspective of social philosophy, there is an asymmetrical relation between the rich possibilities of demonstrating various forms of "degradation"[3] and the philosophical problem of justifying that in which the essential claim to dignity is anchored. Human beings are supposed to be "inviolable" in their dignity. But what does this mean and where does this special status come from? Contrary to the view that any answer to this question must rely on a transcendent, religious justification,[4] in the following brief remarks I will make a plea for a historically reconstructed,[5] yet context-transcending normative understanding of the person as the basis of fundamental moral claims and as the "ground of critique" of social norms. This involves a notion of the person as a justifying being, as a being who uses and "needs" justifications in order to lead a life "fit for human beings" among her fellows.

Recognizing this dignity means seeing persons as beings who are endowed with a *right to justification* of all actions or norms that affect them in morally relevant ways – and acknowledging that every moral person has a duty to provide such justification. In a reflexive turn this right is to be seen as the most basic right because it is the presupposition for being able to orient oneself autonomously in social space as a "space of reasons." This social existence means offering and demanding justifications, and hence being able to live in two or three worlds at the same time: the world of actual normative justifi-cations and the world of normative justifications that must be regarded as correct or more correct (without assuming that normative justifications exist there in some Platonic sense), where the world of criticism and controversy forms the connecting link between these two worlds. To understand societies as *orders of justification* in this sense is not to imply that they do not contain complex and plural contexts and narratives of justification, but it does mean that basic claims exist which point beyond these contexts and call for a new order. To conceive of ourselves as normatively independent within the space of reasons makes us into "critical" beings who never comply with just one given order of justification.[6]

2

Let me begin with some remarks on the phenomenology of dignity. In con-trast to the dignity of a craftsman, who regards it as "beneath his dignity" to perform or be required to perform substandard work, "human dignity" sig-nifies a *status* that applies to human beings as human beings, regardless of their specific identity. What, to put it in negative terms, constitutes the most serious violation of this dignity? Here people's intuitions diverge and they propose such things as living in poverty, suffering social exclusion, or, even worse, being violated in one's bodily integrity. And then it seems natural to assume that human dignity requires having the means that help to avoid poverty, exclusion, and mistreatment. The tendency is to think in terms of basic needs and to infer a substantive social condition that is supposed to make an "existence fit for a human being" possible. However, in concentrating in this way on the passive as opposed to the active component of human dignity something is overlooked. Living in poverty does not violate the dignity of a human being in all cases, such as in the wake of a natural catastrophe that plunges a community into an emergency situation. What violates people's dignity in the first instance is that they *have to* live in poverty, that is that they are *compelled* to do so, in particular that they are compelled by other human beings who have caused this condition, or at least could remedy it but fail to do so, either because they simply ignore the claims of those affected or respond to them in an inadequate fashion. The violation of dignity consists in being ignored, not counting, being "invisible" for the purpose of legitimizing social relations. In issues concerning human dignity, therefore, one should not think in terms of the end, of (objective or subjective) *conditions* or *states of affairs*, but of social *relations*, of processes, interactions, and structures between persons, and of the status of individuals within them. This also explains why certain forms of poverty *relief*, such as mere charity on the part of those who otherwise ignore or even harm the poor, or bureaucratic measures that treat the "needy" in a condescending manner, are no less degrading than poverty itself.[7]

Thus, the central phenomenon of the violation of dignity is not the lack of the necessary means to live a "life fit for a human being" but the conscious violation of the moral status of being a person who is owed justifications for existing relations or specific actions; it is the phenomenon of "invisibility" for the purposes of legitimation,[8] of being subject to rule without adequate justification, and thus of being dominated. This can assume more or less drastic forms, ranging from social exclusion to physical torment. Structurally speaking, however, they remain the same at the core, namely that a person's *right* to justification or, to be more precise, to *reciprocal* justification on a basis of equality, is negated. Being recognized in one's dignity as a human being means, in general terms, not being ignored in questions that concern one in essential ways.

3

This meaning of the concept is also shown by its history. The human being, to whom dignity is attributed, whether on the basis of inner fortitude, as in the Stoics,[9] or with reference to the status of a free citizen of the city, as in republicanism, has always been the individual who is not subject to unauthorized rule, i.e. domination. In other words, it is the human being who determines him or herself, whether personally or politically – in Cicero, paradigmatically both.[10] "Freedom from arbitrariness," both in one's actions and in how one is treated, is the original connotation of dignity. It means being able to act and being recognized as an entity endowed with equal rights and duties to justification.

The stress placed by Christian theology on the idea that all human beings can claim special regard in virtue of being created "in God's image" first acquired its importance for human rights in a *political* context, namely in the conflicts in which people claimed their "divinely endowed" rights against tyrannical forms of domination.[11] Thus the notion that Christianity is historically (as well as normatively) the foundation of the conception of dignity that informs human rights is in need of correction. It first had to undergo extensive reinterpretation (drawing in large part on ancient thought) before the "human being" could emerge as an earthly being in her own right and as a person who can claim unconditional respect. For, traditionally, the chief concern of Christian pastoral care was exclusively with the soul, and not with the dignity of the human being as a free being. Neither Augustine nor

Thomas was in any doubt that earthly death represents by far the lesser evil by comparison with the death of the soul. A new understanding of individuality had to emerge so that the profane human being could appear as morally autonomous and respect-worthy "in itself." "Self-determination without theo-teleological determination," as a central normative idea, is an achievement that cannot be attributed to Christianity, even though Protestantism (and the idea of individual responsibility before God) played a certain (in turn ambivalent) role in this process. It is also important to keep in mind that the conflicts in which the natural law-based claim to freedom and dignity triumphed were to a large extent those which combated traditionally legitimized forms of political-religious rule and domination. In general, it was the "heretics" who discovered freedom.

From a systematic point of view, a religious justification of respect for human beings suffers from the defect that, on the one hand, it can be addressed in the full sense only to those who recognize the other as created in God's image, and hence only to the devout, so that atheists, in particular, would not be able to comprehend why human rights have genuine validity.[12] In addition to the limitation thus placed on the community of active respect, such a jus-tification also potentially restricts the community of those to be respected, for it seems to be an open question whether and why, for instance, the persistent repudiation and undermining of the foundation of morality and law by atheists should be tolerated. Therefore, a religiously founded attribution of human rights, even if it works with universalistic concepts, cannot redeem the uni-versalistic claim that these rights make to be strictly binding across religious boundaries.

As already suggested, the general concept of human dignity is, by contrast, inextricably bound up with that of self-determination[13] in a creative and simultaneously moral sense that already involves a political component. At stake is one's status of not being subject to external forces which have not been legitimized to rule over a person – in other words, being respected in one's autonomy as an independent being.[14] Kant captured this idea in terms of the "worthiness of every rational subject to be a law-giving member in the kingdom of ends."[15] To be such a law-giving member means not being dis-regarded when it comes to legitimizing social rule, and knowing that one should not disregard others in this respect either, that one is subject to the law oneself. This conception of dignity, and correspondingly respect for others as "ends in themselves", means that humans must be regarded as beings who have an unconditional right to justification, a basic right on which all other basic rights are founded. To *possess* human dignity means being an equal member in the realm of subjects and authorities of justification, an attribute, I should add, that does not depend on the active exercise of the capacity of justification, which would exclude infants or disabled persons; correspond-ingly, to *act* with dignity means being able to justify oneself to others; to be *treated* in accordance with this dignity means being respected as such an equal member; to *renounce* one's dignity means no longer regarding oneself as such a member but as inferior; to *treat* others in ways which violate their dignity means regarding them as lacking any justification authority.

4

Some clarifications of the concept of justification may be appropriate at this point.[16] When it comes to justifying morally relevant actions in a social context, the decisive criteria are *reciprocity* and *generality*, since such actions must be justified by appeal to norms which can claim to hold in a reciprocal and general fashion. If one proceeds recursively from the claim to validity of such norms and asks what conditions must be fulfilled in order to redeem it, the criteria of validity of reciprocity and generality become transformed into criteria of discursive justification. It follows that, in justifying or challenging a moral norm (or a mode of action), no one can make specific claims that he denies to others (reciprocity of contents); moreover no one can simply assume that others share his own perspective, evaluations, convictions, interests, or needs (reciprocity of reasons), such that one would claim, for instance, to speak in the "real" interest of others or in the name of an absolutely indubitable truth beyond the reach of justification. And finally, it follows that no affected person may be prevented from raising objections, and that the reasons that are supposed to legitimize a norm must be such that they can be shared by all persons (generality).

In contexts in which what is at stake is safeguarding and recognizing the basic status of justifying beings in the political world, therefore, all fundamental claims on others must be justified in accordance with these same criteria. This results in the possibility of a "moral construction" of certain human rights, namely those which could not be denied to others without violating reciprocity and generality.[17] Such constructions single out a core set of rights, in particular concerning the protection of personality, political participation, and material security; but *prior* to these is the right not to be disregarded whenever it is a question of defining and securing such rights. Once again it becomes apparent that the moral core of human dignity has political relevance. The underlying basic right to justification leads not only to substantive basic rights, but first of all to guarantees of participation in the processes in which such basic rights are formulated and justified. In this sense the right to justification excludes paternalistic stipulations and denials of rights.

Thus, on a second level, in addition to the moral constructivism which is abstract in nature, a more contextualized, discursive "political constructivism" must be conceived which determines the basic rights and claims that should hold in a concrete legal community, always under the proviso that all those who are at risk of suffering disadvantage or discrimination have a reciprocal right of veto. In this way the abstract list of human rights can be embodied in concrete legal and political form as basic rights without sacrificing their essential content, for the right of veto – which, politically speaking, must of course be institutionalized – ensures that this essential content remains intact.

The political and moral stimulus for this conception of dignity is provided by a critique of social power, and this was always also the original inspiration for talk of "human dignity" and "human rights."

5

Against this background, *power* must be regarded primarily as a discursive phenomenon, indeed, however apparently paradoxically, as a noumenal phenomenon.[18] It consists, in particular, in the ability to order and influence, to occupy, and, in extreme cases, to dominate the space of reasons for others, that is, to determine the limits of what can be said and thought and, above all, of what is accepted and acceptable, of what is justified. Thus, exercising power over others – that is, in very general terms, leading them to have thoughts or to perform actions which they would not otherwise have had or have performed – is not primarily a matter of strength and competition of wills, but of the convictions or beliefs which bring persons or groups into a particular social position and anchor them there. Power in general terms does not have a negative connotation, for every space of reasons is a space of the "power of justifications." Power must be constantly regenerated in discourse and thus must be continually renewed; if it degenerates into domination, i.e., rule without adequate justification, it remains effective only if these justifications are accepted, whether through ideology or through fear. Thus, a critique of power ultimately involves problematizing the existing space of reasons and justifications; it consists in breaking open rigid, encrusted justification narratives and reciprocally untenable clusters of reasons.

Here it must be kept in mind that power relations are not uniform but rest on pluralistic and tension-laden justifications that allow for and, if necessary, provoke contradiction (and "counterpower"). Power is situated within a dynamic field of justifications. The transitions to forms of rule [*Herrschaft*] – to sketch a heuristic typology – occur when (religious, traditional, metaphysical, economic, political, etc.) justifications become consolidated into hierarchical systems of thought and action (irrespective of whether the rule in question is legitimate or illegitimate); domination [*Beherrschung*] arises where the closure of the space of justifications permits scarcely any alternatives (whether on account of discursive hegemony or of effective threats) and the right to justification is restricted; the transition to violence occurs when claims to justification are completely rejected and replaced by other means of regulating action. Insofar as this is experienced as "naked violence," of course, the power of the agent resting on recognition dwindles and is reduced to pure physical facticity. Power is an expression of a binding of others through reasons; it collapses, together with the authority on which it is founded, when it no longer rests on acceptance. Whether this marks the end of subjection is a different matter.

The concept of ideology can be reformulated against this background. Ideologies are justifications of relations of rule or domination that insulate themselves from critical challenge by distorting the space of reasons and presenting relations of rule or domination as "natural" (unalterable), "God-given," or in some other way falsely, as sufficiently justified. Thus, they absolve those in power from the effort of justification and offer powerful explanations that prevent criticism from arising. The analysis of "ideological delusion" does not require any problematic concept of "genuine interests" but instead an understanding of the validity claim to reciprocal justification whose satisfaction is thwarted.

6

The idea of the dignity of the human being as a being equipped with the right to justification makes it possible to address and defuse the objection that the central conception of moral autonomy involved is a purely "western," non-universalizable one – a specific aspect of the general problem of cultural immanence versus critical transcendence.

First, we must bear in mind the difference between ethical and moral autonomy. Respecting human dignity means not denying anybody's moral right to justification; but it does not imply that only the life that is "autonomously chosen" (whatever this may mean in concrete terms) is the "good" life. In purely conceptual terms, a life free from demeaning paternalism or domination is one thing, the good life something else. Thus, the argument presented thus far does not involve any specific conception of ethical forms of life or any assertion concerning the good life. Ideological narratives, for instance, may exert their power by means of specific conceptions and realizations of what counts as the "good life." Critique of such narratives can take the form of ethical criticism, but they should be criticized essentially on the grounds that they restrict the justification authority of individuals or particular groups.

Second, the formal pragmatic grounding of the right to justification briefly mentioned above can be supplemented by an immanent grounding.[19] For, assuming that someone were to defend the integrity of his own (let us assume roughly) "non-Western" culture against such "alien" moral conceptions, what would he say? He would appeal to the integrity of his culture as an integral cultural unity, and such an understanding of integrity and integrality would include the assumption that this integration is not maintained by force but implies internal acceptance. This would presuppose, in turn, that nobody would be systematically prevented from adopting a critical stance on this culture and from demanding a right to justification and participation. Such a claim would therefore appeal to this society's own self-understanding; it would be a form of immanent critique. Thus, it becomes apparent that justified social and political structures can very well assume extremely diverse forms and that the project of the political is to discover such forms. However, it also becomes apparent that, notwithstanding this whole wealth of forms, the basic right to justification, and hence a core of basic rights, are indispensable presuppositions for talk of integration, unity, etc., not to mention justice.

7

Up to this point I have discussed the right to justification primarily from the perspective of moral philosophy and in terms of political history. However, a critical theory of social relations calls for a systematic analysis of the practices of justification within a society. Societies should be regarded as orders of justification in several respects. Historically speaking, social institutions rest on certain justification narratives that may in turn be plural in character and provide scope for immanent criticism; sociologically speaking, in any given society there is a plurality of normative spheres in which particular values or expectations concerning justification hold sway – for instance, the spheres of the market, of the family, of education, and of politics – and which can be analyzed as spheres of the good or as contexts of recognition or justification.[20] Then criticism becomes possible in the form of identifying and condemning infringements of certain limits between spheres; but these spheres are also internally by no means normatively homogeneous. Opinions diverge within a given society over the functions of the market or the family and the values they should embody.

From the perspective of political theory, to be sure, a reflexive institutional framework is required whose task is to channel such conflicts and facilitate their solution, namely the political system as a system which generates binding decisions, presupposing that democratic practices of justification have been sufficiently institutionalized, in combination with a discursive public sphere. In this system, criticism can find expression not only with regard to certain social spheres; it can also refer to the conditions of political justification as such. It then assumes the guise of a *critique of relations of justification*.[21] This not only concerns political relations in the narrow sense, however, for social relations and structures in general do not only make participation in justification possible or impossible in a relevant sense; they are also independent contexts of justification in their own right in which disputes over their elaboration are conducted. As I have noted, discursive power[22] must be generated in social-political discourses in order to challenge existing justifications and structures of justification; then social space is revealed as a space of reasons and also a space of struggles over "justification hegemony" (to put it in Gramscian terms).

Thus the "critique of relations of justification" has a number of different meanings. First, it has the meaning of the critical analysis of non-justifiable political and social relations, including those in the economic and cultural dimensions – relations of discrimination, of exclusion, of lack of emancipation or of equality of opportunity. These involve relations that cannot be legitimized in reciprocal and general terms. Second, it means criticism of "false" justifications of such relations that insulate them against challenges and represent them as legitimate, ranging from metaphysical worldviews to arguments concerning factual or empirical constraints.[23] Third, reflexively speaking, it means a critique of the absence of structures and institutions of justification themselves that would be necessary in order to facilitate the first two categories of criticism and to render them effective. The issue here is to expose and rectify the unequal distribution of the resources to generate the "power of justification" in both institutional and informal political spaces. The basic claim of political and social justice with reference to this process is to establish a "basic structure of justification."

8

Challenges to provide justifications – specific forms of social criticism – can avail themselves of different normative languages. "Ethical" criticism, for instance, relates to the quality of existing social conditions in a more or less comprehensive way; it operates with evaluative conceptions of the good or successful life which, however much they diverge from and unmask the pathologies of received notions concerning ways of life, must ultimately be connected back to justification among those affected. For in a social universe of justification there is no place outside of this space of discursive redemption; in Habermas's words, in a process of discursive clarification there are "only participants."[24] This does not compel critique to adopt only thin and formal concepts, though it is compelled to submit itself to criticism as regards its validity. In this way the "moral" form of criticism retains its priority; the central issue is which social structures can be demanded in a reciprocal manner. For instance, actually overcoming "alienation," which is the topic of many ethical forms of criticism, involves the "appropriation" of the social basic structure by those concerned themselves by making it responsive to their demands and subjecting it to their democratic control.[25]

In order to be effective, every form of criticism will combine "immanent" with "transcending" reasons. When the Levellers demanded a "birthright" to political and religious liberty at the time of the English civil war, for instance, they understood by this their rights as free English citizens and their "natural" rights; when in addition they reinterpreted the social contract establishing a system of rule in bourgeois terms as a terminable employment contract, and when they claimed property in themselves as God's will, they combined traditional, revolutionary, bourgeois, and religious arguments and recast the fabric of existing justifications into a new narrative which they regarded as sufficiently powerful to legitimize the overthrow of a system of government.[26] As already mentioned, the alternative between "immanence" and "transcendence" is a false one under such historical conditions; both moments were necessarily involved in the emancipatory demands of the era.

To sum up, structurally speaking, all of these critical languages involve a central reflexive idiom, namely that of the dignity of an autonomous being who can demand and offer justifications; this is the idiom of justice, which does not in the first instance criticize some particular institution or distribution or other but, in a more radical way, the entire structure of an order of justification. To quote Horkheimer: "That is the universal content of the concept of Justice; according to this concept, the social inequality prevailing at any given time requires a rational justification. It ceases to be considered as a good, and becomes something that should be overcome."[27]

The connection between justice and justification is an immanent one: those relations are unjust that are not sufficiently justifiable in reciprocal and general terms, and those relations are profoundly unjust that systematically thwart the practice of justification itself. Putting an end to such relations is the strongest motive of justice driving historical struggles; and the word "dignity" features centrally in such struggles. They aim to create a social structure in which individuals are able to recognize themselves as autonomous in the specifically political sense of being co-creators of the institutions and laws that are binding on them.

Translated by Ciaran Cronin

Notes

1 Ernst Bloch, *Natural Law and Human Dignity*, trans. D.F. Schmidt (Cambridge, MA: MIT Press, 1986), 188; originally *Naturrecht und menschliche Würde* (Frankfurt a.M.: Suhrkamp, 1977), 215.

2 On the issue of utopia that plays a role here, see Rainer Forst, "Utopie und Ironie. Zur Normativität der politischen Philosophie des 'Nirgendwo'," in G. Abel (ed.), *Kreativität* (Hamburg: 20. Deutscher Kongress für Philosophie, 2006).

3 See Avishai Margalit, *The Decent Society* (Cambridge, MA: Harvard University Press, 1996); Axel Honneth, *The Struggle for Recognition: The Moral Grammar of Social Conflicts* (Cambridge, MA: MIT Press, 1996); Axel Honneth, *Unsichtbarkeit* (Frankfurt a.M.: Suhrkamp, 2003).

4 For example, Jeremy Waldron, *God, Locke, and Equality* (Cambridge: Cambridge University Press, 2002); Tine Stein, *Himmlische Quellen und irdisches Recht* (Frankfurt a.M.: Campus, 2007).

5 I provide a reconstruction of the paths along which the concept of the person and his or her dignity developed, in the context of historical and normative conflicts, in conjunction with the issue of toleration in my study *Toleration in Conflict*, trans. Ciaran Cronin (Cambridge: Cambridge University Press, 2013), Part I. Demonstrating the historical context within which such concepts evolved is as important for understanding their conflictual character as the recognition that this does not amount to reducing them to historically relative concepts.

6 For the idea of an order of justification (as employed in the Frankfurt research project on the "The Formation of Normative Orders": www.normativeorders.net) see Rainer Forst and Klaus Günther, "Die Herausbildung normativer Ordnungen. Zur Idee eines interdisziplinären Forschungsprogramms," in Rainer Forst and Klaus Günther (eds.), *Die Herausbildung normativer Ordnungen* (Frankfurt a.M.: Campus, 2011). For an analysis of "contexts of justification" see Rainer Forst, *Contexts of Justice* (Berkeley, CA: University of California Press, 2002).

7 On this see Margalit, *The Decent Society*, chs. 13 and 14.

8 This was given literary expression in Ralph Ellison, *Invisible Man* (New York, NY: Modern Library, 1994).

9 Compare Seneca on the "truly noble man" and the treatment of slaves in *Seneca's Letters to Lucilius* (Oxford: Clarendon Press, 1932), letters nos. 44 and 47.

10 Cicero, *On Duties*, ed. M.T. Griffin and E.T. Atkins (Cambridge: Clarendon Press, 1991), I, 106 (41–42); Cicero, *The Republic*, in *The Republic and the Laws*, ed. J.

Powell (Oxford: Oxford University Press, 1998), II, 29. Philip Pettit takes up this idea underlying republicanism as an emancipatory indictment of domination: "The grievance I have in mind is that of having to live at the mercy of another, having to live in a manner that leaves you vulnerable to some ill that the other is in a position arbitrarily to impose; and this, in particular, when each of you is in a position to see that you are dominated by the other, in a position to see that you each see this, and so on." Philip Pettit, *Republicanism: A Theory of Freedom and Government* (Oxford: Oxford University Press, 1997), 4f. However, the guiding conception of freedom at work here cannot be adequately understood apart from that of dignity as a subject of justification, since it concerns freedom from *arbitrary* rule or domination.

11 On the following see Forst, *Toleration in Conflict*, in particular chs. 3–6.

12 For a clear statement of this position see Robert Spaemann, "Über den Begriff der Menschenwürde," in E.-W. Böckenförde and R. Spaemann (eds.), *Menschenrechte und Menschenwürde: Historische Voraussetzungen – säkuläre Gestalt – christliches Verständnis* (Stuttgart: Klett-Cotta, 1987), 295–313, here 313. Spaemann defends the view that "atheism definitively robs the idea of human dignity of its justification."

13 Thus, Pico della Mirandola, *On the Dignity of Man* (1486), ed. and trans. C.G. Wallis and P.J.W. Miller (Indianapolis, IN: Hackett, 1998), 4, represents God as addressing human beings: "In conformity with thy free judgement, in whose hands I have placed thee, thou art confined by no bounds; and thou wilt fix limits of nature for thyself."

14 On the political component see, in particular, Samuel von Pufendorf, *Of the Duty of Man and Citizen According to Natural Law*, ed. J. Tully (Cambridge: Cambridge University Press, 1991), 61: "Man is an animal which is not only intensely interested in its own preservation but also possesses a native and delicate sense of its own value. To detract from that causes no less alarm than harm to body or goods. In the very name of man a certain dignity is felt to lie, so that the ultimate and most effective rebuttal of insolence and insults from others is 'Look, I am not a dog, but a man as well as yourself'." From this Pufendorf derives principles of equal respect and reciprocal justifiability of claims to justice: "Hence this too is among the common duties of natural law, that no one require for himself more than he allows others, unless he has acquired some special right to do so, but allow others to enjoy their own right equally with him" (62).

15 Immanuel Kant, *Groundwork of the Metaphysics of Morals*, ed. Mary Gregor (Cambridge: Cambridge University Press, 1997), 46.

16 For a more detailed discussion see Rainer Forst, *The Right to Justification*, trans. J. Flynn (New York, NY: Columbia University Press, 2011), especially Part I.

17 See Rainer Forst, "The Justification of Human Rights and the Basic Right to Justification: A Reflexive Approach," *Ethics* 120 (July 2010): 711–740.

18 See Rainer Forst, "Noumenal Power," *Journal of Political Philosophy* 23, no. 2 (June 2015): 111–127.

19 For a more detailed account see Forst, *The Right to Justification*, ch. 9.

20 On the former see Michael Walzer, *Spheres of Justice* (New York, NY: Basic Books, 1983), for the latter see Honneth, *Struggle for Recognition* and Forst, *Contexts of Justice*; for alternative approaches see Luc Boltanski and Laurent Thévenot, *On Justification* (Princeton, NJ: Princeton University Press, 2006), and David Miller, *Principles of Social Justice* (Cambridge, MA: Harvard University Press, 1999).

21 On this see Rainer Forst, "First Things First: Redistribution, Recognition and Justification," *European Journal of Political Theory* 6 (2007): 291–304.

22 In contrast to the communicative conception of power developed by Jürgen Habermas with reference to Hannah Arendt in "Hannah Arendt's Communications Concept of Power" in *Social Research* 44, no. 1 (1977): 3–24, with which I

agree in part, the understanding of discursive power outlined above involves, on the one hand, a more pronounced confrontational component – if you will, the force "to" the better argument. On the other hand, this understanding of power does not have a direct positive or negative connotation; it merely signifies the relations in the social space of justification.

23 Both the present and the next dimension of the critique of relations of justification prevent "established principles" of public justification from imposing narrow limits on what can be criticized. This is a response to an objection of Axel Honneth, "Redistribution as Recognition," in Nancy Fraser and Axel Honneth, *Redistribution or Recognition?* (London: Verso, 2003), 130ff.

24 Jürgen Habermas, *Theory and Practice* (Boston, MA: Beacon Press, 1974), 40; original, *Theorie und Praxis* (Frankfurt a.M.: Suhrkamp, 1971), 45.

25 Here, in my opinion, there is no major difference from the core argument of Rahel Jaeggi, "'Kein Einzelner vermag etwas dagegen': Adornos Minima Moralia als Kritik von Lebensformen," in A. Honneth (ed.), *Dialektik der Freiheit* (Frankfurt a.M.: Suhrkamp, 2005), 115–141.

26 For a more detailed discussion see Forst, *Toleration in Conflict*, § 15.

27 Max Horkheimer, "Materialism and Morality," in *Between Philosophy and Social Science: Selected Early Writings* (Cambridge, MA: MIT Press, 1995), 15–48, here 40.

References

Bloch, Ernst. *Natural Law and Human Dignity*, trans. D.F. Schmidt (Cambridge, MA: MIT Press, 1986), 188; originally in *Naturrecht und menschliche Würde* (Frankfurt a.M.: Suhrkamp, 1977).

Boltanski, Luc and Laurent Thévenot. *On Justification* (Princeton, NJ: Princeton University Press, 2006).

Cicero. *On Duties*, ed. M.T. Griffin and E.T. Atkins (Cambridge: Clarendon Press, 1991).

Cicero. *The Republic* in *The Republic and the Laws*, ed. J. Powell (Oxford: Oxford University Press, 1998).

Ellison, Ralph. *Invisible Man* (New York, NY: Modern Library, 1994).

Forst, Rainer. "Noumenal Power," *Journal of Political Philosophy* 23, no. 2 (June 2015): 111–127.

Forst, Rainer. *Toleration in Conflict*, trans. Ciaran Cronin (Cambridge: Cambridge University Press, 2013).

Forst, Rainer. *The Right to Justification*, trans. J. Flynn (New York, NY: Columbia University Press, 2011).

Forst, Rainer. "The Justification of Human Rights and the Basic Right to Justification: A Reflexive Approach," *Ethics* 120 (July 2010): 711–740.

Forst, Rainer. "First Things First: Redistribution, Recognition and Justification," *European Journal of Political Theory* 6 (2007): 291–304.

Forst, Rainer. "Utopie und Ironie. Zur Normativität der politischen Philosophie des 'Nirgendwo'," in G. Abel (ed.), *Kreativität* (Hamburg: 20. Deutscher Kongress für Philosophie, 2006), 92–103.

Forst, Rainer. *Contexts of Justice* (Berkeley, CA: University of California Press, 2002).

Forst, Rainer and Klaus Günther. "Die Herausbildung normativer Ordnungen. Zur Idee eines interdisziplinären Forschungsprogramms," in Rainer Forst and Klaus Günther (eds.), *Die Herausbildung normativer Ordnungen* (Frankfurt a.M.: Campus, 2011), 11–30.

Habermas, Jürgen. "Hannah Arendt's Communications Concept of Power," *Social Research* 44, no. 1 (1977): 3–24.

Habermas, Jürgen. *Theory and Practice* (Boston, MA: Beacon Press, 1974); original, *Theorie und Praxis* (Frankfurt a.M.: Suhrkamp, 1971).

Honneth, Axel. "Redistribution as Recognition," in Nancy Fraser and Axel Honneth, *Redistribution or Recognition?* (London: Verso, 2003), 110–197.

Honneth, Axel. *Unsichtbarkeit* (Frankfurt a.M.: Suhrkamp, 2003).

Honneth, Axel. *The Struggle for Recognition: The Moral Grammar of Social Conflicts* (Cambridge, MA: MIT Press, 1996).

Horkheimer, Max. *Between Philosophy and Social Science: Selected Early Writings* (Cambridge, MA: MIT Press, 1995).

Jaeggi, Rahel. "Kein Einzelner vermag etwas dagegen': Adornos Minima Moralia als Kritik von Lebensformen," in A. Honneth (ed.), *Dialektik der Freiheit* (Frankfurt a. M.: Suhrkamp, 2005), 115–141.

Kant, Immanuel. *Groundwork of the Metaphysics of Morals*, ed. Mary Gregor (Cambridge: Cambridge University Press, 1997).

Margalit, Avishai. *The Decent Society* (Cambridge, MA: Harvard University Press, 1996).

Miller, David. *Principles of Social Justice* (Cambridge, MA: Harvard University Press, 1999).

Pettit, Philip. *Republicanism: A Theory of Freedom and Government* (Oxford: Oxford University Press, 1997).

Pico della Mirandola, Giovanni. *On the Dignity of Man* (1486), ed. and trans. C.G. Wallis and P.J.W. Miller (Indianapolis, IN: Hackett, 1998).

Seneca. *Seneca's Letters to Lucilius* (Oxford: Clarendon Press, 1932).

Spaemann, Robert. "Über den Begriff der Menschenwürde," in E.-W. Böckenförde and R. Spaemann (eds.), *Menschenrechte und Menschenwürde: Historische Voraussetzungen – säkuläre Gestalt – christliches Verständnis* (Stuttgart: Klett-Cotta, 1987), 295–313.

Stein, Tine. *Himmlische Quellen und irdisches Recht* (Frankfurt a.M.: Campus, 2007).

von Pufendorf, Samuel. *Of the Duty of Man and Citizen According to Natural Law*, ed. J. Tully (Cambridge: Cambridge University Press, 1991).

Waldron, Jeremy. *God, Locke, and Equality* (Cambridge: Cambridge University Press, 2002).

Walzer, Michael. *Spheres of Justice* (New York, NY: Basic Books, 1983).

6 Should we take the "human" out of human rights?

Human dignity in a corporate world

Cristina Lafont

In recent years philosophical discussions of human rights have focused on the question of whether "humanist" and "political" conceptions of human rights are genuinely incompatible or whether some kind of synthesis between them may be possible.[1] Defenders of the humanist conception take human rights to be those rights that we have simply by virtue of being human, and try to ground them on some authoritative conception of human nature or human good. By contrast, defenders of the political conception take contemporary human rights practice as providing an authoritative understanding of human rights; by understanding the purposes of the contemporary practice, one can grasp the concept of human rights that is operative within it.

Many participants in this ongoing debate argue that the supposed incompatibility between these approaches is, in fact, not as dramatic as it may seem, and they identify different ways of combining the most fruitful aspects of both.[2] However, defenses of this compatibility have been largely one-sided, showing that human rights theories that incorporate the central tenets of humanist approaches can also accommodate the core claims of political approaches. But this does not yet answer the question of whether theories using the political approach can incorporate the core claims of humanist approaches without sacrificing their distinctive methodological perspective. Prominent defenders of the political approach answer this question negatively.[3] I think they are wrong. In my view, an account of human rights that disregards the humanist core of human rights practice cannot properly identify its ultimate goal and, as a consequence, lacks the critical distance necessary to provide normative guidance in light of conflicts that can arise within that practice.

If this is indeed the case, then there is a tension between two claims associated with the political approach: on the one hand, the *methodological* claim that a plausible account of human rights must take contemporary human rights practice as authoritative and, on the other, the *substantive* claim that human rights are not rights that we have simply by virtue of being human, but rights that we have by virtue of being subject to political authority. Precisely to the extent that the political approach aims to take contemporary human rights practice seriously, it must provide a plausible account of the practice's humanist core instead of simply rejecting it, as defenders of the political approach do.

In what follows, I defend this claim in four steps. First, I offer a brief overview of the debate between humanist and political approaches in order to show that some of the key functions of the humanist core of human rights practice, most notably those of the concept of human dignity, have not been properly identified. In the next step, I briefly indicate what these key functions are, and illustrate some of the problematic implications of leaving the concept of human dignity out of our account of human rights practice. I focus on the recent extension of legal human rights to corporations. I analyze the negative effects that the distinctive functions of human rights norms – such as limiting state sovereignty, prompting transnational remedial action, and so on – can have upon the human rights of natural persons once corporations are recognized as legal persons bearing human rights. If this legal development continues, human rights practice may be facing two incommensurable paths. To the extent that the political approach endows actual practice with the authority to determine what human rights are, its defenders may find themselves at a crossroads. On the one hand, defenders of the political approach can treat those aspects of the practice that seem to be taking the human out of human rights as authoritative and redefine the practice's ultimate aim as the protection of the urgent interests of all legal subjects, corporations included, no matter the consequences for the fundamental interests of human beings. On the other, they can insist that the protection of human dignity is the ultimate goal of human rights practice, and provide critical guidance concerning legal and institutional mechanisms that may allow the protection of the fundamental interests of human beings to be properly prioritized over those of corporations. I conclude by defending this second alternative, briefly exploring the normative resources that the jurisprudence of dignity may have to offer.

1. The debate between humanist and political conceptions of human rights

A central question within the debate between humanist and political conceptions of human rights is whether the humanist perspective has anything essential to contribute to illuminating or guiding human rights practice. Many defenders of the political conception are skeptical. In their view, the humanist perspective only adds metaphysical baggage that is at best useless and at worst a threat to a practice that aspires to avoid both unnecessary disagreements among different cultures and charges of parochialism that would undermine its key political purposes. The latter concerns underlie John Rawls's project in *The Law of Peoples* of offering an account of human rights without any recourse to the idea that these rights are grounded in some intrinsic moral worth that all human beings possess simply by virtue of being human.[4] This leads him to exclude any reference to human dignity; he argues that references to human dignity as they appear, for instance, in Article 1 of the Universal Declaration of Human Rights – that "all human beings are born free and equal in dignity and rights" – express "liberal aspirations" that are too parochial and contentious to form a properly political basis for a Law of Peoples.

Similarly, in *The Idea of Human Rights*, Charles Beitz rejects attempts to conceive of human rights as rights possessed by all human beings "as such" or "solely by virtue of their humanity" as both useless and unnecessarily contentious. According to him, "human rights are institutional protections against standard threats to urgent interests."[5] The *identity* of these rights, however, does not derive from any grounding value such as "humanity" or "human dignity" but from "their special role as norms of global political life."[6] In contrast to humanist approaches that interpret human rights as an attempt to embody an independently intelligible moral idea (such as human dignity, equal moral worth, and so on) in international law and practice, the political approach infers the nature of human rights from the purposes and modes of action manifested in the ongoing human rights practice itself. In so doing, this approach gives actual practice authority over the answer to the question of what human rights are. From this practical perspective, Beitz concludes that human rights are rights that regulate the behavior of states toward their members and whose infringement is a cause for international concern, which may trigger transnational protective and remedial action.[7]

In addition, Beitz questions whether the *foundationalist* strategy of deriving human rights from a single notion or value (such as human dignity, person-hood, and so on) can be fruitful for generating content, that is, for providing a list of human rights proper. Such accounts are "likely either to be too abstract to settle disagreement about the contents of human rights doctrine or arbitrarily to constrain the doctrine's substantive scope."[8] Defenders of humanist approaches contend that without a robust philosophical conception of their grounds, political approaches lack the resources necessary to deter-mine the substantive content of human rights.[9] Beitz rejects this contention by questioning the ability of humanist approaches to actually generate anything resembling the content of human rights found in current human rights doctrine.[10]

Thus framed, the debate assumes that the concept of human dignity can make a contribution to human rights practice only by *providing a substantive ground sufficient to generate the content of human rights norms*, that is, to generate the list of human rights proper. However, it is not at all clear why human dignity should play such a function. In fact, if foundationalism is as foreign to human rights doctrine as defenders of the political approach con-tend it is, then it seems all the more unlikely that human dignity's prominent presence within the practice of human rights could be explained by the foun-dationalist assumptions of humanist approaches. A different explanation of its presence and function seems to be required. However, two separate questions need to be distinguished here. One is whether the concept of human dignity is necessary for a plausible account of human rights practice and, if so, for what purposes. A different question is whether a single substantive conception of the concept (for example, a theory of human nature or personhood) is also necessary for such an account and, if so, for what purposes.

With respect to the latter question, defenders of the political approach may be correct to doubt that a philosophical conception of human dignity could be articulated that would be able to generate a list of rights sufficiently resembling actual practice. They may also be right in fearing that, even if such a conception could be articulated, it would be too contentious and constraining to serve as a public basis for a global political practice. However, even if these criticisms were true, this says nothing about the prior question, namely, whether the concept of human dignity itself (and not a specific conception of it) is needed in a proper account of human rights practice and, if so, for what purposes.

Christopher McCrudden offers an interesting answer to this question.[11] He argues that the inclusion of human dignity in human rights documents functions as a placeholder that helps to overcome disagreements among members of societies and cultures with different conceptions of the concept. He illustrates this function from a political and a judicial perspective. Commenting on the historical period that gave rise to the Universal Declaration of Human Rights, he indicates that

> the concept of human dignity played a pivotal political role in enabling different cultures with different conceptions of the state, differing views on the basis of human rights, and differing ethical and moral viewpoints, to put aside these deep ideological differences and agree instead to focus on the specific practices of human rights abuses that should be prohibited ... Dignity helped achieve this by enabling all to agree, at a political level, that human rights are founded on dignity and then to move on.[12]

From a judicial perspective, McCrudden claims that the concept of human dignity currently plays a similar role:

> Its role, in practice, is to enable local context to be incorporated in the interpretation of human rights norms ... Dignity, in the judicial context, not only permits the incorporation of local contingencies, it requires it. Dignity remains as a placeholder, but in the judicial context it is a placeholder that allows each jurisdiction to develop its own practice of human rights.[13]

Based on this analysis there is no reason to assume that the role that the concept of human dignity plays in human rights practice is the same that a substantive conception of the concept might be expected to play, namely, offering a philosophical foundation robust enough to generate the content of human rights. In fact, Beitz's observation that the inclusion of the concept of human dignity in the core human rights documents is not based or justified on any further considerations about human nature or the human good, but rather that "it is simply asserted as a fundamental value in its own right,"[14] suggests that its inclusion serves purposes that may not require the additional endorsement of a shared substantive conception of human nature, personhood, and so on.

The analysis so far suggests that rejecting the foundationalism of "humanist" approaches while acknowledging that a theory of human rights must take contemporary human rights practice seriously is perfectly compatible with accepting the view of human rights as those rights that we have by virtue of being human, not by virtue of being subject to political authority, as defenders of the "political" approach propose. Indeed, precisely because the practical approach takes contemporary human rights practice seriously, it should provide some plausible explanation of the sense and justification of the practice's deeply embedded idea that human rights derive from the inherent dignity of the human person, and not from membership in some state or group.

2. What functions does the concept of human dignity play in human rights practice?

Strangely enough, the debate between political and humanist approaches hardly ever mentions the most obvious purpose served by the claim that human rights "derive from the inherent dignity of the human person" – a claim repeatedly stated in most human rights documents.[15] Whatever else it does, this claim serves to identify the ultimate bearers of human rights, namely, *all* and *only* human persons. Since this is so obvious, the tacit assumption might be that defenders of the political approach can justify the demarcation of human rights bearers (that is, the ascription of human rights to all and only human beings) without referencing any concepts such as human dignity, intrinsic moral worth of the human person, and so on. However, as I will show in what follows, it is not clear how this can be done.

References to the inherent dignity of all human beings are prominently included in most human rights documents, and they seem to fulfill at least three important functions. First, as just mentioned, these references help *identify* the bearers of the rights in question. Indeed, without such an indication (typically in the preambles), it would be impossible to convey whether (1) they apply to all human beings or only to some, (2) they apply only to human beings or to other subjects as well, or (3) they apply to all human beings equally (or only to different degrees depending on differences in social or political positions, achievements, and so on). Second, the appeal to human dignity serves to *justify* the demarcation of rights bearers. It makes it clear why this demarcation is not simply an arbitrary stipulation, but instead grounded in something that all and only those bearers have in common, which also has high moral significance.[16] Third, in virtue of this last characteristic, the appeal to human dignity serves to identify the *ultimate aim* of human rights practice, namely, protecting the inherent dignity of all human beings and, in so doing, to convey why having such a practice matters. As a consequence of fulfilling all these important functions, the concept of human dignity imposes *significant constraints* upon generating the proper list of rights,[17] and it can offer some guidance for establishing priorities in cases of conflicts between rights. The question remains whether a theory of human rights can account for these key features without recourse to notions such as human dignity, the intrinsic moral worth of human persons, and so on.[18]

Following Rawls, and in contrast to humanist approaches, Beitz claims that human rights "protect some urgent interests against certain threats,"[19] but that "the distinctive identity and the authority of those rights is not to be found in an underlying value or interest such as human dignity or personhood."[20] To the contrary,

> We understand international human rights better by considering them *sui generis* rather than as instantiations of one or another received idea. Human rights are the constitutive norms of a global practice whose aim is to protect individuals against threats to their most important interests arising from the acts and omissions of their governments (including failures to regulate the conduct of other agents). The practice seeks to achieve this aim by bringing these aspects of the domestic conduct of governments within the scope of legitimate international concern.[21]

Once the identity of human rights is unmoored from any underlying value such as human dignity or personhood, the basis for drawing a distinction between natural and legal persons seems to dissolve. If human rights are not those rights that one has by virtue of being human, but rather those *sui generis* rights that one has by virtue of being subject to state authority, then it seems that human rights should include everyone within a state's jurisdiction who enjoys legal personality rights (that is, has the ability to have rights and obligations) and whose urgent or most important interests can be threatened by the actions and omissions of their government, thereby triggering international concern. Any restriction to the contrary seems rather arbitrary and hard to justify.[22] This difficulty is particularly acute in light of the fact that the political conception rejects any appeal to underlying values such as human dignity or personhood that could otherwise be used to draw a distinction between the sorts of interests of different members.

If, as Beitz contends, the only criteria of evaluation admitted by the political conception are the "urgency" and "importance" of the members' interests threatened by the actions and omissions of their governments, then it should be clear that the existence of corporations and similar entities can be directly threatened by governments. Since no interest can be more "urgent" or "important" than a member's interest in survival, it seems that the political conception can offer no plausible justification for disregarding threats to the existence of corporations.[23]

A perfect example of the latter is the high-profile *Yukos* case that was brought to the European Court of Human Rights (ECtHR). The previously state-owned Yukos Oil Company accumulated tremendous wealth under the leadership of CEO Mikhail Khodorkovsky, who became the wealthiest man in Russia and a politically influential figure. In 2003, Khodorkovsky was arrested and the Russian government expropriated the assets of Yukos on the allegation of unpaid taxes. The company was forcibly broken up and its shares were sold to other companies; it was declared bankrupt in 2006 and liquidated a year later. Yukos ceased to exist and its most lucrative assets ended up with the state-run oil company Rosneft. The case attracted widespread international concern because it was perceived as politically motivated and exhibiting a blatant disregard for due process. In 2004, Yukos lodged an application with the European Court of Human Rights under Article 34 of the Convention. In 2011 the Court ruled that the Russian Federation had violated several human rights of the by then defunct company.

Several aspects of this case are relevant in the present context. First, the Court identified the company itself as possessing human rights. McCrudden explains this point in detail:

> The European Court of Human Rights held recently that the Russia [*sic*] state violated the human rights of the Yukos Oil Company, specifically its right to a fair trial and its right to protection of property. Notice, first, that the Court did not decide only that the rights of the owners of the company had been violated, nor did the Court decide that the rights of the company should be seen as the aggregation of the individual rights of (human) shareholders, nor did the Court decide that Russia was under a legal duty for reasons other than because Yukos had a right. The Court held, rather, that Russia was under a duty because the company itself was the possessor of human rights. Nor is this example exceptional. A significant proportion of claims under the ECHR is now made up of challenges by corporations to alleged violations of their human rights.[24]

The *Yukos* case is also particularly interesting for this discussion because it perfectly matches the political approach's description of the *distinctive functions* fulfilled by international human rights norms in the global political order. The role of international human rights as norms that regulate state behavior toward those within their jurisdiction, that limit their sovereignty, and that potentially trigger transnational protective and remedial action seems to perfectly describe what transpired in this case, wherein state institutions not only failed to protect a legal person's most fundamental rights but were also the perpetrators of the violations in question.[25]

Two legal scholars who favor the extension of human rights to corporations, Winfried van den Muijsenbergh and Sam Rezai, sum up the significance of the *Yukos* case as follows:

The interesting feature of this high profile case entails its potent and compelling demonstration of the importance of the mere availability of the [European Court of Human Rights], as an international independent judicial venue, for a brutalized corporation, which simply had nowhere else to go ... Since Yukos was a Russian corporation (and thus a Russian national), it did not have a (home) State to take up its cause in proceedings against the Russian Federation before the International Court of Justice ... Yukos furthermore could not bring a claim before an international arbitral tribunal under a bilateral investment treaty ... Since Yukos was a Russian corporation (and not a national of any other State), its investment in the Russian Federation could not be governed by any bilateral investment treaty concluded by the Russian Federation with another State. Yukos was thus essentially cut off from all international channels of judicial review because its case simply concerned an internal Russian matter. This is when the European Convention on Human Rights revealed its great significance, namely its establishment of *an international court which (also) adjudicates thoroughly national cases when the values in dispute are of such a fundamental nature that their protection transcends the national legal orders and concerns the international community as a whole.* [26]

As with the *Yukos* case, recent developments in international human rights practice demonstrate institutional support for an inclusionary view.[27] As McCrudden indicates, "human rights in the legal context, at both the national and the international level, protect 'legal' persons as well as 'human' persons."[28] The clearest example of this trend is the European Convention on Human Rights (ECHR).[29] Its first article states that all member states of the Council of Europe shall secure the Convention's rights and freedoms to *everyone* within their jurisdiction. In contrast to other human rights documents, the ECHR does not limit the enumerated rights to natural persons. Article 34, which contains the procedural provision on standing, names "any person, nongovernmental organization or group of individuals" as a potential victim capable of bringing a claim.[30] Moreover, legal persons are explicitly included in the text concerning one of the enumerated rights, the right to property.[31]

In fact, the number of human rights that the European Court has deemed applicable to corporations has steadily grown in recent years due to the high volume of cases they file. The gradual case-by-case extension of human rights to corporations includes rights to privacy,[32] property,[33] due process guarantees,[34] protection against discrimination,[35] freedom of assembly and association,[36] freedom of movement,[37] freedom of religion,[38] freedom of speech,[39] and even the right to compensation for nonpecuniary damages.[40] This expansion has provoked a robust debate among legal scholars, in which opinions are sharply divided between those who reject the inclusion of corporations among human rights bearers on normative grounds[41] and those who offer normative reasons in favor of their inclusion. The latter often bolster their arguments with the observation that the internal dynamics of the legal system are likely to work in favor of expansion.[42] As van den Muijsenbergh and Rezai argue with respect to the ECtHR,

> The Court's case law already concludes that corporations (quite like human beings) can organize themselves, that they are able to express themselves, that they can enjoy their privacy and that they can even suffer non-pecuniary loss. It may not be too far-fetched to assume that the Court's dynamic (snowballing) humanization of corporations, combined with possible future corporate demands, will in due time allow corporations to also enjoy a right to life ... Though the Court currently does not seem willing to expand the right to life to corporations ... it will be interesting to see whether the arguments not to offer this expansion can withstand scrutiny in the face of the inherent dynamics of the Court's own case law.[43]

The European human rights system is by far the most juridically mature of human rights regimes, with an established institutional system in place for the enforcement of its norms, and an authoritative and growing body of human rights jurisprudence generated by the European Court that serves as an inspiration and model for other human rights regimes.[44] Thus, it is not difficult to imagine that this dynamic may soon extend beyond the confines of the European system and decisively shape the future of international human rights law.[45]

If human rights practice itself is beginning to take the human out of human rights in some areas, this would seem to vindicate the political approach to human rights. After all, the political approach contends that theory answers to practice, and that a theory of human rights should therefore treat the practice it aims to explain as authoritative. Moreover, since no one denies that all legal subjects have rights and obligations, what difference does it make whether the rights in question are called "human rights" or just, say, "transnational legal claim rights"?[46] Is there a real distinction behind the difference in terminology? And, in particular, is it a distinction that followers of the political approach must take into account, given their own assumptions? In order to address this question, we need to take a closer look at the distinctive functions of international human rights norms so that we can assess the potential effects of extending *human* rights to corporations.

3. The functions of human rights norms in light of the "human rights" of corporations

Recall that the political approach aims to derive the *identity* of human rights from their distinctive *functions* within human rights practice, and that these functions are in turn inferred from the overall *aims* of that practice. As a result, defenders of the political approach would have no reason to reject the inclusion of corporations among the entities that bear the *sui generis* rights referred to as "international human rights" unless it can be shown that, when attributed to corporate bearers, the distinctive functions of human rights norms may undermine the practice's own aims. However, in this context it would beg the question to assume that the ultimate aim of human rights practice is to protect the equal dignity of all human beings. So, let us simply assume that at least one of the aims of human rights practice is to protect the human rights of natural persons and, from that perspective, look at the potential effects that the distinctive functions of human rights norms might have upon that aim once they are also used to protect the urgent interests of corporations.

As defenders of the political approach are keen to highlight, international human rights norms serve distinctive functions, such as limiting state sovereignty, triggering international concern, or prompting protective and remedial transnational action. Focusing on the first of these functions, there are different senses and ways in which international human rights norms can be said to limit state sovereignty.[47] For present purposes, however, two features of international human rights norms seem especially significant. A key structural difference between human rights treaties and other interstate agreements is that their binding force does not rest on contractual reciprocity. Interstate agreements typically establish rights and obligations among member states that are based on mutual benefit and that rely on reciprocal compliance. By contrast, the primary function of human rights treaties is not to establish rights and obligations between states. Rather, states assume obligations toward all individuals within their jurisdiction, regardless of whether they are the state's own nationals, nationals of other states, or stateless persons. Human rights norms have *erga omnes* application and give rise to universal entitlements, not reciprocal ones. As Turkuler Isiksel puts it,

> The normative force of human rights law does not rest exclusively or even primarily on the reciprocal performance of duties; rather, it rests on alternative considerations such as the status of those norms as derived from universally affirmed moral principles, or each state's act of declaratory self-binding as witnessed by the international community.[48]

A consequence of the self-binding recognition of internationally valid principles is that, in contrast to other types of interstate treaties, states cannot rescind their human rights obligations simply by withdrawing their consent from the treaty that established them. Human rights obligations limit the state's discretion to terminate or renegotiate the terms of the treaties and are understood to have an *irreversible character.* [49] Another important way in which international human rights obligations limit state sovereignty is through state party acceptance of transnational jurisdiction in cases of violations. This can lead to transnational protective or remedial actions that range from the imposition of international economic sanctions (or even military intervention), to juridically imposed remedies (as in the case of regional human rights regimes like the

ECtHR), to diplomatic actions, or to "naming and shaming" by members of the international community when no effective enforcement mechanisms exist.

Now, these different mechanisms for limiting state sovereignty have the explicit purpose of *reinforcing* the ability of states to discharge their primary responsibility for human rights protections. However, if the fundamental interests of corporations are rendered equivalent to those of natural persons, there is no longer any reason to assume that a corporation's ability to use legal human rights instruments that limit state sovereignty would reinforce rather than undermine a state's ability to protect the human rights of natural persons within their jurisdiction. To begin with, the playing field is far from even: corporations have vastly superior resources compared with individual natural persons; they have greater access to the international rule of law; and greater access to effective international remedies.[50] However, none of the above advantages would be such a threat were it not for the crucial differences between the fundamental interests of human beings and those of corporations (whose survival only depends upon their ability to yield profits for their shareholders).

Critics of the extension of human rights to corporations focus their arguments on examples taken from current international economic law and, in particular, from the international investment regime that includes bilateral investment treaties (BITs) and regional free trade agreements. Whereas BITs between states are based on reciprocity, and whereas state parties are free to amend, restrict, or terminate their previous treaty commitments, this ability would be severely restricted if the interests of corporations as third-party beneficiaries were protected under international human rights law. The policy commitments that states have made to one another would become human rights owed to the corporations themselves.[51] This would undermine the ability of states to modify these commitments, even if this were necessary to implement domestic policies that protect the human rights of natural persons within a state's jurisdiction. Since it is in the interests of corporations to constrain state regulatory capacity (which can threaten their profits), the way in which human rights norms function to limit state sovereignty gives corporations the perfect tool to protect their interests, regardless of the effects that this may have on the human rights of natural persons. The ability of foreign investors to challenge states' regulations in international tribunals can seriously undermine the capacity of governments to modify or improve their current levels of human rights protections over time as information changes (for example, about health risks, environmental threats, and so on) or as their willingness to do so increases as a result of citizens' legitimate exercise of their political rights (for example, changing the political party in power).

A well-publicized example of this chilling effect is the recent multibillion dollar Philip Morris lawsuit against Uruguay. The company alleged that Uruguay's antismoking legislation devalues its cigarette trademarks and investments in the country. It is therefore suing Uruguay for compensation under the BIT between Switzerland and Uruguay at the International Centre for Settlement of Investment Disputes.[52] This is by no means an isolated case. Similar arbitration cases that have threatened states' abilities to protect human rights within their jurisdictions include legal challenges to South Africa's attempt to enact domestic affirmative action policies redressing the effects of past racial discrimination[53] and to Germany's recent parliamentary decision to phase out nuclear power in the wake of the Fukushima disaster.[54] Even more worrisome cases concern BITs that allow foreign investors to take over the function of supplying basic commodities, such as water or gas, to large sections of the population. Such takeovers can create conflicts between investors' treaty-rights and the basic human rights of vulnerable populations.[55]

Still, since these conflicts are currently framed as being between the treaty-based rights of corporations and the human rights of natural persons, state parties to BIT agreements can in principle avoid them by modifying or restricting specific provisions. This is something that, for example, South Africa has done in order to ensure that future BITs expressly permit affirmative action policies needed to redress the legacy of racial discrimination.[56] However, if the treaty-based economic rights of corporations were elevated to the status of human rights, then they would be equated with universal entitlements currently guaranteed to natural persons. As a consequence, their scope and level of protection would no longer be seen as derived from and dependent upon state parties' revocable consent and thus subject to their discretion. In this context, the distinctive function that human rights play in limiting state sovereignty would undermine rather than reinforce the ability of states to exercise their primary responsibility to protect the human rights of natural persons within their jurisdiction. If this legal development were to progress along such a path in the future, human rights practice could face a conflict between two very different and potentially incompatible aims: either the protection of the human rights of all human beings or the protection of the urgent interests of all legal subjects, corporations included.

I do not mean to suggest that international human rights practice has already reached such a clash of incompatible aims, nor that it is clear which of these two aims best describes the future of international human rights practice. The purpose of presenting this hypothetical scenario is to help us assess the resources that a theory of human rights that incorporates the concept of human dignity has at its disposal for offering practical guidance, and which a theory that excludes the practice's humanist core lacks. If we focus on the "jurisprudence of dignity" as a distinctive category within human rights jurisprudence in general, we can see how it contains normative resources that can offer support to the practice's aim of protecting the human rights of all natural persons, even in the face of a pervasive extension of legal human rights to corporations.

4. Jurisprudence of dignity: the last resort?

There is a certain tension between the political approach's aim of explaining contemporary human rights practice and its decision to discard the humanist core that so ubiquitously and prominently figures in that practice. A possible explanation for this mismatch is offered by McCrudden, who argues that it is part of a broader and even more puzzling oversight, namely, the failure of defenders of the political approach to engage with human rights jurisprudence despite its key role in human rights practice.[57] Had they taken the juridical component of legal human rights practice seriously, McCrudden argues, it would have been much harder for them to ignore how human dignity plays a central organizing role. It is certainly plausible to claim that the inclusion of human dignity in the preambles of human rights documents primarily served a rhetorical role insofar as it papered over deep disagreements in order to enable a global political consensus. However, once judges began to engage in judicial interpretation of the rights in question, they had to account for the claim that human rights derive from the inherent dignity of the human person within the reasoned justifications backing their decisions.[58] In other words, the concept of dignity has been put to use precisely in a context wherein conflicts and disagreements are resolved on the basis of reasoned arguments. From this perspective, the development of human rights adjudication offers the perfect context for an analysis of the functions of human dignity within human rights practice.

According to McCrudden, the concept of human dignity contains at least three elements, which constitute what he calls its "minimum core": that each human being possesses an intrinsic worth, simply by virtue of being human; that some forms of conduct are inconsistent with respect for this intrinsic worth; and that the state exists for the sake of the individual human being, and not vice versa.[59] Beyond this minimum core there is disagreement on what such intrinsic worth consists of, the sorts of treatment that are inconsistent with it, and their implications for the proper understanding of the role of the state vis-à-vis individuals. Different conceptions of human dignity give different and even mutually incompatible answers to these questions. However, recognizing the indeterminacy of the concept should not lead us to underestimate its importance. McCrudden distinguishes three distinctive *institutional* functions that human dignity fulfills to help address certain difficulties that arise during human rights adjudication. We can call them the *prioritizing, contextualizing*, and *extending* functions. For present purposes, the first function is the most significant.[60]

The aim of protecting human dignity justifies the *prioritization* of particular rights in cases involving conflict between different rights or between rights and other values or societal goals – "collision cases." Interpreting human rights through the lens of human dignity has an impact upon how the analysis of such conflicts is structured. First, it justifies the application of *strict scrutiny* when assessing acceptable restrictions upon any right that is understood to engage human dignity. Second, it justifies the attribution of *considerable* (even, in some cases, *overwhelming) weight* to the right in question. By contrast, if dignity is not a factor, then less weight can be attributed to the interest protected by the right in question and stronger restrictions might be considered justified.

It is important to notice that in collision cases the prioritizing effect of human dignity does not mean that a fixed priority is established once and for all, such that one right always trumps an inherently less weighty right. This could hardly be the case. If what singles rights out as human rights is that they are necessary for protecting human dignity, then that means that all of them can, in principle, affect human dignity or, to use Dieter Grimm's expression, all of them have a *dignity core*. [61] Grimm explains this idea in the context of interpreting the role of human dignity in proportionality analysis of constitutional rights: "Every right has a dignity core and this can become relevant when the principle of proportionality is applied. The closer the restriction of a right comes to its dignity core the higher the weight of the right in the balancing process."[62] In other words, when there is a collision between rights in a specific situation, the question to be determined is which of them more directly touches upon human dignity and thereby justifies stricter protection. This remains the case even if human dignity is understood to be at stake on both sides of the conflict. Even in such cases, human dignity plays a key role in justifying the application of strict scrutiny to the conflict, and in tipping the scales in favor of the right understood to bear more strongly on its protection in that particular case. Needless to say, in cases in which only one of the rights in the conflict is considered to engage human dignity, its prioritizing function is all the more obvious.

In our context, this last type of case is the most relevant. The extension of human rights to corporations by no means requires that we ascribe human dignity to them. Even from a purely legal perspective, these are two separate steps subject to separate dynamics. Yet even if legal dynamics were to lead to the extension of the concept of dignity to corporations in specific cases, the jurisprudence of dignity still seems to contain the conceptual resources for properly prioritizing the protection of the human rights of natural persons over those of corporations.[63] If we can establish the correct priorities in collision cases involving only natural persons – by distinguishing the kinds of interests at stake and their differential impacts on human dignity – then nothing prevents us from doing the same for collision cases involving both natural and legal persons. As long as corporations lack the intrinsic worth of human persons, the prioritizing function of the "thin" concept of human dignity should still enable human rights practice to defend its moral aims against a hostile takeover by corporate interests.[64] By contrast, an approach to human rights that rejects the humanist core expressed by the concept of human dignity would seem to lack any conceptual resources that could fulfill the *prioritizing* function needed to protect the human rights of all natural persons.

Acknowledgments

An earlier version of this chapter was presented at a workshop on human rights and human dignity at the University of Chicago in May 2015 and at a workshop on the philosophical justification of human rights at the University of Frankfurt in June 2015. I would like to thank the audiences of both events as well as the anonymous reviewers of *Ethics & International Affairs* for their insightful comments. I am also grateful to Ceyda Erten for her excellent research assistance.

Notes

1 Different authors refer to these methodological approaches with different names. What I am calling "humanist" approaches are also referred to as "traditional," "orthodox," or "natural-law" approaches and are usually identified with the work of authors such as Alan Gewirth, James Griffin, John Tasioulas, etc. Political approaches are also called "practical" and are defended by authors such as John Rawls, Charles Beitz, Joseph Raz, etc.

2 E.g., Pablo Gilabert, "Humanist and Political Perspectives on Human Rights," *Political Theory* 39, no. 4 (2011): 439–467; S. Matthew Liao and Adam Etinson, "Political and Naturalistic Conceptions of Human Rights: A False Polemic?" *Journal of Moral Philosophy* 9, no. 3 (2012): 327–352; Erasmus Mayr, "The Political and Moral Conceptions of Human Rights – A Mixed Account," in Gerhard Ernst and Jan-Christoph Heilinger (eds.), *The Philosophy of Human Rights* (Berlin: De Gruyter, 2011), 73–106. There are considerable differences between the accounts given by each of these authors, and the distinction between these two approaches is by no means exhaustive. For examples of approaches that do not fit well under either description, see Jürgen Habermas, *Between Facts and Norms* (Cambridge, MA: MIT Press, 1999); Seyla Benhabib in *Dignity in Adversity: Human Rights in Troubled Times* (Cambridge: Polity Press, 2011); and Allen Buchanan in *The Heart of Human Rights* (New York, NY: Oxford University Press, 2013).

3 E.g., John Rawls, *The Law of Peoples* (Cambridge, MA: Harvard University Press, 1999), and Charles Beitz, *The Idea of Human Rights* (New York, NY: Oxford University Press, 2009).

4 This aim is crisply expressed in Allen Buchanan's characterization of the Rawlsian approach as one that is "taking the human out of human rights" (in *Human Rights, Legitimacy, and the Use of Force* [New York, NY: Oxford University Press, 2010], 31–49). It is also what motivates the title of my chapter. For a critique of the way in which the political approach severs the internal connection between human rights and human dignity, see Jürgen Habermas, "The Concept of Human Dignity and the Realistic Utopia of Human Rights," *Metaphilosophy* 41, no. 4 (2010): 464–480, esp. 478ff.

5 Beitz, *The Idea of Human Rights*, 111.

6 Ibid., 128.

7 Ibid., 65.

8 Ibid., 138.

9 See, e.g., Liao and Etinson, "Political and Naturalistic Conceptions of Human Rights."

10 See Charles Beitz, "Human Dignity in the Theory of Human Rights: Nothing But a Phrase?" *Philosophy & Public Affairs* 41, no. 3 (2013): 276–277.

11 See Christopher McCrudden, "Human Dignity and Judicial Interpretation of Human Rights," *European Journal of International Law* 19, no. 4 (2008): 655–724; and Christopher McCrudden, "Jurisprudence of Dignity" (paper presented at the conference "Justification Beyond the State: Philosophy and International Law" at Yale University, New Haven, CT, December 5, 2014).

12 McCrudden, "Jurisprudence of Dignity," 4.

13 Ibid., 13. Notice that this interpretation of the function of human dignity in human rights practice is more congenial with a dynamic view of human rights than

with a foundationalist view that assumes that the content of human rights can be derived once and for all from a philosophical theory of human nature or personhood.

14 Beitz, *The Idea of Human Rights*, 20.

15 The explicit link between human rights and human dignity can be found in a majority of human rights documents, most notably in the preambles of the UN Charter, the Universal Declaration of Human Rights, the International Covenant on Civil and Political Rights, and the International Covenant on Economic, Social and Cultural Rights. Multiple references to human dignity are also present in the American Convention on Human Rights (1969), the Helsinki Final Act (1975), the African Charter of Human and People's Rights (1986), the Vienna Declaration (1993), the Arab Charter on Human Rights (1994), etc. In addition, in 1986 the UN General Assembly passed a resolution indicating that new human rights instruments should "derive from the inherent dignity and worth of the human person" (Resolution 41/120, December 1986).

16 As David Luban puts it, human dignity implies that "every human being has high status and rank." ("Human Rights Pragmatism and Human Dignity," in Rowan Cruft, S. Matthew Liao, and Massimo Renzo (eds.), *Philosophical Foundations of Human Rights* [New York, NY: Oxford University Press, 2015], 277.) Consequently, the inclusion of the concept of "equal human dignity in human rights instruments is a commitment to equalizing up" (ibid.). On the internal connection between the concept of dignity and the idea of high rank, see Jeremy Waldron, *Dignity, Rank, & Rights* (New York, NY: Oxford University Press, 2012), 34, 47ff.

17 To claim that the concept imposes *significant* constraints does not mean that it imposes *sufficient* constraints upon generating the proper list of rights. It is indeed plausible that the latter function could only be fulfilled by a substantive *conception* of the concept of human dignity. However, this does not mean that the *concept itself* is empty. There are at least three types of constraints internally related to the "thin" core meaning of the concept: (1) constraints related to the *moral significance* of the rights in question, namely, that they protect those conditions that are essential for a life with human dignity. However sketchy this claim may be, it is certainly not empty. This becomes clear if we contrast it with alternatives offered by theories of human rights that appeal instead to concepts such as "urgent" interests or conditions necessary for a "minimally decent" life – concepts that cannot be found in any of the actual human rights documents. In contrast to notions such as "urgency" or "minimal decency," the notion of human dignity is patently more demanding (as are the human rights actually enumerated in international human rights documents). This is due to two other types of constraints internally related to its core meaning, namely, (2) *equal status* (e.g., all bearers have the same set of rights, with the same scope and weight, no possibility of discrimination in its application, and requiring equally effective remedies, etc.), and (3) *high status* (e.g., in cases of conflict human dignity may *trump* other considerations and its protection requires quite *demanding* conditions). On the last two aspects of the notion of dignity see the prior note. I am thankful to an anonymous reviewer for pressing the need to clarify the limited functions of the concept of human dignity in contrast to those of a full-blown conception.

18 In general, I refer to human dignity because it is the concept that is used in human rights documents to express the humanist core of human rights *practice*. However, similar notions such as "common humanity," "equal moral status," etc. could serve the same function in a *theory* of human rights. My critique targets human rights theories that purport to eliminate *all* such humanist notions and not just the notion of human dignity in particular. For a defense of the claim that the notion of "equal moral status" is better suited than the notion of "dignity" for a theory of

human rights, see, e.g., Samantha Besson, "The Egalitarian Dimension of Human Rights," *Archiv für Rechts- und Sozialphilosophie,* Beiheft 136 (2013): 19–52.

19 Beitz, *The Idea of Human Rights,* 111.

20 Ibid., 128.

21 Ibid., 197.

22 I see two options here but both seem problematic. On the one hand, in order to provide a nonarbitrary justification for ascribing human rights only to human beings (and not to other legal subjects, other animals, etc.) defenders of the political conception would need to appeal to something that only human beings have in common. This line of argument, however, would seem to support rather than undermine the view that human beings have human rights by virtue of being human. On the other hand, defenders of the political conception could stipulate that, per definition, only human beings have human rights. However, including such a stipulation in their theories would seem to directly conflict with their methodological contention that a theory of human rights ought to give authority to human rights practice in determining what human rights are. The ascription of legal human rights to corporations within current human rights practice would seem in direct conflict with such an arbitrary stipulation.

23 In this chapter I focus on business corporations, but it should be clear that similar tensions might arise from the recognition of other types of collective entities as human rights bearers (e.g., indigenous peoples, families, churches, unions). An analysis of such additional cases is beyond the scope of this text. However, it is important to note that the difficulties I am focusing on here do not arise merely from the fact that human rights *practice* may recognize collective entities as beneficiaries of human rights. So long as human rights practice accepts that human rights derive from the dignity of the human person, establishing priorities on that normative basis in order to resolve potential conflicts between different types of rights and of rights bearers seems in principle possible. For an example, see James Nickel, *Making Sense of Human Rights,* 2nd edition (Oxford: Blackwell, 2007), 154–168. The difficulties I discuss here arise specifically for a theory of human rights that aims to eliminate any reference to the humanist core of human rights practice (i.e., any appeal to underlying values such as human dignity, equal moral worth of the human person, etc.). I am thankful to an anonymous reviewer for pressing the need to clarify this point.

24 McCrudden, "Jurisprudence of Dignity," 19. For an in-depth analysis, see Marius Emberland, *The Human Rights of Companies: Exploring the Structure of ECHR Protection* (Oxford: Oxford University Press, 2006).

25 In fact, it should come as no surprise that an approach explicitly refraining from humanist assumptions can offer little assurance that the resulting theory will end up underwriting them. Beitz explicitly cautions against treating humanist inferences about the content and basis of international human rights as analytic (see Beitz, *The Idea of Human Rights,* 72). If so, it may also be a mistake to regard the claim that only human beings have human rights as analytic. Instead, the authority for determining what human rights are should be left to the practice itself.

26 Winfried van den Muijsenbergh and Sam Rezai, "Corporations and the European Convention on Human Rights," *Global Business & Development Law Journal* 25, no. 1 (2012): 62, 67–68; my italics.

27 It is important to note that the political conception may not only be over-inclusive (insofar as it may include all legal subjects as human rights bearers). More problematically, it may also be under-inclusive. If human rights are those rights that one has by virtue of being subject to state authority, it would seem that stateless persons who find themselves in international waters do not have human rights (e.g., Palestinians crossing the Mediterranean Sea to flee from Syria or Rohingya people fleeing Myanmar by boat).

28 McCrudden, "Jurisprudence of Dignity," 19.
29 European Convention on Human Rights (ECHR), 213 UNTS 222.
30 Ibid., Art. 34.
31 See Art. 1 of Protocol 1.
32 E.g., *Société Colas Est* v. *France* (2004) 39 EHRR 17.
33 See Art. 1 of Protocol 1 to the ECHR; the *Yukos* case is an obvious example.
34 E.g., *Agrotexim* v. *Greece* (1996) 21 EHRR 250; *Immobiliare Saffi* v. *Italy* 30 (1999) EHRR 756; Application No. 7261/06 *Stavebná* v. *Slovakia.*
35 E.g., *National and Provincial Building Society* v. *U.K.* (1997) 25 EHRR 127.
36 E.g., Application No. 9905/82 *Association A and H* v. *Austria* (1984) 36 DR 187; Application No. 41579/98 *AB Kurt Kellermann* v. *Sweden* (2004) (both cases concerned nonnatural legal persons that were not companies). See Anat Scolnicov, "Lifelike and Lifeless in Law: Do Corporations Have Human Rights?" (May 2013), University of Cambridge Faculty of Law Research Paper No. 13/2013, 4, https://papers.ssrn.com/abstract=2268537 (accessed on September 4, 2017).
37 E.g., Application No. 16163/90 *Eugenia Michaelidou Developments Ltd and Michael Tymvios* v. *Turkey* (2008).
38 E.g., Application No. 18147/02 *Church of Scientology Moscow* v. *Russia* (2007) ECHR 258. This and other such cases concern organizations (i.e., churches) and not companies.
39 E.g., *Autronic AG* v. *Switzerland* (1990) 12 EHRR 485. This case is particularly contentious because it protects commercial speech. See Scolnicov, "Lifelike and Lifeless in Law," 17–19.
40 *Comingersoll S.A.* v. *Portugal*, 2000-IV European Court of Human Rights (ECtHR) 355.
41 See, e.g., Scolnicov, "Lifelike and Lifeless in Law"; Anna Grear, "Challenging Corporate 'Humanity': Legal Disembodiment, Embodiment and Human Rights," *Human Rights Law Review* 7, no. 3 (2007): 511–543; Upendra Baxi, *The Future of Human Rights* (Oxford: Oxford University Press, 2002), 234–275.
42 See, e.g., van den Muijsenbergh and Rezai, "Corporations and the European Convention on Human Rights."
43 Ibid., 60.
44 See, e.g., Grear, "Challenging Corporate 'Humanity,'" 536.
45 However, it should be noted that the European human rights system differs from other regional human rights systems as well as the UN treaty monitoring bodies in that it accepts applications from corporate entities whereas the latter only accept petitions or complaints submitted by groups or organizations insofar as they concern alleged violations of the rights of individual human beings.
46 I take this expression from David Luban, although he uses it for a different line of argument. See Luban, "Human Rights Pragmatism and Human Dignity," 269.
47 I discuss this issue at length in "Sovereignty and the International Protection of Human Rights," *Journal of Political Philosophy* 24, no. 1 (2015), and "Human Rights, Sovereignty and the Responsibility to Protect," *Constellations* 22, no. 1 (2015): 68–78.
48 Turkuler Isiksel, "The Rights of Man and the Rights of the Man-Made: Corporations and Human Rights: Corporations and Human Rights," *Human Rights Quarterly* 38, no. 2 (May 2016): 294–349; 329.
49 For an overview of the key differences between treaty-based rights and human rights, see Isiksel, "The Rights of Man and the Rights of the Man-Made," 306–314, 331.
50 For an overview of these important differences, see Jose E. Alvarez, "Are Corporations 'Subjects' of International Law?" *Santa Clara Journal of International Law* 9, no. 1 (2011): 19–21.
51 See Isiksel, "The Rights of Man and the Rights of the Man-Made," 316.

52 See *Philip Morris Products S.A. and Abal Hermanos S.A.* v. *Oriental Republic of Uruguay*, International Centre for Settlement of Investment Disputes (ICSID) Case No. ARB/10/7, at www.italaw.com/cases/460 (accessed on September 2, 2017).

53 See Isiksel, "The Rights of Man and the Rights of the Man-Made," 339–340; also, Alvarez, "Are Corporations 'Subjects' of International Law?" 21.

54 Ongoing arbitration proceedings against Germany at the ICSID were initiated by the Swedish company Vattenfall, which owns two nuclear plants in Germany. According to media reports, Vattenfall is claiming compensation of USD 5.8 billion, plus 4 percent interest, for both past and future lost profits.

55 E.g., the well-publicized conflict on the right to water in Bolivia. See *Aguas del Tunari S.A.* v. *Bolivia* ICSID Case No. ARB/02/03. See Alvarez, "Are Corporations 'Subjects' of International Law?", 21.

56 Alvarez, "Are Corporations 'Subjects' of International Law?" 21.

57 McCrudden, "Jurisprudence of Dignity," 29ff.

58 See McCrudden, "Human Dignity and Judicial Interpretation of Human Rights," 669.

59 Ibid., 679; McCrudden, "Jurisprudence of Dignity," 5.

60 Let me briefly summarize McCrudden's account of the extending and contextualizing functions of human dignity. Accepting the protection of human dignity as the purpose of human rights practice offers a justification for *extending* the list of rights actually enumerated in human rights documents to include additional rights that are deemed necessary for the effective protection of human dignity. This can involve *expanding* the scope of rights already included in human rights law (e.g., the decision by the Inter-American Court of Human Rights to expand the right to life to include basic socioeconomic rights), *importing* rights that may have been intentionally excluded from specific human rights instruments (e.g., the appeal to freedom of religion as protecting human dignity by the Israeli Supreme Court, a right that was not included in the Basic Law), or *generating new* rights in light of social, political, and technical developments (e.g., new reproductive rights). The aim of protecting human dignity also justifies the *contextualization* of human rights in response to the threats that are most salient in different countries due to their specific social circumstances and historical experiences (e.g., restrictions of freedom of speech related to denial of the Holocaust as upholding human dignity in German law in contrast to the less restricted understanding of that right that is prevalent in the United States).

61 Dieter Grimm, "Dignity in a Legal Context: Dignity as an Absolute Right," in Christopher McCrudden (ed.), *Understanding Human Dignity* (New York, NY: Oxford University Press, 2013), 381–391.

62 Ibid., 390.

63 I have not been able to find any cases from global or regional human rights courts that ascribe human dignity to corporations. However, nothing in my argument turns on excluding the possibility of a legal extension of the concept of dignity to corporations. If priorities based on considerations of human dignity can be established in conflicts between rights that only concern natural persons, the same would hold true in conflicts that concern both natural and legal persons. The same applies to the possible extension of the concept of dignity to animals. For some legal examples of the latter, see McCrudden, "Human Dignity and Judicial Interpretation of Human Rights," 708.

64 In fact, the ECtHR offers some examples. See, e.g., *Tatar* v. *Romania*, ECtHR, App. No. 67021/01 (2009).

References

AB Kurt Kellermann v. *Sweden*, 41579/98, § 44 ECHR (2004).
Agrotexim v. *Greece*, 21 EHRR 250 (1996).

Aguas del Tunari S.A. v. Bolivia, ARB/02/03 ICSID IIC 8 (2005).

Alvarez, Jose E. "Are Corporations 'Subjects' of International Law?" *Santa Clara Journal of International Law* 9, no. 1 (2011): 19–21.

Association A and H v. Austria, 9905/82, 36 DR 187 (1984).

Autronic AG v. Switzerland, 12 EHRR 485 (1990).

Baxi, Upendra. *The Future of Human Rights* (Oxford: Oxford University Press, 2002).

Beitz, Charles. "Human Dignity in the Theory of Human Rights: Nothing But a Phrase?" *Philosophy & Public Affairs* 41, no. 3 (2013): 276–277.

Beitz, Charles. *The Idea of Human Rights* (New York, NY: Oxford University Press, 2009).

Benhabib, Seyla. *Dignity in Adversity: Human Rights in Troubled Times* (Cambridge: Polity Press, 2011).

Besson, Samantha. "The Egalitarian Dimension of Human Rights," *Archiv für Rechts- und Sozialphilosophie*, Beiheft 136 (2013): 19–52.

Buchanan, Allen. *The Heart of Human Rights* (New York, NY: Oxford University Press, 2013).

Buchanan, Allen. *Human Rights, Legitimacy, and the Use of Force* (New York, NY: Oxford University Press, 2010).

Church of Scientology Moscow v. Russia, 18147/02 ECHR 258 (2007).

Comingersoll S.A. v. Portugal, 35382/97 ECHR 355 (2000).

Emberland, Marius. *The Human Rights of Companies: Exploring the Structure of ECHR Protection* (Oxford: Oxford University Press, 2006).

Eugenia Michaelidou Developments Ltd and Michael Tymvios v. Turkey, 16163/90 ECHR (2008).

European Convention on Human Rights (ECHR), 213 UNTS 222.

Gilabert, Pablo. "Humanist and Political Perspectives on Human Rights," *Political Theory* 39, no. 4 (2011): 439–467.

Grear, Anna. "Challenging Corporate 'Humanity': Legal Disembodiment, Embodiment and Human Rights," *Human Rights Law Review* 7, no. 3 (2007): 511–543.

Grimm, Dieter. "Dignity in a Legal Context: Dignity as an Absolute Right," in Christopher McCrudden (ed.), *Understanding Human Dignity* (New York, NY: Oxford University Press, 2013), 381–391.

Habermas, Jürgen. "The Concept of Human Dignity and the Realistic Utopia of Human Rights," *Metaphilosophy* 41, no. 4 (2010): 464–480.

Habermas, Jürgen. *Between Facts and Norms* (Cambridge, MA: MIT Press, 1999).

Immobiliare Saffi v. Italy, 30 EHRR 756 (1999).

Isiksel, Turkuler. "The Rights of Man and the Rights of the Man-Made: Corporations and Human Rights: Corporations and Human Rights," *Human Rights Quarterly* 38, no. 2 (May 2016): 294–349.

Lafont, Cristina. "Human Rights, Sovereignty and the Responsibility to Protect," *Constellations* 22, no. 1 (2015): 68–78.

Lafont, Cristina. "Sovereignty and the International Protection of Human Rights," *Journal of Political Philosophy* 24, no. 1 (2015): 427–445.

Liao, S. Matthew and Adam Etinson. "Political and Naturalistic Conceptions of Human Rights: A False Polemic?" *Journal of Moral Philosophy* 9, no. 3 (2012): 327–352.

Luban, David. "Human Rights Pragmatism and Human Dignity," in Rowan Cruft, S. Matthew Liao, and Massimo Renzo (eds.), *Philosophical Foundations of Human Rights* (New York: Oxford University Press, 2015), 263–278.

Mayr, Erasmus. "The Political and Moral Conceptions of Human Rights – A Mixed Account," in Gerhard Ernst and Jan-Christoph Heilinger (eds.), *The Philosophy of Human Rights* (Berlin: De Gruyter, 2011), 73–106.

McCrudden, Christopher. "Jurisprudence of Dignity" (paper presented at the conference "Justification Beyond the State: Philosophy and International Law" at Yale University, New Haven, CT, December 5, 2014).

McCrudden, Christopher. "Human Dignity and Judicial Interpretation of Human Rights," *European Journal of International Law* 19, no. 4 (2008): 655–724.

National and Provincial Building Society v. U.K., 25 EHRR 127 (1997).

Nickel, James. *Making Sense of Human Rights*, 2nd edition (Oxford: Blackwell, 2007), 154–168.

Philip Morris Products S.A. and Abal Hermanos S.A. v. Oriental Republic of Uruguay, ARB/10/7 ICSID (2016), at www.italaw.com/cases/460 (accessed on September 2, 2017).

Rawls, John. *The Law of Peoples* (Cambridge, MA: Harvard University Press, 1999).

Scolnicov, Anat. "Lifelike and Lifeless in Law: Do Corporations Have Human Rights?" (May 2013), University of Cambridge Faculty of Law Research Paper No. 13/2013, 4, https://papers.ssrn.com/abstract=2268537 (accessed on September 4, 2017).

Société Colas Est v. France, 39 EHRR 17 (2004).

Stavebná v. Slovakia, 7261/06 ECHR (2011).

Tatar v. Romania, 67021/01 ECHR (2009).

United Nations General Assembly. *Resolution* 41/120*Setting International Standards in the Field of Human Rights* (December 4, 1986) UN Doc A/RES/41/120.

van den Muijsenbergh, Winfried and Sam Rezai. "Corporations and the European Convention on Human Rights," *Global Business & Development Law Journal* 25, no. 1 (2012): 43–68.

Waldron, Jeremy. *Dignity, Rank, & Rights* (New York, NY: Oxford University Press, 2012).

7 Dignity, communicative freedom, and law

Eduardo Mendieta

1. Introduction

In order to introduce the theme of this chapter, I want us to consider the following cases. During the early 1980s, Brazilian photographer Sebastião Salgado spent several months, over a year, photographing the victims of the famines in Africa unleashed by droughts and civil wars. Some of the pictures were published in two-page spreads and on the cover of the *New York Times* Sunday Magazine. To say the least, the pictures were harrowing, unsettling, beyond anything most of us dare to stare at.[1] I will attempt to describe one. A child is being weighed from a hanging weight. The child is incredibly thin and weak. His limbs are thin as sticks. He is so thin and weak that he can't support his head, which hangs back. His mouth is distorted in pain. His hands are trying to hang on to the rope that is holding him, but his fingers are giving way. The hand on the weight points at the 3 o'clock position. Is it 15 pounds, 15 kilograms?

The other pictures are as haunting. These pictures were eventually published in a book with the title of *Sahel: The End of the Road* (2004).[2] I want to quote from the description of the book one can find on amazon.com:

> In 1984 Sebastião Salgado began what would be a fifteen-month project of photographing the drought-stricken Sahel region of Africa in the countries of Chad, Ethiopia, Mali, and Sudan, where approximately one million people died from extreme malnutrition and related causes. Working with the humanitarian organization Doctors Without Borders, Salgado documented the *enormous suffering and the great dignity* of the refugees. This early work became a template for his future photographic projects about other afflicted people around the world. Since then, Salgado has again and again sought to give visual voice to those millions of human beings who, because of military conflict, poverty, famine, overpopulation, pestilence, environmental degradation, and other forms of catastrophe, teeter on the edge of survival.

I want you to note "enormous suffering and the great dignity" in this description. Had you seen the photos, the last thing you would think of would be of their "dignity." Their condition was the most abject, devastating, dehumanizing, soul-freezing form of poverty. How could someone about to be food for vultures have dignity, when we consider that it is part of dignity to have one's remains properly disposed so that they are not carrion. The people in Salgado's pictures languished, neither living nor dying. They were below dignity. Yet, many pictures of these human beings on the edge of the living do present and exemplified a dignified carriage. Like the mother, also famished, holding her dying child, tenderly, trying to feed him, although her body has nothing to give. She refused to slip below some invisible line of dignity. She held tenaciously to her dignity as mother in the most extreme of moments when her own life was at stake. Some of the faces in these pictures with their piercing eyes seemed to say: "I would rather die than lose my dignity."

Let me now turn to another set of images. Many have seen the pictures from the torture and abuse at Abu Ghraib.[3] These pictures are also deeply troubling, but for slightly different reasons than those Salgado took in Africa. Here we see acts of humiliation and shaming perpetrated by other human beings. There are victims and perpetrators, in the same frame. The degradation of the prisoners at Abu Ghraib was not brought about by the forces of nature, but by other human beings. I like to suggest that these pictures are more shocking because the suffered indignity was brought about by acts of undignified behavior. In other words, humans were undignified by the undignifying behavior of other human beings. In many of those pictures, many of which we now know were taken in order to document the abject conditions in which US soldiers found themselves in Iraq, show a process of *self-undignification*, a process of lowering oneself below the threshold of a certain level of dignified comportment.[4]

Let me divert your mind's eye away from disturbing images and let us consider the publication of a document, while still holding on to the fact that human dignity was doubly violated at Abu Ghraib. I have in mind the 2008 publication of the President's Council on Bioethics report titled *Human Dignity and Bioethics.* [5] This is a 555-page report, chaired by Leon Kass, a well-known conservative bioethicist. The report, in sum, put forward a rejection of many contemporary biomedical techniques that aim to remedy or eliminate congenital diseases. The general basis of this attack on medical innovation was a heavily religiously sanctioned conception of human dignity. I am bringing this report, which incidentally had efficacy inasmuch as it resulted in a series of policies that have either halted or delayed all kinds of gene therapies, because of the pivotal role dignity played in it. One would assume that given the weight and traction given to the concept of "human dignity" that the authors would have offered an unambiguous and clear definition. But, as Steven Pinker noted in his excellent essay on this report, published in *The New Republic*, and I quote:

> how well do the essayists clarify the concept of dignity? By their own admission, not very well. Almost every essayist concedes that the concept

remains slippery and ambiguous. In fact, it spawns outright contradictions at every turn. We read that slavery and degradation are morally wrong because they take someone's dignity away. But we also read that nothing you can do to a person, including enslaving or degrading him, can take his dignity away. We read that dignity reflects excellence, striving, and conscience, so that only some people achieve it by dint of effort and character. We also read that everyone, no matter how lazy, evil, or mentally impaired, has dignity in full measure. Several essayists play the genocide card and claim that the horrors of the twentieth century are what you get when you fail to hold dignity sacrosanct. But one hardly needs the notion of "dignity" to say why it's wrong to gas six million Jews or to send Russian dissidents to the gulag.[6]

Which is why Pinker thinks that "dignity" is a "squishy, subjective notion, hardly up to the heavyweight moral demands assigned to it."[7] Pinker lays out why the concept of dignity is unusable, at least as it was deployed by the authors of this report, delineating three features that make the concept highly messy and hazardous. For Pinker, "dignity" should be referred to with caution because: first, "dignity is relative," not only with reference to culture, but also to time: someone's dignity is someone else's shame, and what we found dignifying at one time is beyond the pale of human decency today; second, "dignity is fungible," that is, we are willing to negotiate its boundaries or threshold, take for instance the kinds of "undignifying" treatments we are willing to submit at airports, at the doctors, and gyms. Third, "dignity can be harmful."[8] Calls to respect "dignity" can lead to violence, as was the case with Rushdie, who offended the dignity of Islam.

Let me turn to another case. The same year that the President's Council on Bioethics published its report, in the shadow of Abu Ghraib and Guantanamo, many legal scholars, philosophers, ethicists, and political theorists were celebrating the sixtieth anniversary of the Universal Declaration of Human Rights. As legal scholar Christopher McCrudden wrote in his magisterial "Human Dignity and Judicial interpretation of Human Rights":

> Due significantly to its centrality in both the United Nations Charter and the Universal Declaration of Human Rights, the concept of "human dignity" now plays a central role in human rights discourse ... Dignity is becoming commonplace in the legal texts providing for human rights protections in many jurisdictions. It is used frequently in judicial decision, for example justifying the removal of restrictions on abortion in the United States, in the imposition of restrictions on dwarf throwing in France, in overturning laws prohibiting sodomy in South Africa, and in the consideration of physician-assisted suicide in Europe.[9]

But then, he goes on to ask a series of key questions, which will guide the rest of my considerations: "what does dignity mean in these contexts? Can it be a basis for human rights, a right in itself, or is it simply a synonym for human rights? In particular, what role does the concept of dignity play in the context of human rights adjudication?"[10]

The concept of dignity has been as squishy as it has been efficacious. The last half-century of development in the area of human rights, in their specification and their securing has been enabled and accelerated by the incorporation of the "dignity" discourse in international law, as well as within constitutional and civil law. In the following I will articulate and defend a "constructivist" conception of dignity that dispenses with anthropocentrism or what we can call metaphysical chauvinism on the part of *Homo sapiens*. I will develop this conception, relying on the work of Jeremy Waldron, Michael Rosen, and Jürgen Habermas. In order to lay out this "constructivist" conception of dignity, I will articulate a conception of human freedom that overcomes the ontological atomism, or moral individualism, that has characterized the political morality of most modern political philosophy. The key claim is that a constructivist conception of dignity requires a proper understanding of human freedom, one that is provided by a discourse ethics conception of communicative freedom. Freedom, however, is something secured by what Dworkin has called "Law's empire." I will, therefore, in a third section, talk about "Freedom's Law," or what German philosopher Axel Honneth has called *Das Recht der Freiheit*, or freedom's right. In fact, what I am doing is bringing three key themes of our time: the theme of disrespect and degradation as an assault on human dignity,[11] the theme of reflexive, or communicative, freedom that overcomes the aporias of political liberalism, and the theme of the normativity of juridification, or better yet of the normativity of jurisgenerativity, or perhaps more accurately, to paraphrase Seyla Benhabib, the normativity of jurisgenerative iterations.[12]

2. Building the pedestal of dignity

The oldest meaning of dignity is related to the status, standing, or office of someone who has by merit, delegation, or appointment been raised to that height.[13] Dignity in this sense then refers to a hierarchical distinction. There are those who look up and those who look down from either a symbolic or real pedestal of distinction. Cicero took this notion of dignity and turned it into more substantive and universal concept when he referred to the "dignity of the human race." Extending the Socratic notion that the "unexamined life is not worth living for a human being," Cicero argued that there are activities unworthy of the dignity of humans. For Cicero, however, this dignity of the human is intricately related to the place humans occupy in the cosmos. Human dignity is thus related to a certain ontological place that humans occupy in the great chain of being. Cicero's horizontal expansion of the reach of dignity, however, is gained at the expense of a vertical elevation of humans above all other creatures in nature. It is this notion of dignity that is taken up by the Judeo-Christian tradition and expanded, further elevating humans above all other animals, and anything that can be deemed beastly. In the Judeo-Christian tradition, a new aspect of dignity is elaborated. The dignity of the human being is a function of its "creaturely" existence, that is, our having been created by God. We are created, not made. Our dignity depends on our being precisely God's elect created creature. The Judeo-Christian vertical elevation of human dignity has now placed us above all other created creatures, as their master and stewards. Here, however, dignity has acquired a new connotation. It is something endowed, gifted, granted, and assigned to us by God, and thus, it is inalienable. The sanctity of our being is the ground of our dignity, and for this reason it is something that can be neither diminished nor taken away from us. The sanctity of our being is also the ground of its pricelessness, or better invaluableness, to use Kantian language. The sacrosanct dignity of the human being is its infinite worth, one that is beyond calculation.

Before I summarize the different meanings and connotations of dignity, I need to highlight two moments in the semantic enrichment of the concept. In the transition from the Middle Ages, with its theological conceptions of dignity, to the modern secularized conceptions of dignity, there are two key figures that extended a bridge between these two conceptual schemes. There is first Giovanni Pico della Mirandola (1463–1494), who wrote probably one of the most important texts contributing to what I called "building the pedestal of dignity" at the heading of this section. His famous *Oratio de hominis dignitate* (1486) introduces what I would call a de-ontologization and de-theologization of the concept of human dignity. Let me quote the relevant passage. Pico della Mirandola begins by describing God's creation of the world, until he gets to the creation of humans. He writes:

> Therefore, He took up man, a work of indeterminate form; and placing him at the midpoint of the world, He spoke as follows: "We have given to thee, Adam, no fixed seat, no form of thy very own, no gift peculiarly thine, that thou mayest feel as thine own, have as thine own, possess as thine own the seat, the form, the gifts from which thou thyself shalt desire. A limited nature in other creatures is confined within the laws written down by Us. In conformity with thy free judgment, in whose hands I have placed thee, thou art confined by no bounds; and thou wilt fix limits of nature for thyself. I have placed thee at the center of the world, that form there thou mayest more conveniently look around to see whatsoever is in the world. Neither heavenly nor earthly, neither mortal nor immortal have We made thee. Thou, like a judge appointed for being honorable, art the molder and maker of thyself; thou mayest sculpt thyself into whatever shape thou dost prefer. Thou canst grow downward into the lower natures which are brutes. Thou canst again grow upward from thy soul's reason into the higher nature which are divine."[14]

This is a wildly innovative reading of the Judeo-Christian doctrine of *imago dei*, namely that we are created in the likeness of God, thus sharing some resemblance or substance with him. Here, what makes us like God is neither our countenance, nor that we share in some divine essence, *ousia*, nor that we participate fully in divine reason. For Pico della Mirandola what makes us like God is that we are creators, and above all, we are creators of ourselves. We are God's most elevated creature because we create ourselves. Our dignity, then, resides in that we are like God, creators, and above all, creators of our humane dwelling and the limits of our own nature. If we think of dignity as both a status and the adscription of a certain incalculable worth, then Pico della Mirandola enables us to think of this status as something we construct. Dignity then is not a substantive quality. It is also not a metaphysical or ontological aspect of our being, but rather the name for an abode or dwelling under construction.

The second moment takes place almost three centuries later, and goes by the name of Immanuel Kant (1724–1804), who is the *de rigueur* point of reference for all modern conceptions of dignity. There are of course several places where Kant discusses dignity, but the key place is in the *Grundlegung zur Metaphysik der Sitten* (1785). Let me go directly to the relevant passages.

> In the kingdom of ends everything has either a *price* or a *dignity* [*Würde*]. What has a price can be replaced by something else as its *equivalent*; what on the other hand is raised [*erhaben*] above all price and therefore admits of no equivalent has dignity.
>
> (4:434)[15]

This passage is important when we pair it with the discussion of the king-dom of ends earlier in Kant's text. One of the versions of the categorical imperative refers to our being members of a kingdom of ends. Kant writes:

> A rational being belongs as a *member* to the kingdom of ends when he gives universal laws in it but it is also himself subject to these laws. He belongs to it *as a sovereign* when, as lawgiving, he is not subject to the will of any other.
>
> (4:433)

Thus, what Kant is arguing is that to be a member of the kingdom of ends means that one is both sovereign and subject, lawgiver and law-abiding sub-ject, but who addresses himself as a lawgiver, as someone who has dignity, but no price. To be a member of the kingdom of ends is to have dignity. Or rather, we have dignity because we are universal legislators of the moral law. In Kant's own words:

> Now, morality is the condition under which alone a rational being can be an end in itself, since only through this is it possible to be a law-giving member in the kingdom of ends. Hence morality, and humanity insofar as it is capable of morality, is that which alone has dignity. Skill and

diligence in work have a market price; wit, lively imagination and humor have a fancy price; on the other hand, fidelity in promises and benevolence from basic principles (not from instinct) have an inner worth.

Kant then summarizes it in a succinct formulation:

Autonomy is therefore the ground of the dignity [*Würde*] of human nature and of every rational nature.

(4:435)

Autonomy, however, is something that we achieve, and not something that is given to us as a substance. Our dignity resides, for Kant, in that we exercise our free will guided by reason to legislate the moral law. It is the legislating of moral law, the source of our autonomy, or what is equivalent, namely our sovereignty in the kingdom of ends, which is the source or ground of our dignity. This dignity, or worth beyond price and calculation, commands our respect and our admiration. In fact, as Kant argues three years later in the *Critique of Practical Reason*:

It is something very sublime in human nature to be determined to actions directly by a pure rational law, and even the illusion that takes the subjective side of this intellectual determinability of the will as something aesthetic and the effect of a special sensible feeling (for an intellectual feeling would be a contradiction) is sublime.

(5:117)

If we remember that for Kant sublime is that which is "absolutely large," and that in comparison "with which everything is small," and therefore, sublime "is what even to be able to think proves that the mind has a power surpassing any standard of sense" (*Critique of Judgment*, § 25), then we could surmise that for Kant the ground of our dignity is our autonomy but it is also the ground of our sublimity, as that which raises us above anything and in the shadow of which everything is absolutely small. The sublime has an additional meaning for Kant, namely the sublime is that which leads us to surpass our sensibility while stretching the reach of reason. The sublime is the aesthetic education of reason is as much as it leads us to surpass our concepts. Be that as it may, what is relevant in Kant's transformation of the concept of dignity is that like Pico della Mirandola he thinks our dignity resides in something we do, and not in something we are. But, unlike Pico della Mirandola, it is the ceaseless striving towards our autonomy that incites in us a feeling of the sublime. Another way of putting it would be to say that for Kant, we are sublime when we are legislating the moral law.

We are now in the position to offer a typology of the different ways in which we talk about dignity. First, there is the classical sense of dignity as a social status, office, or title. Second, there is the sense of dignity as a value, or worth, that is sometimes exclusively assigned to humans, although sometimes we do talk about the dignity of all creation. This worth, or incalculable value, is thought to be intrinsic to humans, because it is granted to them by nature or God. There is a third sense that is made clear with Pico della Mirandola and Immanuel Kant, as that is the idea of dignity as respect for what it commands in us. Michael Rosen refers to this sense of dignity as "respect as observance."[16] So, dignity commands our respect because of our moral freedom, that is, because we are all morally free, our dignity must be respected. There is a fourth sense of dignity, and that is the one intimated by some of the people portrayed by Salgado in his pictures from Sahel, and that is dignity as a comportment, as the upright carriage of the individual who preserves himself or herself even in the most extreme of circumstances. Rosen calls this "respect as respectfulness."[17] These two senses of dignity, as observance and as respectfulness, are implicit in Kant's linking the dignity of autonomy and the sublimity of autonomy. We should note that we can divide these four senses of dignity into two categories: ontological and relational. So, dignity as value is ontological, the other three senses are relational.[18]

Let me now return to the pictures from Abu Ghraib. The pictures of the abuse, torture, and degradation of the prisoners there was accompanied by the self-degradation and self-abuse of US soldiers, who were either compelled or volunteered to engage in those acts. This is why it is perhaps impossible to retrieve any sense of dignity from those pictures. This is why many of us were scandalized and revolted by them: not simply because someone had suffered this degradation but because one of us, someone just like us, had done these acts of shaming, dehumanization, and bestialization. The point I am making is that dignity is relational in the sense that dignity demands observance and respect as a form of behaving towards that which is dignified. For this reason, I want to claim that in as much as dignity is relational it is also reflexive. Observing the dignity of humanity commands in us a certain type of behavior, a stance, a comportment, an upright carriage, to use Ernst Bloch's beautiful expression, which in turn reflects back the light of reverence and respect. Dignity becomes the mirror in which our sublimity reflects new visions of humanity.

3. Reflexive freedom

We should begin with one of the most well-known formulations on freedom that we have and it comes from Hobbes. Chapter XXI of the *Leviathan* begins:

> Liberty, or Freedom, signifieth (properly) the absence of opposition (by opposition, I mean external impediments of motion) and may be applied no less to irrational and inanimate creatures than to rational.
>
> (II.XXI, 136)[19]

Or, as he puts it in the second paragraph of this same section:

> A Free-Man is *he that in those things which by his own strength and wit he is able to do is not hindered to do what he has a will to.*
>
> (II.XXI, 136)

This absence of opposition or hindrance to pursue our aims is now called "negative freedom." This means that we are free to the degree that no other human or entity interferes with our plans. When there is some opposition, interference, blockage, constraint, we have in fact some coercion. To be free then is not to be coerced. Here, then freedom is a letting be, or being left alone. Negative freedom is freedom *from* some sort of constrain and inter- ference. As Isaiah Berlin put it: "By being free in this sense I mean not being interfered with by others. The wider area of non-interference the wider my freedom."[20] The use of "area" in Berlin's formulation is extremely suggestive. Freedom is indeed a horizon. There is a geography of freedom. There are *topoi* of freedom. In fact, I want to talk about the topology of freedom.

In this vein, then, we ought to note that this non-interference and non-coercion is a negativity, a withdrawal, within a larger space of relationality. Negative freedom is a positive space of absence. This ought to reveal to us that while we assume the historical and ontological priority of negative freedom, positive freedom has priority. What this means is that "negative freedom" exists only within the larger horizon of positive freedom as the positive affirmation of a refusal of coercion.

Positive freedom, on the other hand, is as Berlin put it: "the wish on the part of the individual to be his own master. I wish my life and decisions to depend on myself, not on external forces of whatever kind."[21] Positive freedom is what Kant calls autonomy. This is the freedom to be one's own master, to set goals for oneself, and to be able to carry them out and accomplish them. Positive freedom is freedom *to* live our lives by the light of our reason. *Prima facie* negative and positive freedom seem the same, or rather their difference seems to be matters of degree. Historically, however, what at first blush may seem hardly distinct, has gone in two very different directions. In fact, con- stitutions and bills of rights, or charters of rights, address negative and positive freedom in different orders of priority, specifying for each a different set of rights. Thus, and in very sketchy fashion, negative freedom is what we call subjective rights, or civil rights, basic rights to be left alone by the state. These are what we can call rights of privacy, property, conscience, belief, etc. These core "subjective rights" secure negative freedom. Positive freedom, in con- trast, is protected, or better yet, enabled, by what we generally call rights of participation, or rights to political agency. These rights include right of assembly, right to vote, right to office, right to publish, etc. These rights secure positive right because they enable individuals to participate in their political community and set goals and pursue them collectively. Since the work of T.H. Marshall on citizenship, we have come to recognize that these positive rights have to be buttressed, or given force, with what are called social rights: rights to a minimum wage, to education, to health, to work, to retirement, in general to a dignified existence that enables my political agency. In the last half a century, and in the shadow of Auschwitz, we have also come to recognize what are called fourth generation rights, or rights to culture, which include language rights, rights to our own cultural inheritance, and cultural and/or religious practices. Here, however, we are getting ahead of ourselves.

In a lecture delivered before the British Academy in November 2001, intellectual historian Quentin Skinner articulated what he called "A Third Concept of Liberty."[22] This lecture, appropriately enough named after Isaiah Berlin, offered a very insightful historization of Berlin's and by way of Berlin, of Hobbes's preoccupation with "negative liberty." For Hobbes, the background was the emergence in the early seventeenth century of a "republican conception" of freedom. For Berlin, the background was World War II, the rise of totalitarianism, which was taken to be a pathological version of republicanism. The essay, published in the Proceedings of the British Academy, exhibits a profound and comfortable knowledge of the evolution of British political thinking through the last five hundred years. In reconstructing this fascinating history, which includes the impact of translations of Roman historians by English scholars, Skinner wanted to show that there was another conception of "negative freedom" that Hobbes was attempting to subvert and counter. In Skinner's words, this other conception of negative freedom should be analyzed thusly:

> The essence of the argument is that freedom is restricted by dependence. To be free as a citizen, therefore, requires that the actions of the state should reflect the will of all its citizens, for otherwise the excluded will remain dependent on those whose will move the state to act. The outcome is the belief – crucial alike to the English revolution of the 17th century and to the American and French revolutions a century later – that it is possible to enjoy our individual liberty if and only if we live as citizens of self-governing republics. To live as subjects of a monarch is to live as slaves.[23]

According to Skinner, behind Hobbes's arguments for articulating freedom as non-interference are the arguments by seventeenth-century English thinkers that freedom is non-dependence. Thus, Skinner argued, we should recognize that there are three different conceptions of freedom, and not just two. As important as Skinner's historiography is, and his arguments make Berlin's argument subtler and historically more precise, I want to show that both still are missing something very important, and that is that positive freedom has both historical and conceptual priority. In order to recognize this, we have to retain the semantics of three conceptions of freedom, for heuristic reasons, but that freedom properly understood, should be thought of as reflexive freedom, to use the language of Axel Honneth, or communicative freedom, to use Habermas's language, which entails the notion of reflexivity.[24]

Let me elaborate this point by quoting Honneth directly:

> Whereas the idea of negative freedom has hardly any precursors in antiquity or the Middle Ages, the notion of reflexive freedom reaches all the way back to the intellectual prehistory of modernity. Ever since Aristotle, a number of thinkers and philosophers have claimed that in order for individuals to be free, they must be able to arrive at their own decisions and influence their own will. The historical asymmetry between these two concepts of freedom demonstrates that the idea of reflexive freedom cannot be viewed merely as an expansion or more profound version of the ideal of negative freedom. It would be careless of us to regard the notion of an externally secured free-space as a merely preliminary stage of a model of freedom which then resolutely focuses on the internal. Negative freedom is an original and indispensable element of modernity's moral self-understanding; it conveys the demand that all individuals be entitled to act in accordance with their own preferences, without external restrictions and without having to submit their motives to rational judgment, provided they do not violate the right of their fellow citizens to do the same. By contrast, the idea of reflexive freedom focuses solely on the subject's relationship-to-self; according to this notion, individuals are free if their actions are solely guided by their own intentions.[25]

There are three key ideas in Honneth's passage that I need to highlight now. First, that reflexive freedom is both historically and conceptually prior to negative freedom. Second, that "negative freedom" cannot be the basis for a reflexive conception of freedom. Third, that "negative" freedom is in fact enabled by reflexive freedom. I think this last point is partly acknowledged by Berlin when he wrote that "a frontier must be drawn between the area of private life and that of public authority."[26] Freedom, not simply as the negative of the absence of constraint and hindrance, but as most fundamentally the ability to be one's own master is at base, as Honneth puts it, a reflexive relation. To want to be one's own master, sovereign in the house of one's own subjectivity and agency, means that I have to ask, "who is it that I want to be," "who is it that I want to become." To be free means to reflect on who we want to fashion ourselves as. We are projects, as Jean Paul Sartre put it, because our freedom is something we are continuously living out in the process of constructing our moral persona. As projects, we are also a performance, both in the sense of something that is enacted and as something that is a staged drama. To be free is dramatic. Therefore, we ought to speak of the drama of freedom.

Hannah Arendt had something like this in mind, when she wrote: "The Greek polis once was precisely that 'form of government' which provided men with a space of appearances where they could act, with a kind of theater where freedom could appear."[27] The Greek polis with its *agora*, provided the stage for freedom to be performed. In fact, Arendt had written as much a page earlier when she appealed to Machiavelli's concept of *virtù*, the excellence with which a person takes up *fortuna*, the opportunities offered by the world to him or her. Arendt argues that *virtù* should be more appropriately translated as "virtuosity." She writes:

> virtuosity ... an excellence we attribute to the performing arts ... where the accomplishment lies in the performance itself and not in an end product which outlasts the activity that brought it into existence and become independent of it ... Since all acting contains an element of virtuosity, and because virtuosity is the excellence we ascribe to the performing arts, politics has often been defined as an art.[28]

The drama that is freedom, thus, also means that when we perform our freedom when can do so with virtuosity. Here, I would not want to pass up a reference back to Kant's notion of the sublimity of our autonomy.

Reflexive freedom, however is *ipso facto*, relational, discursive, dialogic, or more emphatically "communicative." I will provide you with Habermas's definition, knowing in advance that it may be a bit too obtuse:

> I understand "communicative freedom" as the possibility – mutually presupposed by participants engaged in the effort to reach an understanding – of responding to the utterances of one's counterpart and to the concomitantly raised validity claims, which aim at intersubjective recognition.[29]

What is relevant in this formulation is that freedom involves trying to reach an agreement, whose conditions of possibility are framed by always already presupposed validity claims in every speech act, which also involved, per definition, intersubjective recognition. Behind this formulation is also the basic insight that freedom is not simply something one has, but something one does.[30] As Arendt argued: "Men *are* free – as distinguished from their possessing the gift of freedom – as long as they act, neither before nor after; to *be* free and to act are the same."[31] Habermas, builds on this insight and links freedom, as action, to a process of what has been called by Robert Brandom "score keeping in the game of reason giving and reason taking." What this means is that freedom always involves taking into account a point of view, i.e. someone's reason for acting. Freedom without reasons does not lead to acting, but mere behaving, or mere having reflex reactions. Action that is voluntary and can be given an account is freedom guided by reason. What is key here is that articulating freedom as communicative freedom foregrounds that to be free means to be free in relation to how others would respond to my actions, and how, in turn, I would have to respond. To be free means to always have to recognize that your actions have consequences. Freedom is thus a power over yourself, but for this very same reason, over others. Freedom thus generates what Habermas called, following Arendt, "communicative power," i.e. that kind of power that arises when humans act together on the basis of the mutual recognition of their reasons, their point of view, and the attempts to fashion themselves through the drama of their freedom.

4. The legal orthopedics of human dignity

At the beginning of this chapter I spoke about dignity as both a comportment and as pedestal to which we elevate our humanity. I mentioned Ernst Bloch's concept of the "upright carriage" of the human standing tall with dignity. Dignity is precisely this upright carriage of humanity. As I indicated, however, this upright carriage is something we have to continuously wrest from conditions of abjection, degradation, privation, and debasement. It is something we build. Ernst Bloch referred to this process of the construction of dignity as the "orthopedia of the upright carriage of human pride, and of humanity."[32] We can speak with Bloch of the moral orthopedics of human dignity, which take place through the many struggles against conditions where humans are: dispirited, discouraged, disheartened, dejected, debased, and denigrated. Following Bloch, however, I want to argue that there is also a legal orthopedics of human dignity. This orthopedics takes place through *jurisgenesis*, the creation of law, either through constitutional processes or through the generation of rights by constructive legal interpretation of the law that is already extant, as well as of the legal norms that are implicit in the Universal Declaration of Human Rights. Without law, dignity and freedom are mere shibboleths, empty catchphrases. Without being grounded in dignity and freedom, law is blind. I am now making explicit that dignity and freedom are two sides of what I have called the *humanum*. This means that there are co-dependences and cross-fertilizations between two types of traditions: the tradition of natural law, which crystallized in the concept of human dignity as the foundational pillar of human rights; and the tradition of "social utopias" that aim to liberate humans from any type of oppression, exploitation, and dependence.

Ernst Bloch articulated the interdependence of these two traditions in the following way:

> Social utopias and natural law have mutually concerns within the same human space; they marched separately but, sadly, did not strike together. Although they were in accord on the decisive issue, a more humane society, there nevertheless arose important differences between the doctrines of social utopia and natural law. Those differences can be formulated as follows. Social utopian thought directed its efforts toward human happiness, natural law was directed towards human dignity. Social utopias depicted relations in which *toil* and *burden* ceased, natural law constructed relations in which *degradation* and *insult* ceased.[33]

Or, as he puts it elsewhere:

> Social utopias want to clear away all that stands in the way of the
> *eudaemonia* of *everyone*; natural law wants to do away with all that
> stands in the way of *autonomy* and its *euonomia* [the good law].[34]

Bloch establishes here not only a mutuality of concern between social utopias
and natural law, but also between the concept of dignity and what he calls
euonomia, good law. The *telos* of the struggle for rights is the creation of a
just law, a moral law, a law that aims to respect the moral equality of all
human beings at the same time that it enables a just social order in which we
can all live our liberty. Law, which is actualized in rights, is the means for the
transformation of communicative power, which is reflexive freedom, into a
collective wherewithal to elevate our humanity to the pedestal of human dignity.
Habermas has articulated this process beautifully in this way:

> The idea of human dignity is the conceptual hinge which connects the
> morality of equal respect for everyone with positive law and democratic
> lawmaking in such a way that their interplay could give rise to a poli-
> tical order founded upon human rights … Because the moral promise
> of equal respect for everyone is supposed to be cashed out in legal
> currency, human rights exhibit a Janus face turned simultaneously to
> morality and to law. Notwithstanding their exclusive moral *content*,
> they have the *form* of positive, enforceable subjective rights which
> guarantee specific liberties and claims. They are designed to be *spelled
> out in concrete terms* through democratic legislation, to be *specified*
> from case to case in adjudication and to be *enforced* with public
> sanction.[35]

I want to direct your attention to the phrase at the end: "to be *enforced* with
public sanction." Rights are the means through which force is transformed
into legitimate authority. *Jurisgenesis* is the transformation of coercion into a
form of collective power that regulates our interactions, our collective actions.
Or, in other words, the creation of law is the means for reflexive freedom to be
cashed out into collective agency with efficacy.

Jurisgenesis, however, departs from a *topos*, a specific cultural context in
the face of specific challenges that were both thrown at us as such by specific
cultural traditions and that have to be met with the resources that can speak
to that cultural context. When we think about the jurisgenerative dimension
of human rights, which is what I am particularly interested in here when I
focus on "freedom's law," we have to think also about the relationship
between different conceptions of human dignity and the ways such conceptions are a rich reservoir and pedagogical germinal for the development of
broader and deeper understandings of human rights. I think legal and social
theorist Boaventura de Sousa Santos has given us some wonderful tools to

work through these issues. Santos makes a very useful distinction between globalization from above (which takes place through the form of globalized localisms and localized globalisms), and globalization from below (which takes place through the interaction between cosmopolitanism and the movements for recognition and protection of "the common inheritance of humanity"). Santos eloquently argues that the expansion of the discourse of human rights in the last 50 years has taken place because of what he calls globalization from below. Here I would like to quote Santos:

> In the area of human rights and dignity, the mobilization and support of the emancipatory claims that they potentially contain, can only be attained if such claims have been appropriated in the local cultural context. For this, we require a transcultural dialogue and a diatopic hermeneutics.[36]

By diatopic hermeneutics Santos means that type of hermeneutics that intensifies cultural awareness about the incompleteness of self-reflection on one's own culture's blind spots. One cannot see one's own blind spot without the aid of another eye that can see where we cannot. Thus, we not only have to engage in a "transcultural" dialogue in which we attempt to translate key ideas from one hermeneutical horizon into another horizon, but we must also become aware of the partiality of our point of view. By combining transcultural dialogue and diatopic hermeneutics, we are able to bypass the misleading and sterile debate whether human rights are globalized localisms (specific cultural creations that do not have global applicability), or localized globalisms (global struggles that require the imposition of a global lingua franca). Human rights claims always begin from a local cultural context that then unleashes a series of hermeneutical enlightenments that are more than globalization from above, as they are always local vindications requiring local discursive and practical applications.[37]

I will conclude by quoting one of the United States' most important legal thinkers, Ronald Dworkin:

> We live in and by the law. It makes us what we are: citizens and employees and doctors and spouses and people who own things. It is sword, shield, and menace: we insist on our wage, or refuse to pay our tent, or are forced to forfeit penalties, or are closed up in jail, all in the name of what our abstract and ethereal sovereign, the law, has decreed. And we *argue* about what it has decreed, even when the books that are supposed to record its commands and directions are silent; we act then as if law had muttered its doom, too low to be heard distinctly. We are subjects of law's empire, liegemen to its methods and ideals, bound in spirit while we debate what we must therefore do.[38]

Note the "in" in the first sentence. We dwell in the house of law. Ultimately, law builds up the canopy in which humans can dwell in equal freedom and sublime dignity. There can be no human dignity without rights, and no rights without the abolition of conditions of exploitation and debasement, but just the same there is no end to exploitation and debasement without the establishment of rights. An alternative formulation, in the spirit of Axel Honneth's thinking, would be to aver that freedom's right is the "right to have rights" – to use Arendt's pregnant formulation – but this is nothing more and no less than the right to human dignity, the right to the upright carriage.

Acknowledgments

An earlier version of this chapter was written for the "Freedom, Personhood, and Justice Forum" at Muhlenberg College, September 18, 2013. I want to give special thanks to Professor Morgan for the invitation and her hospitality during my visit at Muhlenberg.

Notes

1 When I first drafted this chapter, I began with a description of a picture of a child who is dragging herself, or seems to have collapsed on herself. In the background is a vulture, menacingly leaning forward, ready to attack the child. I have been haunted by this picture, which had burnt itself somewhere in my mind. I saw this picture at the same time I saw Salgado's pictures. So, I had originally thought this picture was also Salgado's, but in fact, it belonged to Kevin Carter, who won a Pulitzer Prize for this and similar photographs. Kevin Carter committed suicide shortly after receiving this prize. According to close friends, he was consumed by the guilt that he should have picked up the child, instead of taking the picture, although he had been expressly ordered by UN personnel not to touch anyone, due to the possibility of the transmission of disease. See: http://safaisal.wordpress.com/2013/05/30/iconic-photo-vulturestalking-a-child/.

2 Sebastião Salgado, *Sahel: The End of the Road* (Berkeley, CA: University of California Press, 2004).

3 I treated these photographs somewhere else; see Eduardo Mendieta, "'Moral Optics': Biopolitics, Torture and the Imperial Gaze of War Photography," in José-Manuel Barreto (ed.), *Human Rights from a Third World Perspective: Critique, History, and International Law* (Newcastle upon Tyne: Cambridge Scholars Press, 2012), 117–139.

4 See Philip Gourevitch and Errol Morris, *Standard Operating Procedure* (New York, NY: Penguin Press, 2008).

5 Accessible online at: http://bioethics.georgetown.edu/pcbe/reports/human_dignity/.

6 Steven Pinker, "The Stupidity of Dignity: Conservative Bioethics's Latest, Most Dangerous Ploy," *The New Republic* 238, no. 9 (May 28, 2008): 28–31; here 30.

7 Pinker, "The Stupidity of Dignity," 28.

8 It should be noted that a lot of Pinker's criticisms of the concept of dignity were already articulated by Arthur Schopenhauer, who wrote: "But that expression, dignity of man, once uttered by Kant, afterwards became the shibboleth of all the perplexed and empty-headed moralists who concealed behind that imposing expression their lack of any real basis of morals, or, at any rate, of one that had any meaning ... For we should then find that it too is only a hollow hyperbole in which the *contradictio in adjecto* lurks like a gnawing worm. Every worth or value is the estimation of one thing in comparison; consequently, it is relative, and this relativity constitutes the very essence of the concept of worth" (Arthur

Schopenhauer, *On the Basis of Morality* [Indianapolis, IN: Hackett, 1995], 100–101). Later in the same text, Schopenhauer is even more mordant, when he writes: "Whoever thinks that it is not sufficiently fashionable, doctrinaire, and academic, may return to the categorical imperatives, to the shibboleth of the 'dignity of man,' to the hollow phrases, the brain-webs and soap bubbles of the schools, to principles ridiculed at every step by experience, to principles whereof no one outside the lecture halls knows anything or has ever had any experience" (Schopenhauer, *On the Basis of Morality*, 130).

9 Christopher McCrudden, "Human Dignity and Judicial Interpretation of Human Rights," *The European Journal of International Law* 19, no. 4 (2008): 655–724.

10 McCrudden, "Human Dignity and Judicial Interpretation of Human Rights," 656.

11 Evidently, the key texts are Axel Honneth, *The Struggle for Recognition: The Moral Grammar of Social Conflicts*, trans. J. Anderson (Cambridge, MA: MIT Press, 1996), especially chs. 5 and 6; and Axel Honneth, *Disrespect: The Normative Foundations of Critical Theory* (Cambridge: Polity, 2007).

12 In particular, Honneth's *The Pathologies of Individual Freedom: Hegel's Social Theory*, trans. L. Löb (Princeton, NJ: Princeton University Press, 2010). I am also taking the concept of jurisgenerative from Seyla Benhabib, as she has developed it in her Tanner Lectures. See Seyla Benhabib, *Another Cosmopolitanism* (Oxford: Oxford University Press, 2006), especially the second lecture "Democratic Iterations," 45–81.

13 In the following I have been inspired and guided by Waldron's work; see Jeremy Waldron, "Dignity and Rank," *European Journal of Sociology* 48, no. 2 (August 2007): 201–37, as well as his Tanner Lecture, "Dignity, Rank, and Rights," delivered at the University of California, 2009, accessible online at: http://tannerlec tures.utah.edu/_documents/a-to-z/w/Waldron_09.pdf.

As well, see the following works: George Kateb, *Human Dignity* (Cambridge, MA: Belknap Press, 2011), and Aurel Kolnai, "Dignity," *Philosophy* 51, no. 197 (July 1976): 251–271. I came across this fantastic book after I had finished my chapter, and wished I had been able to incorporate some key insight in it: Peter Bieri, *Eine Art zu Leben. Über die Vielfalt menschlicher Würde* [A Form of Life: On the Plurality of Human Dignity] (München: Carl Hanser Verlag, 2013).

14 Pico della Mirandola, *On the Dignity of Man* (Indianapolis, IN: Hackett, 1998), 5.

15 Henceforth I am using the *Cambridge Edition of the Works of Immanuel Kant, Practical Philosophy*, ed. and trans. Mary J. Gregor (Cambridge: Cambridge University Press, 1996) and providing references to this edition in parentheses.

16 Michael Rosen, *Dignity: Its History and Meaning* (Cambridge, MA: Harvard University Press, 2012), 57.

17 Rosen, *Dignity*, 57 and 61–62.

18 See McCrudden, "Human Dignity and Judicial Interpretation," 679.

19 Thomas Hobbes, *Leviathan, with selected variants from the Latin edition of 1668*, ed. E. Curley (Indianapolis, IN: Hackett, 1994). Henceforth I am giving the references to *Leviathan* by chapter and paragraph numbers in parentheses.

20 Isaiah Berlin, *Liberty: Incorporating Four Essays on Liberty*, ed. Henry Hardy (Oxford: Oxford University Press, 2002), 170.

21 Berlin, *Liberty*, 178.

22 Quentin Skinner, "A Third Concept of Liberty," *Proceedings of the British Academy* 117 (2002): 237–268. A very abbreviated version of this essay was published in the *London Review of Books* 24. no. 7 (April 4, 2002): 16–18; accessible online at: www.lrb.co.uk/v24/n07/quentin-skinner/a-third-concept-of-liberty.

23 Here I am quoting from the *London Review of Books* version, at p. 8 of the online version.

24 These thoughts are also informed by Albrecht Wellmer's work; see Albrecht Wellmer, *Endgames: The Irreconcilable Nature of Modernity. Essays and Lectures*,

trans. D. Midgley (Cambridge, MA: MIT Press, 1998), especially ch. 1, "Models of Freedom in the Modern World (1989)," 3–38.

25 Axel Honneth, *Das Recht Der Freiheit: Grundriß einer demokratischen Sittlichkeit* (Frankfurt a.M.: Suhrkamp Verlag, 2011), 58. A translation has appeared as *Freedom's Right: The Social Foundations of Democratic Life* (New York, NY: Columbia University Press, 2014).

26 Berlin, *Liberty*, 171.

27 Hannah Arendt, *Between Past and Future* (New York, NY: Penguin Books, 1993 [1961]), 154. I am quoting from her essay "What is Freedom?", 142–169.

28 Arendt, *Between Past and Future*, 153.

29 Jürgen Habermas, *Between Facts and Norms: Contributions to a Discourse Theory of Law and Democracy*, trans. W. Rehg (Cambridge, MA: MIT Press, 1998), 119.

30 I have developed this idea further in Eduardo Mendieta, "Freedom as Practice and Civic Genius: On James Tully's Public Philosophy," in Robert Nichols and Jakeet Singh (eds.), *Freedom and Democracy in an Imperial Context: Dialogues with James Tully* (London and New York, NY: Routledge, 2014), 32–47.

31 Arendt, *Between Past and Future*, 153.

32 Ernst Bloch, *Natural Law and Human Dignity*, trans. D.J. Schmidt (Cambridge, MA: MIT Press, 1986), 174.

33 Bloch, *Natural Law and Human Dignity*, xxix.

34 Bloch, *Natural Law and Human Dignity*, 205.

35 Jürgen Habermas, *The Crisis of the European Union: A Response*, trans. C. Cronin (Cambridge: Polity, 2013), 81–82. The essay first appeared as "The Concept of Human Dignity and the Realistic Utopia of Human Rights," *Metaphilosophy* 41, no. 4 (July 2010): 464–480.

36 Boaventura de Sousa Santos, *De la mano de Alicia: Lo Social y lo Político en la Posmodernidad* [By Alice's Hand: The Social and the Political in Postmodernity] (Santafé de Bogotá: Siglo del Hombre Editores, Facultad de Derecho de los Andes, Ediciones Uniandes, 1998), 357; my translation.

37 See Seyla Benhabib's wonderful essay "Utopia and Dystopia in Our Times," which advances similar ideas under the heading of cosmopolitanism, in her book *Dignity in Adversity: Human Rights in Troubled Times* (London: Polity, 2011), 184–95.

38 Ronald Dworkin, *Law's Empire* (Cambridge, MA: Belknap Press, 1986), vii.

References

Arendt, Hannah. *Between Past and Future* (New York, NY: Penguin Books, 1993 [1961]).

Benhabib, Seyla. *Dignity in Adversity: Human Rights in Troubled Times* (London: Polity, 2011).

Benhabib, Seyla. *Another Cosmopolitanism* (Oxford: Oxford University Press, 2006).

Berlin, Isaiah. *Liberty: Incorporating Four Essays on Liberty*, ed. Henry Hardy (Oxford: Oxford University Press, 2002).

Bieri, Peter. *Eine Art zu Leben. Über die Vielfalt menschlicher Würde* [A Form of Life: On the Plurality of Human Dignity] (München: Carl Hanser Verlag, 2013).

Bloch, Ernst. *Natural Law and Human Dignity*, trans. D.J. Schmidt (Cambridge, MA: MIT Press, 1986).

Dworkin, Ronald. *Law's Empire* (Cambridge, MA: Belknap Press, 1986).

Gourevitch, Philip and Errol Morris. *Standard Operating Procedure* (New York, NY: Penguin Press, 2008).

Habermas, Jürgen. *The Crisis of the European Union: A Response*, trans. C. Cronin (Cambridge: Polity, 2013).

Habermas, Jürgen. "The Concept of Human Dignity and the Realistic Utopia of Human Rights," *Metaphilosophy* 41, no. 4 (July 2010): 464–480.

Habermas, Jürgen. *Between Facts and Norms: Contributions to a Discourse Theory of Law and Democracy*, trans. W. Rehg (Cambridge, MA: MIT Press, 1998).

Hobbes, Thomas. *Leviathan, with selected variants from the Latin edition of 1668*, ed. E. Curley (Indianapolis, IN: Hackett, 1994).

Honneth, Axel. *Freedom's Right: The Social Foundations of Democratic Life* (New York, NY: Columbia University Press, 2014); German as *Das Recht Der Freiheit: Grundriß einer demokratischen Sittlichkeit* (Frankfurt a.M.: Suhrkamp Verlag, 2011).

Honneth, Axel. *The Pathologies of Individual Freedom: Hegel's Social Theory*, trans. L. Löb (Princeton, NJ: Princeton University Press, 2010).

Honneth, Axel. *Disrespect: The Normative Foundations of Critical Theory* (Cambridge: Polity, 2007).

Honneth, Axel. *The Struggle for Recognition: The Moral Grammar of Social Conflicts*, trans. J. Anderson (Cambridge, MA: MIT Press, 1996).

Kant, Immanuel. *Practical Philosophy [Cambridge Edition of the Works of Immanuel Kant]*, ed. and trans. Mary J. Gregor (Cambridge: Cambridge University Press, 1996).

Kateb, George. *Human Dignity* (Cambridge, MA: Belknap Press, 2011).

Kolnai, Aurel. "Dignity," *Philosophy* 51, no. 197 (July 1976): 251–271.

McCrudden, Christopher. "Human Dignity and Judicial Interpretation of Human Rights," *The European Journal of International Law* 19, no. 4 (2008): 655–724.

Mendieta, Eduardo. "Freedom as Practice and Civic Genius: On James Tully's Public Philosophy," in Robert Nichols and Jakeet Singh (eds), *Freedom and Democracy in an Imperial Context: Dialogues with James Tully* (London and New York, NY: Routledge, 2014), 32–47.

Mendieta, Eduardo. "'Moral Optics': Biopolitics, Torture and the Imperial Gaze of War Photography," in José-Manuel Barreto (ed.) *Human Rights from a Third World Perspective: Critique, History, and International Law* (Newcastle upon Tyne: Cambridge Scholars Press, 2012), 117–139.

Pico della Mirandola. *On the Dignity of Man* (Indianapolis, IN: Hackett, 1998).

Pinker, Steven. "The Stupidity of Dignity: Conservative Bioethics's Latest, Most Dangerous Ploy," *The New Republic* 238, no. 9 (May 28, 2008): 28–31.

Rosen, Michael. *Dignity: Its History and Meaning* (Cambridge, MA: Harvard University Press, 2012).

Salgado, Sebastião. *Sahel: The End of the Road* (Berkeley, CA: University of California Press, 2004).

Schopenhauer, Arthur. *On the Basis of Morality* (Indianapolis, IN: Hackett, 1995).

Skinner, Quentin. "A Third Concept of Liberty," *London Review of Books* 24, no. 7 (April 4, 2002): 16–18, accessible online at: www.lrb.co.uk/v24/n07/quentin-skinner/a-third-concept-of-liberty.

Skinner, Quentin. "A Third Concept of Liberty," *Proceedings of the British Academy* 117 (2002): 237–268.

Sousa Santos, Boaventura de. *De la mano de Alicia: Lo Social y lo Político en la Posmodernidad* [By Alice's Hand: The Social and the Political in Postmodernity] (Santafé de Bogotá: Siglo del Hombre Editores, Facultad de Derecho de los Andes, Ediciones Uniandes, 1998).

The President's Council on Bioethics. *Human Dignity and Bioethics* [chaired by Leon Kass], last accessed on September 27, 2017 at: http://bioethics.georgetown.edu/pcbe/reports/human_dignity/.

Waldron, Jeremy. "Dignity, Rank, and Rights," Tanner Lecture delivered at the University of California, 2009, last accessed online on September 17, 2017 at: http://tannerlectures.utah.edu/_documents/a-to-z/w/Waldron_09.pdf.

Waldron, Jeremy. "Dignity and Rank," *European Journal of Sociology* 48, no. 2 (August 2007): 201–237.

Wellmer, Albrecht. *Endgames: The Irreconcilable Nature of Modernity. Essays and Lectures*, trans. D. Midgley (Cambridge, MA: MIT Press, 1998).

8 Human dignity and plurality in justifications of human rights

Amos Nascimento

This chapter relies on a Kantian approach and discourse-ethical version of Critical Theory to consider how a plurality of perspectives on human dignity may contribute to the justification of human rights. First, I introduce a variety of positions worldwide with their respective challenges and contributions to human rights. Second, I show various religious, moral, political, and legal perspectives on human dignity. Third, I argue that the missing link between human dignity and human rights is provided by human duties that prompt us to act and establish new practices and institutions. By connecting human dignity, human duties, and human rights in a horizontal and complementary way, we can have a conduit for values that contribute to the process of justifying human rights. In this process, plurality is not simply a description, but it has a normative function. It makes us aware of a multiplicity of expressions of humanity, encourages us to dialogue with a greater variety of theoretical positions and practical experiences, and prompts us to act in promoting human rights worldwide.

1. Critical Theory as a point of departure

Is human dignity a necessary and sufficient foundation or justification for human rights? This question can be expressed and interpreted in different ways. Let me break this statement into three other subordinate questions that bring us to the heart of contemporary discussions on the philosophy of human rights.

A first point to consider is whether a justification of human rights is necessary. Because the Universal Declaration of Human Rights and other documents have been ratified by many members of the United Nations, we assume that there is a consensus on human rights and further justifications are unnecessary. Contrary to this assumption, however, human rights discourses have become controversial. For instance, Asian governments have questioned the very concept of human rights because it claims universality but seems unavoidably limited by Western culture, individualism, and lack of emphasis on duties.[1] Similarly, member states of the Organization of the Islamic Conference affirm that they already possess a repertoire of rights dictated by the *Qur'an*. [2] In Africa, the focus is on peoples, communities, and collective identities.[3] In Latin America, there is a suspicion that human rights discourses are often used to project Eurocentric values and imperialistic economic interests.[4] Even within the European and North American contexts, there is a growing wariness that human rights may be contaminated by old metaphysical, essentialist, or idealistic narratives that are no longer tenable.[5] These examples point toward a clear answer: new justifications for human rights are needed as a response to contemporary challenges.[6]

A second concern is whether existing proposals provide sufficient answers to these challenges. Philosophies that rely on natural rights postulate that core beliefs provide an ontological basis upon which all human rights can be grounded. However, there are strong arguments against this position: the ontological premise of innate rights implies some untenable metaphysical assumptions based on foundationalism. Other philosophical positions negate the possibility of a single metaphysical or epistemic justification for human rights and prefer to appeal to existing practical forms of moral, historical, social, political, or legal considerations. Thus, they rely on concrete practices, institutions, or regimes to define the origins, justification, and implementation of human rights.[7] However, this kind of proposal often relies on some kind of reductionism that downgrades the human dimension.

A third consideration concerns the plausibility of resorting to human dignity to justify human rights.[8] Yet human dignity can be seen as another way of importing metaphysical foundationalism into the discussion by appealing to the *imago Dei* and other theological reasons. Even a more empirical perspective on human dignity, based on prudential considerations by states, can be criticized as being merely a convenient arbitrary threshold to constrain ontological issues. A more political definition of humanity, dignity, and rights in terms of citizenship has limitations as well as because it may also imply that non-citizens of a given nation-state or stateless persons are non-bearers of rights and, consequently, not worthy of being considered fully humans. Finally, a strict appeal to juridification may constrain the concept of human dignity to positive and enforceable legal categories within a particular constitutional framework, but here there is still a risk of downplaying the importance of wider moral reflections, social contexts, or political processes that may enable or hinder inclusive interpretations of human dignity.[9]

The difficulty with these positions is that they seem to fall on extremes that need to be avoided: the temptation to define human dignity according to metaphysical abstractions, the attempt to naturalize categories, and the allure to rely on expediently vague definitions as placeholders. The discourse-ethical contribution to a Critical Theory of Human Rights is a robust framework that has the potential to address these issues.[10] However, this philosophical program needs to be in dialogue with a greater variety of theories and positions worldwide and consider their practical implications in real lives because it is precisely when we talk about real human lives that the concept of human dignity becomes tangible and central. In this sense, human dignity is the entry point for efforts to conceive of "humanity" as a supplement to the language of "rights."[11] Today, not all lives seem to matter, not everybody is considered as a full human being, and not all people enjoy basic rights. Critical Theory needs to recognize the concrete plurality of ways of being human and reject the multiple unjust practices that disregard human dignity and, therefore, deny human rights to all.

2. Avoiding extremes in human rights

In contemporary philosophy, there is no need to be apologetic when affirming the importance of plurality, diversity, locality, contextuality, heterogeneity, or particularity. These and other terms once dismissed as relativism or post-modernism are now acceptable as related to the "fact of pluralism."[12] Conversely, it has become more difficult to emphasize foundations without a proper justification.[13] The main challenge to philosophical justifications of human rights is to find a way of affirming the compatibility between plural contexts and universally acceptable norms without falling into the extremes of foundationalism or reductionism.[14]

Moving beyond foundationalism and reductionism

Foundationalism is a serious philosophical problem that emerged in mathematics at the beginning of the twentieth century and later influenced other philosophical fields, including ethics and politics, mainly through the influence of Ludwig Wittgenstein[15] and his interpreters. Philosophers related to postmodernism, poststructuralism, and neopragmatism were the main responsible for connecting this critique of foundationalism to issues in human rights. Three examples based on Jean-François Lyotard, Jacques Derrida, and Richard Rorty suffice to show how plurality, multiplicity, and heterogeneity emerge as alternatives to foundationalism in human rights.

Lyotard presents his views in various ways. In *The Postmodern Condition*[16] he states that appeals to modern metadiscourses have lost their legitimacy, in "Grundlagenkrise" he describes a crisis of foundations in ethics,[17] and in *L'Enthousiasme: la critique kantienne de l'histoire*[18] he acknowledges the possibility of defending human rights without universalism. In his view, this requires respect for cultural boundaries, attention to concrete cases, and an ethical criterion based on a multiplicity that inhibits terror and other forms of inhumanity.[19] This also implies rejecting the marginalizing of heterogeneous traditions and avoiding the claim that a sole form of politics, culture, or norm has a universal status and can be imposed upon others. Although Jürgen Habermas and Karl-Otto Apel have shown that many of Lyotard's provocative claims were performative contradictions,[20] we can still appreciate a critical intention in his initiative of revealing what is often occluded in philosophical discourse. In the semiological analysis of the "human rights" concept we need to identify what we mean when we say "human," what is implied by our definition of "rights," and what disappears or emerges in the gap between these two terms.

Similar considerations are developed by Derrida, who talks about cosmopolitanism and human rights, but puts more emphasis on particular meanings, contextual interpretations of norms, and identification of gaps or interstices in our conceptions of humanity and rights. Applying deconstruction, he is particularly critical of humanitarian interventions and defends a non-foundational conception of human rights that could be more inclusive of real-life experiences worldwide:

> Just as the concept of human rights has slowly been determined over the course of centuries through many socio-political upheavals (whether it be a matter of the right to work or economic rights, of the rights of women and children, and so forth), likewise international law should extend and diversify its field to include, if at least it is to be consistent with the idea of democracy and of human rights it proclaims, the *worldwide* economic and social field.[21]

Echoes of these positions can be heard in Richard Rorty's critique of human rights. In his Oxford Amnesty Lecture, "Human Rights, Rationality, and Sentimentality," he quotes Derrida approvingly and addresses the problem of foundationalism by describing dehumanization:

> Serbians murderers and rapists do not think of themselves as violating human rights. For they are not doing this to fellow human beings, but to *Muslims*. They are not being inhuman, but rather are discriminating between true humans and pseudo-humans. They are making the same sort of distinction the Crusaders made between humans and infidel dogs, and Black Muslims make between humans and blue-eyed devils. The founder of my university [Thomas Jefferson, founder of the University of Virginia] was able to both own slaves and to think it is self-evident that all men are endowed by their creator with certain inalienable rights.[22]

Rorty shows more explicitly that the meaning of human rights depends directly on cultural and social processes that emerge in that gap between humanity and rights. He then goes on to show that philosophers have tried different strategies to define what counts as human, but invariably fall prey to "human rights foundationalism," as exemplified by the essentialism of Platonic philosophy, Thomas Aquinas' naturalism, and Immanuel Kant's rationalism. Against these philosophies, Rorty provocatively states that "the most philosophy can hope to do is to summarize our culturally influenced intuitions about the right thing to do in various situations."[23] Therefore, he proposes to replace "human rights foundationalism" with an aesthetic emphasis on sentimentality.

These philosophers have been criticized, but their points elicit a series of important reflections. First, it is necessary to identify and criticize the foundationalist affirmation that there is a univocal, objective, and unimpeachable basis for human rights. Second, there is a gap between the concepts of "human" and "rights," through which all kinds of extraneous considerations can emerge. Third, it is necessary to see discussions about human rights as invariably tied to arbitrary conceptions of humanity that need to be spelled out. Fourth, it is possible to avoid these problems by affirming plurality and using an aesthetic sensibility to reveal what is occluded. By adding these components to human rights, Lyotard, Derrida, and Rorty ask for more attention to cultural, historical, and social experiences. Through this, new human actors emerge and become more visible. Plurality, therefore, does not merely mean to describe dynamic facts, events, processes, and narratives in terms of diversity, difference, or contingency, but it becomes normative as a duty, a processual requirement, an obligation to consider many possibilities to define human agency instead of arbitrarily reducing them to a single factor.

In fact, we already accept plurality when talking about rights. The Universal Declaration of Human Rights lists thirty rights. Similarly, we ought to be "required" to think about plurality when considering humanity. From a Kantian perspective, humanity is not necessarily a singularity, but rather a community of multiple beings who may share common abilities such as freedom and rationality, albeit in different ways. Categorically, Kant conceives of humans as a plurality of persons with equality because he wants to safeguard the distinctiveness of individual autonomy.[24] Similarly, Wittgenstein insists on the multiplicity and heterogeneity of language-games and forms-of-life at the cultural level in order to identify collective markers and consider the possibility of transitions, linkages, and aesthetic ways of recognizing the variety of anthropological arrangements and philosophical methods.[25] Therefore, plurality can help reveal the multiplicity of individual and collective human experiences.

Affirming the plurality in conceptions of human dignity

Based on the considerations above, we can relate a duty to plurality to issues regarding human dignity. Using multiple lenses, we can observe a variety of appeals to human dignity and ask about what is forgotten or excluded when we apply this concept.

The first article of the Universal Declaration of Human Rights states that "all human beings are born free and equal in dignity and rights." The validity of this statement is generally taken for granted and from there one goes on to talk in more detail about basic and specific rights that should be valid for all humans. However, statements like these leave a series of unanswered questions. Does this mean that freedom, autonomy, and equality are foundations upon which dignity and rights rest? Or does dignity justify freedom, autonomy, and equality? Do we have dignity and then rights or is there a more fundamental right that grants us both? Can we grant, suppress, or increase dignity and rights at different stages in life? These and other questions are very serious and deserve our attention, but I want to focus on a simpler point: How can we apply plurality to the understanding of human dignity and human rights?

Theologically, the reference to human dignity is generally supported on revelation, but this recourse to metaphysics can be criticized as foundationalism. This line of argument can be seen especially in the theological doctrine of *betzelem Elohim* or *imago Dei* – i.e., the assumption that all humans are created in the image of G-d, thus having human dignity as an ontological substantiation. This doctrine became central to Catholic theology in 1891 through Pope Leo XIII in the encyclical *Rerum Novarum*, was reaffirmed during the Vatican II Council in the document *Dignitatis Humanae*, and is now used to back the social teachings of many Christian churches.[26] Although this position has been criticized, it is still recognized as the cultural expression of many religious communities in the Abrahamic traditions.

Morally, assumptions about human dignity are pervasive. Alan Gewirth, for example, says that "for human rights to exist there must be valid moral criteria or principles that justify that all humans, qua humans, have the rights and hence also the correlative duties."[27] He then goes on to analyze the structure of rights in detail, taking humanity and human dignity for granted. Similar considerations occur at the level of social and political institutions. Jack Donnelly begins his book *Universal Rights in Theory and Practice* by saying that human rights "are the rights one has because one is a human,"[28] and then goes on to describe the international human rights regime built upon this premise. Other authors justify human dignity by adding the Kantian proviso that humans have dignity "by virtue of their humanity,"[29] without explaining what this means. In all these approaches, there is an axiomatic postulate of human dignity as an unjustified justification that is expected to play a key role in defining duties and establishing human rights institutions.

Politically, one can go back to the concept of *dignitas* in Stoic philosophy, especially in Cicero, who defines human dignity as a "status" or rank defined according to a certain hierarchy that places certain entities above others – such as humans above animals and virtuous persons above criminals as well as office-holders above common citizens.[30] In this sense, human dignity is an entitlement granted by the established political power. For sure, in many cultures and at different times, human dignity was made more secular and related to the image of a king or chief, and then transferred to others according to honor codes.[31] Adapting this approach to contemporary views on liberal rights, Jeremy Waldron proposes that this concept has evolved and been freed from its metaphysical and non-egalitarian baggage. In *Dignity, Rank, and Rights* [32] he shows that through legal and political initiatives many political communities now define human dignity as a "high ranking status" for every individual, simply based on one's humanity.[33] In Waldron's view, this is guaranteed today as a "dignity of citizenship" in secularized democratic societies and as a condition for securing human rights. This approach has been criticized because Waldron proposes a gradual "leveling-up" process through law – in which any individual could be promoted in rank toward full humanity – instead of criticizing arbitrary social, economic, economic, and political impediments. As a result, he pays less attention to the possibility of dignity being denied to humans located outside of arbitrary legal-political boundaries.

Legally, we can also find a justification of human rights based on human dignity, generally by means of an appeal to the normative authority of first principles. According to this view, human dignity is a basic norm that remains unquestioned, as seen in the Universal Declaration of Human Rights, whose first article states that "all human beings are born free and equal in dignity and rights." The European Convention on Human Rights makes a comparable move in its Protocol 13, concerning the abolition of the death penalty in all circumstances. It states that "the abolition of the death penalty is essential for the protection of this right [to life] and for the full recognition of the inherent dignity of all human beings",[34] but it nowhere spells out the meaning of this inherent human dignity.

Similarly, in several national constitutions, human dignity is affirmed as an absolute right. The German Constitution or Basic Law [*Grundgesetz*] of 1949 is a celebrated example, as in its Bill of Rights it states on its Article 1, that "human dignity is inviolable" [*unantastbar*].[35] Similar provisions can be seen in the Brazilian Constitution of 1988, the Tenth Basic Law of Israel in 1992, the South African Constitution of 1996, and many other contemporary constitutions that insist of the foundational legal role of human dignity. The difficulty in these cases is the expectation that this proposition can support the positivization and enforcement of a principle to curb cruelty, torture, death penalty, and other practices defined as degrading. Therefore, jurisprudential and rhetorical strategies have emerged, such as seeing the concept of human dignity as an "empty placeholder" or as a "non-interpreted thesis" that uses the definition of human dignity on a case-by-case basis. However, the assumptions of historical, cultural, and philosophical perspectives that influence legal interpretation are often left out of consideration.

It seems obvious, therefore, that there is a plurality of theological, moral, political, and legal references to human dignity, which rely on assumptions that do not seem to be properly introduced or justified in critical philosophical terms. A growing literature has generated lively polemic debates that should motivate the reflection of a Critical Theory of Human Rights, although some of their polemic and rhetoric devices needs to be questioned. For instance, in *The Last Utopia* Samuel Moyn has described the emergence of human rights discourses as a mere instrumental tool of powerful states during the Cold War,[36] and he used the same strategy to show how the concept of human dignity – as first enshrined onto the Constitution in Ireland in 1937[37] – has been instrumentalized systematically for conservative purposes since 1945.[38] Similarly, Michael Rosen has written a provocative book, *Dignity: Its History and Meaning*, in which he presents strong criticisms against various ways how the idea of dignity is presented arbitrarily.[39]

This leads to the conclusion that there are various approaches to human dignity in relation to human rights, but they have a limited scope and fail to address the gap between conceptions of what counts as human and what is valid as rights. If we insist on plurality, reveal underlying assumptions and pay attention to gaps, we can differentiate various usages of the term, identify problems, and evaluate potentials. In what follows, I will consider how a Critical Theory of Human Rights provides an alternative perspective on the appeal to human dignity as a justification for human rights.

3. Critical perspectives on human dignity and human rights

Philosophers connected to Critical Theory have offered some positive approaches to questions about the relationship between human dignity and human rights. This can be seen in various authors, but I would like to concentrate on Jürgen Habermas, Rainer Forst, and Seyla Benhabib as examples, since they engage in a dialogue with some of the issues raised thus far.

Jürgen Habermas assesses human rights in light of his discourse theory. As early as in *Structural Transformation of the Public Sphere* [40] he briefly referred to human rights in relation to the European Enlightenment and modern citizenship, but in *Between Facts and Norms* [41] he developed a new discourse-theory of law and politics that dealt with the system of rights within contemporary national democratic states. However, his focus initially remained domestic and, at most, restricted to North-Atlantic examples. Later, however, Habermas turned his attention to international human rights in texts such as "The Intercultural Discourse on Human Rights"[42] and "Remarks on Legitimation through Human Rights."[43] He then assessed the concept of human dignity more directly in "The Concept of Human Dignity and the Realist Utopia of Human Rights,"[44] where he provides a brief historical overview of recent discussions on this issue and discusses the tension between morality and law. In this text, Habermas hints at the gap between "human" and "rights" when he raises awareness of the fact that only after World War II a philosophical concept of human dignity was enshrined into texts of international law and national constitutions. He notes a dislocation between the historical discussions about human dignity and those about human rights.[45] However, he defends the thesis that "an intimate, if initially only implicit, conceptual connection has existed from the very beginning" because human rights have always been the product of resistance to despotism, oppression, and humiliation.[46] Reflecting on discussions about this concept in Germany, he presents legal reasons for human dignity to be seen as the "the moral 'source' from which all of the basic rights derive their sustenance."[47]

For Habermas, this moral source has always been there in many legal documents, but only in light of historical events such as the Holocaust we actually realize its moral power. In eloquent statements, Habermas affirms that "'human dignity' performs the function of a seismograph that registers what is constitutive for a democratic legal order, namely just those rights that the citizens of a political community must grant themselves if they are to be able to *respect* one another as members of a voluntary association of free and equal persons."[48] He also shows sensibility to human rights struggles in China, Africa, and Russia as well as the deportation of asylum seekers in Europe,[49] but in the end he insists that this moral promise needs to be translated directly and implemented positively through the legal language of a democratic constitution:

> Because the *moral promise* is supposed to be cashed out in *legal currency*, human rights exhibit a Janus face turned simultaneously to morality and to law. Notwithstanding their exclusively moral *content*, they have the *form* of enforceable subjective rights that grant specific liberties and claims. They are designed to be *spelled out in concrete terms* through democratic legislation, to be *specified* from case to case in adjudication, and to be *enforced* in cases of violation. Thus, human rights circumscribe precisely that part of morality which *can* be translated into the medium of coercive law and become political reality in the robust shape of effective civil rights.[50]

Habermas's strategy avoids both foundationalism and reductionism by establishing a horizontal dimension based upon which he defines both terms as "co-original," so that human dignity and human rights complement each other without establishing a vertical or hierarchical relation. However, he has been criticized for being dualist in his approach,[51] playing morality against law in an ambiguous way without spelling out the mediating role of cultural, social, or political processes or giving much space for other types of consideration on human rights. Social and political practices and institutions emerge in the gap between morality and legality, but he seems to disregard this point in this text. Another point concerns the applicability of his proposal on a global scale, especially because he constructs the system of law and the juridification of human rights based on Western, North Atlantic examples, avoiding the tricky issues that emerge from a plurality of multicultural experiences, Non-Western cultures, or different socio-political conditions worldwide. Because Habermas's intention is to conceive of human rights in a global perspective, these missing points certainly need to be addressed.[52]

Rainer Forst may offer some alternatives. Building on his previous work on "contexts of justice,"[53] he allows for more plurality, thus addressing some points that Habermas leaves underdeveloped. In *Toleration in Conflict*, he expands the discourse-theoretical approach to address the question about human dignity in relation to the concept of "person," showing how dignity emerges in relation to historical conflicts about toleration. Forst's discussion of this issue is presented more succinctly in "The Ground of Critique: On the Concept of Human Dignity in Social Orders of Justification," where he starts with a reference to Ernst Bloch's classic study, *Natural Law and Human Dignity*, thus rescuing some of the original intentions of Critical Theory.[54]

Moving beyond Habermas, Forst provides a phenomenology of dignity which still relies on Waldron's view of human dignity as political *status*, but expands this definition to include moral and political aspects of dignity which complement each other. Differently from Habermas, Forst does not simply say that a moral conception of dignity must be translated into a legal concept of rights, but – in dialogue with Michel Foucault and Axel Honneth – he makes room for considerations about power, social relations, and cultural processes. In the end, however, he states that "the central phenomenon of the violation of dignity is not the lack of the necessary means to live a 'life fit for a human being' but the conscious violation of the moral status of being a person who is owed justifications for existing relations or specific actions."[55]

Forst is not necessarily worried about the problem of foundationalism, but he seems to avoid this charge by paying attention to a conceptual plurality of contexts in which claims about human rights and human dignity are raised. However, in the end he makes a strong claim to subsume or reduce various possible interpretations of human dignity – theological, moral, political, and legal – to the idea of a fundamental moral "right to justification." There are some ambiguities here. For example, on the one hand he finds the theological doctrine of *imago Dei* unacceptable because it is valid only for those who share the same religious belief; but on the other, he rejects the dichotomy between immanence and transcendence because religious categories may express critical insights on human dignity. In any case, Forst clearly proposes that human dignity could mean "not denying anybody's moral right to justification."[56] The positive aspect of this proposal is to expand the discussion beyond the legal approach privileged by Habermas and to include more explicit moral, political, and even theological considerations about dignity. However, the social dimension of human dignity seems less developed in his argument. Finally, when he subsumes human dignity to a moral right to justification, he appears to be moving in circularity – by defining human dignity as an outcome of justification processes. Therefore, a question remains unanswered: do we derive our human dignity from a right to justification or rather claim our right to justification because we have – or are entitled to – human dignity?

Seyla Benhabib helps us correct some of these shortcomings, especially as she emphasizes the concreteness and situatedness of humans whose human dignity are violated daily, especially women, immigrants, refugees, and asylum seekers. She follows Critical Theory and its cosmopolitan project – from Kant to Habermas – but rejects metaphysical, epistemic, and cultural limits she finds in this tradition. Thus, she expands the framework and dialogues with other positions. For instance, the concept of "concrete others" was spelled out by Benhabib in *Situating the Self: Gender, Community, and Postmodernism in Contemporary Ethics*, [57] where she also establishes a dialogue with postmodern and feminist positions – such as Linda Nicholson, Nancy Fraser, Judith Butler, and others – to offer a "situated criticism" of generalities and affirm the humanness of a "concrete other."[58] This dimension of human situatedness is key for a better understanding of "others," in a process that is sensitive to the plurality of ways in which people claim human dignity. This idea is spelled out in *The Rights of Others: Aliens, Residents, and Citizens* and *Another Cosmopolitanism: Hospitality, Sovereignty, and Democratic Iterations,* [59] where Benhabib sides with Habermas but acknowledges that he has been unable to enlarge the scope of what counts as human. In her critique of Habermas she adds that discourse ethics "cannot limit the scope of the *moral conversation* only to those who reside within nationally recognized boundaries; it views the moral conversation as potentially including all of *humanity.*"[60] Expanding on this point in *Dignity in Adversity: Human Rights in Troubled Times,* [61] Benhabib reaffirms the importance of critical cosmopolitanism by reassessing Hannah Arendt's legacy, reflecting on the Jewish experience in Europe, and mapping different forms of exclusion in order to show that otherness emerges anyway and anywhere by means of "democratic iterations" and "jurisgenerative politics," whenever those who do not have rights dare to affirm their dignity and raise their claims to recognition in the public sphere.

In this process, Benhabib is well aware of the gap between "human" and "rights" as well as the variety of issues that emerge through this interstice. In her analysis of Muslim women wearing a scarf in France and Germany, Benhabib borrows the term "iteration" from Derrida and shows that when discriminated individuals insist on affirming their identity and contingencies in order to assert their human dignity – as many Muslim women in Europe did – they exercise "democratic iterations" that augment the *"meaning of rights claims"* and promote the *"growth of the political authorship by ordinary individuals,"* thus extending human rights to others.[62] "Democratic iterations" is a communicative process of raising claims, reiterating them, and making them visible and audible, so that change may eventually happen. This perspective complements what we find in Forst. Benhabib shows that a right to justification is exercised by means of cultural and political processes in which we reiteratively appeal to our humanity. In the case of Muslim women in France and Germany, they were discriminated for crossing borders and maintaining their cultural identity, rejecting assimilation, and affirming their right to freedom of religion. However, they were able to translate their religious views into moral claims that are updated to legal rights by means of *democratic iterations* that expanded their initial appeal to humanity. The most relevant point is Benhabib's focus on the *humanity* of those who move beyond their original locations and the *plurality* of their predicament, as they find themselves situated in dislocated contexts and as victims of discrimination, especially due to their gender and religious identity. Relying on Hannah Arendt's views on *human plurality*, Benhabib questions the power of state-centric institutions that impose very limiting citizenship conditions for the granting and exercise of rights or go to the extreme of promoting genocide in order to eliminate those who are different.[63] In her view, rights are not dispensations from state structures, but rather the achievement of legitimate and inalienable political victories of individual and collective agents who affirm and reaffirm their dignity in situations of adversity.[64]

This brief review of key authors indicates that there are already some initial aspects for a systematic consideration of human dignity in relation to a justification for human rights in the perspective of a Critical Theory. Based on a Critical Theory of Human Rights, we can argue more forcefully that the question of plurality – in both its descriptive and normative sense – has to be addressed more systematically when discussing human dignity in relation to human rights.

4. Plurality in justifications of human rights

In attempting to address a few controversial questions on the justification of human rights in relation to human dignity, we have found many perspectives. Some would suggest that we should give up on the search for necessary and sufficient justifications of human rights and disregard altogether the possibility of grounding human rights on human dignity. Others emerged with important contributions that point toward a plurality of justificatory approaches. In what follows, I would like to affirm "plurality" and articulate the points discussed so far.

The normative importance of plurality

Recent discussions in the philosophy of human rights offer a clearer recognition of plurality. The expression "philosophical foundations or justifications of human rights" – in plural – is now used to demarcate an emerging area of studies.[65] This new field refers to multiple historical, social, and political experiences by "humans," various moral and legal "rights," and alternative "justifications" of their relations.

John Tasioulas offers a sophisticated account of a pluralist foundation for human rights which is very helpful. In his publications, he gradually addresses the relationship between human dignity and human rights in terms of a non-foundationalist strategy. In "Towards a Philosophy of Human Rights" he differentiates between foundationalist and functionalist approaches.[66] Then, in "On the Nature of Human Rights"[67] he defends an orthodox conception that equates human rights to natural rights.[68] In another article, on "Human Dignity and the Foundations of Human Rights," he acknowledges different ways in which political activists, lawyers, philosophers, and ordinary citizens talk about human dignity, but then states that "what is to be justified are 'human rights',"[69] not necessarily human dignity. However, he then goes on to defend the moral idea of human dignity from many of its detractors in order to define a "human nature conception of human dignity," a conception that accounts for various features (embodiment, lifespan, psychological capacities, rationality, and others) inherent to a human being from the moment of coming into existence, independent of variations in capacity.

These features are related to a special value and grounded on a basic moral equality.[70] Nonetheless, in another text, "On the Foundations of Human Rights," he states that human dignity refers to the "intrinsically valuable status equally possessed by all human beings."[71] Tasioulas's pluralist approach can be put in dialogue with Critical Theory and the positions discussed thus far.

I would like to focus on this last article, for here Tasioulas argues that Rorty disregards justification processes and fails to distinguish between foundationalist views that ground human rights on metaphysical assumptions about human nature, agency or values and the idea of pluralist foundations of human rights that can be justified by reference to human interests and human dignity.[72] For Tasioulas, human rights need to be grounded "in a plurality" of human interests. Moreover, he adds that "human dignity characteristically operates in intimate union with a profile of universal human interests in generating human rights."[73] This leads him to a double assumption: first, that foundationalism emerges only when one grounds the morality of human rights independently of human interests and the duties they generate, so this problem can be avoided; second, that "human rights are grounded in the universal interests of human beings each and every one of whom possesses an equal moral status arising from their common humanity."[74] Based on these views, Tasioulas proposes a pluralistic scheme that necessarily links interests, rights, duties, and historical contexts in order to establish and justify any human right: (i) there must be an interest common to all humans; (ii) this interest not only generates very specific rights but also justifies duties on others; (iii) duties are constrained by at a particular historical time and context; (iv) under these conditions, rights are granted to all humans within that time and context.[75]

The proposed scheme is very dynamic and recognizes different accounts of human dignity, but one problem seems to be Tasioulas's strong claim that moral status arises from common humanity, without acknowledging the various forms of being human. Despite his emphasis on human dignity, humanity remains underdetermined. Also, as Onora O'Neil rightly notes, he does not say much about who are the duty-bearers under (iii).[76] By comparing him to Critical Theory, we can identify other problems. He is not pluralist enough about types of interests – a task that Habermas performs in *Knowledge and Human Interests* by differentiating among technical, practical, and emancipatory interests;[77] he does not differentiate the contexts in which right claims are made – a task partially accomplished by Forst;[78] and he does not spell out the plurality in humanity – a task fulfilled by Benhabib when she identifies different types of people whose human rights are violated due to gender, cultural, racial, and other forms of discrimination.[79] Yet Tasioulas provides an important methodological proposal to attach plurality and human dignity as underlying components in the justification of human rights. This proposal can be useful to Critical Theory.

How can we connect Critical Theory and Tasioulas's pluralist approach to the justification of human rights? First, we need to recognize that plurality applies to both human dignity and human rights. Second, the concept of "human" in *human rights* serves as an entry point for considerations on human dignity, which can be related to the various meanings of "rights." Third, we need to be cognizant of the gap between "human" and "rights" – through which questions about human duties can be introduced, especially as we refer to the plurality of interests, forms of agency, and practices that generate rights. Fourth, we can establish a horizontal connection among human dignity, human duties, and human rights in a mediating process through which each concept functions as a correction and complement to each other – an affirmation of human dignity is the point of departure in this chain of deliberations and human duties offer a bridge leading to the institutionalization of human rights.[80] This is a way of expanding Habermas's suggested co-originality of human dignity and human rights by adding the obligation to consider a variety of moral, cultural, social, and political as well as practical considerations. Combining Tasioulas's scheme with Critical Theory, we can have a framework that envisions humanity being affirmed and reaffirmed, duties being defined, and rights claimed in a way that allows for enforcement mechanisms.

The duty of plurality in human dignity, human duties, and human rights

Human dignity is a necessary starting point, but not a sufficient basis for the justification of human rights. We need to add the normative importance of "plurality" and the mediating roles of "duties." With this double supplement we are prompted to consider, at each juncture, the variety of contexts, the possible theological, moral, political, or legal perspective on duties or obligations, and their relation to interests, forms of agency, and practices that generate rights. A focus on plurality allows us to see the generation and transfer of values, it unlocks and unleashes multiple connections, and it reveals the diversity occluded by foundationalist or reductionist views that "do not mind the gap" between humanity and rights.

The emphasis on plurality reveals the many possibilities in the concept of human dignity and expands the framework of a Critical Theory of Human Rights. For instance, it considers not only a right to justification, as Forst would put it, but also calls for an explicit duty to respond. It reaffirms the importance of "democratic iterations," as defined by Benhabib, not necessarily as repetitions of the same story, but as a reaffirmation and enlargement of an emancipatory interest in upholding human dignity, imposing specific duties, and exploring the potential to enforce and institutionalize rights. These three dimensions are not necessarily co-original, as Habermas suggests, but rather complementary and expandable. By asking more directly who counts as human and are entitled to rights, we are prompted to take into account the various ways in which human dignity is affirmed or violated and, therefore, are encouraged to exercise the moral duty to oppose these violations – individually or collectively; collaborate in the establishment and oversight of corresponding institutions – cultural, social, political or legal; and create the necessary frameworks in which rights are enforceable – through rules of several institutions in civil society or constitutional arrangements within and beyond nation-states.

One result of this strategy is to avoid many of the challenges discussed in this chapter, especially the threat of simplistic views on foundationalism and reductionism. Another result is the possibility of providing stronger justifications for human rights by revealing instead of occluding diversity. Yet another result is the suggestion to see plurality more explicitly as a justification method and, expanding on Tasioulas's proposal, have a clearer structure that prompts us to acknowledge, from the beginning, how real people assert their humanity through multiple iterations, leading to the emergence of duties that are transformed and defined institutionally to justify, in the end, full-fledged rights. All this is implicit in the term "human rights," but the duty to plurality makes explicit the many dimensions implicit in the concepts of "human" and "right." Moreover, human rights are justified not by means of foundationalist claims or reductive strategies, but by expandable horizontal relations in which each one of these dimensions corrects and expands on each other.

A Critical Theory of Human Rights should serve as a tool to counter the temptation to downplay or neglect the multifarious dimensions of human life. By affirming plurality, a Critical Theory of Human Rights reminds us that the cry for human dignity serves as a starting point and as a warning system against inequalities, exploitation, and exclusion, thus motivating us to recognize our duties to reveal those expressions of humanity that are forgotten or negated, to express solidarity with them, and to create the necessary means to promote their rights.

Notes

1   Fred Dallmayr, "'Asian Values' and Global Human Rights," *Philosophy East & West* 52, no. 2 (April 2002): 173–189; Joanne Bauer and Daniel Bell (eds.), *The East Asian Challenge for Human Rights* (Cambridge: Cambridge University Press, 1999).
2   Abdulaziz Sachedina, *Islam and the Challenge of Human Rights* (Oxford: Oxford University Press, 2009).
3   Francis Deng, "Human Rights in the African Context", in Kwasi Wiredu (ed.), *A Companion to African Philosophy* (Malden, MA: Blackwell, 2004), 499–508; Thaddeus Metz, "*Ubuntu* as a Moral Theory and Human Rights in South Africa," *African Human Rights Law Journal* 11 (2011): 532–339.
4   Walter Mignolo, "Who Speaks for the 'Human' in Human Rights?" in Ana Forcinito, Raúl Marrero Fente, and Kelly McDonough (eds.), *Human Rights in Latin American and Iberian Cultures* [Hispanic Issues On Line] 5, no. 1 (2009): 7–24; Oscar Guardiola-Rivera, "Human Rights and Latin American Voices," in Upendra Baxi, Abdul Paliwala, and Christopher McCrudden (eds.), *Law's Ethical, Global and Theoretical Contexts: Essays in Honour of William Twining* (Cambridge: Cambridge University Press, 2015), 1–38.
5   These types of critique can be seen since Karl Marx's "On the Jewish Question." More recently, see Maurice Cranston, *What Are Human Rights?* (London: Bodley Head, 1973); Costas Douzinas, *The End of Human Rights* (Oxford: Hart Publishing, 2000); Samuel Moyn, *The Last Utopia: Human Rights in History* (Cambridge, MA: Harvard University Press, 2010); and Eric Posner, *The Twilight of Human Rights Law* (Oxford: Oxford University Press, 2014).

6 José-Manuel Barreto (ed.), *Human Rights from a Third World Perspective: Critique, History, and International Law* (Newcastle upon Tyne: Cambridge Scholars Publishing, 2013).

7 For example, Allen Buchanan, *The Heart of Human Rights* (Oxford: Oxford University Press, 2013).

8 Rowan Cruft, S. Matthew Liao, and Massimo Renzo (eds.), *Philosophical Foundations of Human Rights* (Oxford: Oxford University, 2015).

9 Christopher McCrudden, "Human Dignity and Judicial Interpretation of Human Rights," *European Journal of International Law* 19, no. 4 (2008): 655–724.

10 See Jürgen Habermas, *The Inclusion of the Other: Studies in Political Theory*, trans. C. Cronin (Cambridge, MA: MIT Press, 1998), *The Postnational Constellation*, trans. M. Pensky (Cambridge, MA: MIT Press), 166, *The Divided West*, trans. C. Cronin (Cambridge: Polity, 2007), and *Europe: The Faltering Project*, trans. C. Cronin (Cambridge: Polity, 2009); Seyla Benhabib, *The Rights of Others: Aliens, Residents, and Citizens* (Cambridge: Cambridge University Press, 2004), *Another Cosmopolitanism* (Oxford: Oxford University Press, 2006), *Dignity in Adversity: Human Rights in Troubled Times* (Cambridge: Polity Press, 2011); Cristina Lafont, *Global Governance and Human Rights* (Amsterdam: Van Gorcum, 2012); Amos Nascimento, *Building Cosmopolitan Communities* (New York, NY: Palgrave Macmillan, 2013); Matthias Lutz-Bachmann and Amos Nascimento (eds.), *Human Rights, Human Dignity, and Cosmopolitan Ideals: Essays on Critical Theory and Human Rights* (Surrey: Ashgate, 2014); Lars Rensmann, "Critical Theory of Human Rights," in Michael Thompson (ed.), *The Palgrave Handbook of Critical Theory* (New York: Palgrave Macmillan, 2017), 631–653; and Rainer Forst, "A Critical Theory of Human Rights: Some Groundwork," in Penelope Deutscher and Cristina Lafont (eds.) *Critical Theory in Critical Times* (New York, NY: Columbia University Press, 2017), 74–88.

11 Nascimento, *Building Cosmopolitan Communities*. See also Lutz-Bachmann and Nascimento, *Human Rights, Human Dignity, and Cosmopolitan Ideals*.

12 John Rawls, *Political Liberalism* (New York: Columbia University Press, 1993).

13 William Talbott, *Which Rights Should Be Universal?* (Oxford: Oxford University Press, 2005).

14 Joseph Raz, "Human Rights without Foundations," in Samantha Besson and John Tasioulas (eds.), *The Philosophy of International Law* (Oxford: Oxford University Press, 2010), 321–338.

15 Ludwig Wittgenstein, *Remarks on the Foundations of Mathematics* (Cambridge: Cambridge University Press, 1939) and *On Certainty* (Cambridge: Cambridge University Press, 1969).

16 Jean-François Lyotard, *The Postmodern Condition: A Report on Knowledge*, trans. Geoffrey Bennington and Brian Massumi (Minneapolis, MN: University of Minnesota Press, 1984).

17 Jean-François Lyotard, "Grundlagenkrise," *Neue Hefte für Philosophie* 26, no. 1 (1986): 1–33.

18 Jean-François Lyotard, *Enthusiasm: The Kantian Critique of History* (Palo Alto, CA: Stanford University Press, 2009).

19 Jean-François Lyotard, *The Inhuman: Reflections on Time* (Palo Alto, CA: Stanford University Press, 1992).

20 Jürgen Habermas, *The Philosophical Discourse of Modernity: Twelve Lectures*, trans. Frederick Lawrence (Cambridge, MA: MIT Press, 1987); Karl-Otto Apel, *Diskurs und Verantwortung: Das Problem des Übergangs zur postkonventionellen Moral* (Frankfurt a.M.: Surhkamp, 1988).

21 Jacques Derrida. "Wears and Tears (Tableau of an Ageless World)," cited in Patrick Hayden (ed.), *The Philosophy of Human Rights* (St. Paul, MN: Paragon Press, 2001), 265.

22 Richard Rorty, "Human Rights, Rationality, and Sentimentality", in Stephen Shute and Susan Hurley (eds.) *On Human Rights: The Oxford Amnesty Lectures* (New York, NY: Basic Books, 1993), 111–134, here 111.

23 Rorty, "Human Rights, Rationality, and Sentimentality," 113.

24 Immanuel Kant, *Groundwork to the Metaphysics of Morals* (4:436). See Allen Wood, *Kant's Ethical Thought* (Cambridge: Cambridge University Press, 1999), 185–186.

25 Ludwig Wittgenstein, *Philosophical Investigations* (Cambridge: Cambridge University Press, 1980), § 133: "There is not a philosophical method, though there are indeed methods, like different therapies." The corresponding reference here is to Kant's aesthetics and his proposal of transitions [*Übergänge*] to and from distinct domains. Se Immanuel Kant, *Critique of the Power of Judgment* (Cambridge: Cambridge University Press, 2011); original, *Kritik der Urteilskraft* (1790) in *Kants Gesammelte Schriften* (Berlin: Königliche Akademie der Wissenschaften, 1900–), § 23.

26 Alexander Altmann, "*Homo imago Dei* in Jewish and Christian Theology," *The Journal of Religion* 48, no. 3 (July 1968), 235–259; Walter Abbott and Joseph Gallagher (eds.), *The Documents of Vatican II* (New York, NY: America Press, 1966).

27 Alan Gewirth, *Human Rights: Essays on Justification and Applications* (Chicago, IL: University of Chicago Press, 1982) 42.

28 Jack Donnelly, *Universal Human Rights in Theory and Practice* (Ithaca, NY: Cornell University Press, 2002), 7.

29 Immanuel Kant. *Groundwork to the Metaphysics of Morals* (4:429–431, 435) and *Metaphysics of Morals* (6:237).

30 Cicero, *De officiis* [*On Duties*, Loeb Classical Library, Vol. 30] (Cambridge, MA: Harvard University Press, 1913), I.

31 Anthony Appiah, *The Honor Code: How Moral Revolutions Happen* (New York, NY: Norton, 2011).

32 Jeremy Waldron, *Dignity, Rank, and Rights* (Oxford: Oxford University Press, 2012).

33 Waldron, *Dignity, Rank, and Rights,* 57.

34 Council of Europe, *European Convention on Human Rights* [Supplemented by Protocols 1, 4, 6, 7,12 and 13] (Strasbourg: European Court of Human Rights, 2010), 52.

35 Dieter Grimm, "Dignity in a Legal Context: Dignity as an Absolut Right" in Christopher McCrudden (ed.) *Understanding Human Dignity* (Oxford: Oxford University Press, 2013), 381–391.

36 Moyn, *The Last Utopia.*

37 Moyn, "The Secret History of Constitutional Dignity" in Christopher McCrudden (ed.), *Understanding Human Dignity* (Oxford: Oxford University Press, 2013), 95–111.

38 Samuel Moyn, *Christian Human Rights* (Philadelphia, PA: University of Pennsylvania Press, 2015).

39 Michael Rosen, *Dignity: Its History and Meaning* (Cambridge, MA: Harvard University Press, 2012).

40 Jürgen Habermas, *The Structural Transformation of the Public Sphere*, trans. T. Burger (Cambridge, MA: MIT Press, 1989), 117–121.

41 Jürgen Habermas, *Between Facts and Norms: Contributions to a Discourse Theory of Law and Democracy*, trans. W. Rehg (Cambridge, MA: MIT Press, 1996).

42 Jürgen Habermas, "Der Interkulturelle Diskurs um Menschenrechte," in M. Lutz-Bachmann et al. (eds.), *Recht auf Menschenrechte* (Frankfurt a.M.: Suhrkamp, 1996).

43 Published, respectively, in Habermas, *The Inclusion of the Other*, trans. Ciaran Cronin and Pablo De Greiff (Cambridge: Polity, 2000) and *The Postnational Constellation.*

44 Jürgen Habermas, *The Crisis of the European Union*, trans. C. Cronin (Cambridge: Polity, 2012), 71–100.

45 Habermas, *The Crisis of the European Union*, 73–74.

46 Habermas, *The Crisis of the European Union*, 74–75.

47 Habermas, *The Crisis of the European Union*, 75.

48 Habermas, *The Crisis of the European Union*, 81.

49 Habermas, *The Crisis of the European Union*, 94.

50 Habermas, *The Crisis of the European Union*, 82.

51 See Jeffrey Flynn, "Habermas on Human Rights: Law, Morality, and International Dialogue," *Social Theory and Practice* 29, no. 3 (2003): 431–457.

52 Nascimento, *Building Cosmopolitan Communities.*

53 Rainer Forst, *Contexts of Justice: Political Philosophy beyond Liberalism and Communitarianism*, trans. John M. Farrell (Berkeley, CA: University of California Press, 2002).

54 Ernst Bloch, *Natural Law and Human Dignity*, trans. D.J. Schmidt (Cambridge, MA: MIT Press, 1986).

55 Rainer Forst, "The Ground of Critique: On the Concept of Human Dignity in Social Orders of Justification," in *Justification and Critique* (Cambridge: Polity, 2013), 98.

56 Forst, "The Ground of Critique," 99.

57 Seyla Benhabib, *Situating the Self: Gender, Community, and Postmodernism in Contemporary Ethics* (London: Routledge, 1992).

58 Benhabib, *Situating the Self*, 225–228.

59 Benhabib, *The Rights of Others* and *Another Cosmopolitanism.*

60 Benhabib, *Another Cosmopolitanism*, 18 (emphasis in original).

61 Benhabib, *Dignity in Adversity.*

62 Benhabib, *Another Cosmopolitanism*, 49 (emphasis in original).

63 Benhabib, *Another Cosmopolitanism*, 171–175.

64 Benhabib, *Dignity in Adversity*, 15–19, 124–125.

65 Cruft et al., *Philosophical Foundations of Human Rights.*

66 John Tasioulas, "Towards a Philosophy of Human Rights," *Current Legal Problems* 65 (2012): 1–30.

67 John Tasioulas, "On the Nature of Human Rights," in Gerhard Ernst and Jan-Christoph Heilinger (eds.), *The Philosophy of Human Rights: Contemporary Controversies* (Berlin: De Gruyter, 2012), 17–59.

68 Tasioulas, "On the Nature of Human Rights," 43–56.

69 John Tasioulas, "Human Dignity and the Foundations of Human Rights," in Christopher McCrudden (ed.) *Understanding Human Dignity* (Oxford: Oxford University Press, 2013), 293–314, here 293.

70 Tasioulas, "Human Dignity," 304–306.

71 John Tasioulas, "On the Foundations of Human Rights," in Cruft et al., *The Philosophical Foundations of Human Rights*, 45–70, here 53.

72 Tasioulas, "On the Foundations of Human Rights," 45–50.

73 Tasioulas, "On the Foundations of Human Rights," 50.

74 Tasioulas, "On the Foundations of Human Rights," 50.

75 Tasioulas, "On the Foundations of Human Rights," 50–51.

76 Onora O'Neil. "Response to John Tasioulas," in Cruft et al., *The Philosophical Foundations of Human Rights*, 71–78.

77 Jürgen Habermas, *Knowledge and Human Interests*, trans. Jeremy J. Shapiro (Boston, MA: Beacon Press, 1971).

78 Forst, *Contexts of Justice* and *The Right to Justification*, trans. J. Flynn (New York, NY: Columbia University Press, 2011).

79 Benhabib, *Dignity in Adversity*, vi–vii, 35–36, 119f.

80 Amos Nascimento, "Human Duties," in Fathali Moghaddam (ed.), *Encyclopedia of Political Behavior* (Thousand Oaks, CA: SAGE, 2017), 358–361.

References

Abbott, Walter and Joseph Gallagher (eds.). *The Documents of Vatican II* (New York, NY: America Press, 1966).

Altmann, Alexander. "*Homo imago Dei* in Jewish and Christian Theology," *The Journal of Religion* 48, no. 3 (July 1968): 235–259.

Apel, Karl-Otto. *Diskurs und Verantwortung: Das Problem des Übergangs zur postkonventionellen Moral* (Frankfurt a.M.: Surhkamp, 1988).

Appiah, Anthony. *The Honor Code: How Moral Revolutions Happen* (New York, NY: Norton, 2011).

Barreto, José-Manuel (ed.). *Human Rights from a Third World Perspective: Critique, History, and International Law*(Newcastle upon Tyne: Cambridge Scholars Publishing, 2013).

Bauer, Joanne and Daniel Bell (eds.). *The East Asian Challenge for Human Rights* (Cambridge: Cambridge University Press, 1999).

Benhabib, Seyla. *Dignity in Adversity: Human Rights in Troubled Times* (Cambridge: Polity Press, 2011).

Benhabib, Seyla. *Another Cosmopolitanism* (Oxford: Oxford University Press, 2006).

Benhabib, Seyla. *The Rights of Others: Aliens, Residents, and Citizens* (Cambridge: Cambridge University Press, 2004).

Benhabib, Seyla. *Situating the Self: Gender, Community, and Postmodernism in Contemporary Ethics* (London: Routledge, 1992).

Bloch, Ernst. *Natural Law and Human Dignity*, trans. D.J. Schmidt (Cambridge, MA: MIT Press, 1986), published originally in German as *Naturrecht und menschliche Würde* (Frankfurt a.M.: Suhrkamp, 1977).

Brown, Garrett. "The Laws of Hospitality, Asylum Seekers, and Cosmopolitan Right: A Kantian Response to Jacques Derrida", *European Journal of Political Theory* 9, no. 3 (2010): 1–10.

Buchanan, Allen. *The Heart of Human Rights* (Oxford: Oxford University Press, 2013).

Cicero. *De officiis* [*On Duties*, Loeb Classical Library, Vol. 30] (Cambridge, MA: Harvard University Press, 1913).

Council of Europe. *European Convention on Human Rights* [Supplemented by Protocols 1, 4, 6, 7,12 and 13] (Strasbourg: European Court of Human Rights, 2010).

Cranston, Maurice. *What Are Human Rights?* (London: Bodley Head, 1973).

Cruft, Rowan, S. Matthew Liao, and Massimo Renzo (eds.). *Philosophical Foundations of Human Rights* (Oxford: Oxford University, 2015).

Dallmayr, Fred. "'Asian Values' and Global Human Rights," *Philosophy East & West* 52, no. 2 (April 2002): 173–189.

Deng, Francis. "Human Rights in the African Context", in Kwasi Wiredu (ed.), *A Companion to African Philosophy* (Malden, MA: Blackwell, 2004), 499–508.

Donnelly, Jack. *Universal Human Rights in Theory and Practice* (Ithaca, NY: Cornell University Press, 2002).

Douzinas, Costas. *The End of Human Rights* (Oxford: Hart Publishing, 2000).

Flynn, Jeffrey. "Habermas on Human Rights: Law, Morality, and International Dialogue," *Social Theory and Practice* 29, no. 3 (2003): 431–457.

Forst, Rainer. "A Critical Theory of Human Rights: Some Groundwork," in Penelope Deutscher and Cristina Lafont (eds.), *Critical Theory in Critical Times* (New York, NY: Columbia University Press, 2017), 74–88.

Forst, Rainer. *Justification and Critique: Towards a Critical Theory of Politics*, trans. Ciaran Cronin (Cambridge: Polity, 2013).

Forst, Rainer. *The Right to Justification*, trans. J. Flynn (New York, NY: Columbia University Press, 2011).

Forst, Rainer. *Contexts of Justice: Political Philosophy beyond Liberalism and Communitarianism*, trans. John M. Farrell (Berkeley, CA: University of California Press, 2002).

Gewirth, Alan. *Human Rights: Essays on Justification and Applications* (Chicago, IL: University of Chicago Press, 1982).

Grimm, Dieter. "Dignity in a Legal Context: Dignity as an Absolut Right," in Christopher McCrudden (ed.), *Understanding Human Dignity* (Oxford: Oxford University Press, 2013), 381–391.

Guardiola-Rivera, Oscar. "Human Rights and Latin American Voices," in Upendra Baxi, Abdul Paliwala, and Christopher McCrudden (eds.), *Law's Ethical, Global and Theoretical Contexts: Essays in Honour of William Twining* (Cambridge: Cambridge University Press, 2015), 1–38.

Habermas, Jürgen. *The Crisis of the European Union*, trans. C. Cronin (Cambridge: Polity, 2012).

Habermas, Jürgen. *Europe: The Faltering Project*, trans. C. Cronin (Cambridge: Polity, 2009).

Habermas, Jürgen. *The Divided West*, trans. C. Cronin (Cambridge: Polity, 2007).

Habermas, Jürgen. *The Inclusion of the Other*, trans. Ciaran Cronin and Pablo De Greiff (Cambridge: Polity, 2000).

Habermas, Jürgen. *The Inclusion of the Other: Studies in Political Theory*, trans. C. Cronin (Cambridge, MA: MIT Press, 1998).

Habermas, Jürgen *The Postnational Constellation*, trans. M. Pensky (Cambridge, MA: MIT Press, 1998).

Habermas, Jürgen. *Between Facts and Norms: Contributions to a Discourse Theory of Law and Democracy*, trans. W. Rehg (Cambridge, MA: MIT Press, 1996).

Habermas, Jürgen. "Der Interkulturelle Diskurs um Menschenrechte," in M. Lutz-Bachmann et al. (eds.), *Recht auf Menschenrecht* (Frankfurt a.M.: Suhrkamp, 1996).

Habermas, Jürgen. *The Philosophical Discourse of Modernity: Twelve Lectures*, trans. Frederick Lawrence (Cambridge, MA: MIT Press, 1987).

Habermas, Jürgen. *Knowledge and Human Interests*, trans. Jeremy J. Shapiro (Boston, MA: Beacon Press, 1971).

Habermas, Jürgen. *The Structural Transformation of the Public Sphere*, trans. T. Burger (Cambridge, MA: MIT Press, 1989).

Hayden, Patrick (ed.). *The Philosophy of Human Rights* (St. Paul, MN: Paragon Press, 2001).

Kant, Immanuel. *Critique of the Power of Judgment*, trans. Paul Guyer and Eric Matthews (Cambridge: Cambridge University Press, 2011); German original as *Kritik der Urteilskraft* (1790) in *Kants Gesammelte Schriften* (Berlin: Königliche Akademie der Wissenschaften, 1900–).

Kant, Immanuel. *Groundwork to the Metaphysics of Morals*, ed. and trans. M. Gregor (Cambridge: Cambridge University Press, 1998).

Lafont, Cristina. *Global Governance and Human Rights* (Amsterdam: Van Gorcum, 2012).

Lutz-Bachmann, Matthias and Amos Nascimento (eds.). *Human Rights, Human Dignity, and Cosmopolitan Ideals: Essays on Critical Theory and Human Rights* (Surrey: Ashgate, 2014).

Lyotard, Jean. *Enthusiasm: The Kantian Critique of History* (Palo Alto, CA: Stanford University Press, 2009); in French as *L'Enthousiasme: la critique kantienne de l'histoire* (Paris: Galilée, 1986).

Lyotard, Jean. *The Inhuman: Reflections on Time* (Palo Alto, CA: Stanford University Press, 1992); originally in French as *L'Inhumain: causeries sur les temps* (Paris: Galilée, 1991).

Lyotard, Jean. Grundlagenkrise," *Neue Hefte für Philosophie* 26, no. 1 (1986): 1–33.

Lyotard, Jean-François. *The Postmodern Condition: A Report on Knowledge*, trans. Geoffrey Bennington and Brian Massumi (Minneapolis, MN: University of Minnesota Press, 1984); French as *La condition postmoderne* (Paris: Minuit, 1979).

McCrudden, Christopher (ed.). *Understanding Human Dignity* (Oxford: Oxford University Press, 2013).

McCrudden, Christopher. "Human Dignity and Judicial Interpretation of Human Rights," *European Journal of International Law* 19, no. 4 (2008): 655–724.

Metz, Thaddeus. "Ubuntu as a Moral Theory and Human Rights in South Africa," *African Human Rights Law Journal* 11 (2011): 532–559.

Mignolo, Walter. "Who Speaks for the 'Human' in Human Rights?" in Ana Forcinito, Raúl Marrero Fente, and Kelly McDonough (eds.), *Human Rights in Latin American and Iberian Cultures* [Hispanic Issues On Line] 5, no. 1 (2009): 7–24.

Moyn, Samuel. *Christian Human Rights* (Philadelphia, PA: University of Pennsylvania Press, 2015).

Moyn, Samuel. "The Secret History of Constitutional Dignity," in Christopher McCrudden (ed.), *Understanding Human Dignity* (Oxford: Oxford University Press, 2013), 95–111.

Moyn, Samuel. *The Last Utopia: Human Rights in History* (Cambridge, MA: Harvard University Press, 2010).

Nascimento, Amos. "Human Duties," in Fathali Moghaddam (ed.), *Encyclopedia of Political Behavior* (Thousand Oaks, CA: SAGE, 2017).

Nascimento, Amos. *Building Cosmopolitan Communities* (New York, NY: Palgrave Macmillan, 2013).

O'Neil, Onora. "Response to John Tasioulas," in Rowan Cruft, S. Matthew Liao, and Massimo Renzo (eds.), *Philosophical Foundations of Human Rights* (Oxford: Oxford University, 2015), 71–78.

Posner, Eric. *The Twilight of Human Rights Law* (Oxford: Oxford University Press, 2014).

Rawls, John. *Political Liberalism* (New York, NY: Columbia University Press, 1993).

Raz, Joseph. "Human Rights without Foundations," in Samantha Besson and John Tasioulas (eds.), *The Philosophy of International Law* (Oxford: Oxford University Press, 2010), 321–338.

Rensmann, Lars. "Critical Theory of Human Rights," in Michael Thompson (ed.), *The Palgrave Handbook of Critical Theory* (New York, NY: Palgrave Macmillan, 2017), 631–653.

Rorty, Richard. "Human Rights, Rationality, and Sentimentality," in Stephen Shute and Susan Hurley (eds.) *On Human Rights: The Oxford Amnesty Lectures* (New York, NY: Basic Books, 1993), 111–134.

Rosen, Michael. *Dignity: Its History and Meaning* (Cambridge, MA: Harvard University Press, 2012).

Sachedina, Abdulaziz. *Islam and the Challenge of Human Rights* (Oxford: Oxford University Press, 2009).

Talbott, William. *Which Rights Should Be Universal?* (Oxford: Oxford University Press, 2005).

Tasioulas, J. "On the Foundations of Human Rights," in Rowan Cruft, S. Matthew Liao, and Massimo Renzo (eds.), *Philosophical Foundations of Human Rights* (Oxford: Oxford University, 2015), 45–70.

Tasioulas, J. "Human Dignity and the Foundations of Human Rights," in Christopher McCrudden (ed.), *Understanding Human Dignity* (Oxford: Oxford University Press, 2013), 293–314.

Tasioulas, J. "On the Nature of Human Rights," in Gerhard Ernst and Jan-Christoph Heilinger (eds.), *The Philosophy of Human Rights: Contemporary Controversies* (Berlin: De Gruyter, 2012), 17–59.

Tasioulas, J. "Towards a Philosophy of Human Rights," *Current Legal Problems* 65 (2012): 1–30.

Waldron, Jeremy. *Dignity, Rank, and Rights* (Oxford: Oxford University Press, 2012).

Wittgenstein, Ludwig. *Philosophical Investigations* (Cambridge: Cambridge University Press, 1980).

Wittgenstein, Ludwig. *On Certainty* (Cambridge: Cambridge University Press, 1969).

Wittgenstein, Ludwig *Remarks on the Foundations of Mathematics* (Cambridge: Cambridge University Press, 1939).

Wood, Allen. *Kant's Ethical Thought* (Cambridge: Cambridge University Press, 1999).

Index

abilities 28, 34, 94, 115; as described by Marsilio Ficino in *Theologia Platonica* 27; to exercise a person's own rationality 34; of foreign investors to challenge states' regulations in international tribunals 94; to have rights and obligations 89; of human beings to understand what is rational or good 33; of the humanist approaches rejected by Charles Beitz 86; to order and influence, to occupy, and to dominate the space of reasons for others 76; to protect human rights 95; to self-legislate as a moral subject 43

abolition 53, 67, 120, 131; of conditions of exploitation and debasement 120; of the death penalty 53, 131; of war 67

Abu Ghraib prison 106–7, 112

actions 27–29, 34, 44, 58, 63, 72–73, 75–76, 89, 93–94, 111, 114–16, 118, 126, 134; collective 118; diplomatic 94; individual 48; inter-subjective 44; legal 58; political xiv; regulating 76; remedial 85–86, 90, 93; remedial transnational 93

Adorno, Theodor W. xiii, 2–5

Africa xii, 8, 62, 95, 99n15, 105–7, 126, 131, 133; and deaths from extreme malnutrition and related causes 105; famines in 105; and the focus on peoples, communities, and collective identities 126

African Charter of Human and People's Rights 99n15

Alvarez, Jose E. 101–2

American Convention on Human Rights 99n15

Anderson, Joel 3

Apel, Karl-Otto xiii, 5, 7

Aquinas, Thomas 32, 42, 128

The Arab Charter on Human Rights 99n15

Arendt, Hannah xiii, 4, 6–7, 66, 81, 115–16, 135

Asian governments 125

autonomy 2, 6, 11, 24, 43, 58, 60, 74, 111–13, 116, 118, 129; individual 57, 129; informational 54; moral 77

basic rights 5, 45, 49, 52, 54–56, 61, 64–65, 67, 74, 77, 81, 113, 127, 132; competing 48; derived 2; substantive 75

Baynes, Kenneth 63

Beitz, Charles 86, 89

Benhabib, Seyla xiii, 6–7, 11, 98, 108, 121–22, 132, 134–35, 137–38

Benjamin, Walter xiii, 3, 33

Berlin, Isaiah 113–14

Besson, Samantha 99–100

Between Facts and Norms 6

bioethics 10, 42, 45, 47, 106–7

Bloch, Ernst xiii, 4, 71, 117–18, 133

Bohman, James xiii, 6

Boltanski, Luc 81

Bonaparte, Napoleon 2

bourgeois terms 79

Buchanan, Alan 98

Butler, Judith 134

capacity 25, 34, 60, 74, 94, 136; natural 45; psychological 136; regulatory 94

Carter, Kevin 120

cases 47, 55, 57–58, 62, 64, 72, 89–91, 93, 95–97, 99–102, 107, 118, 131, 133; arbitration 95; concrete 127; isolated 95; national 91; single 63